Goodbye to THES

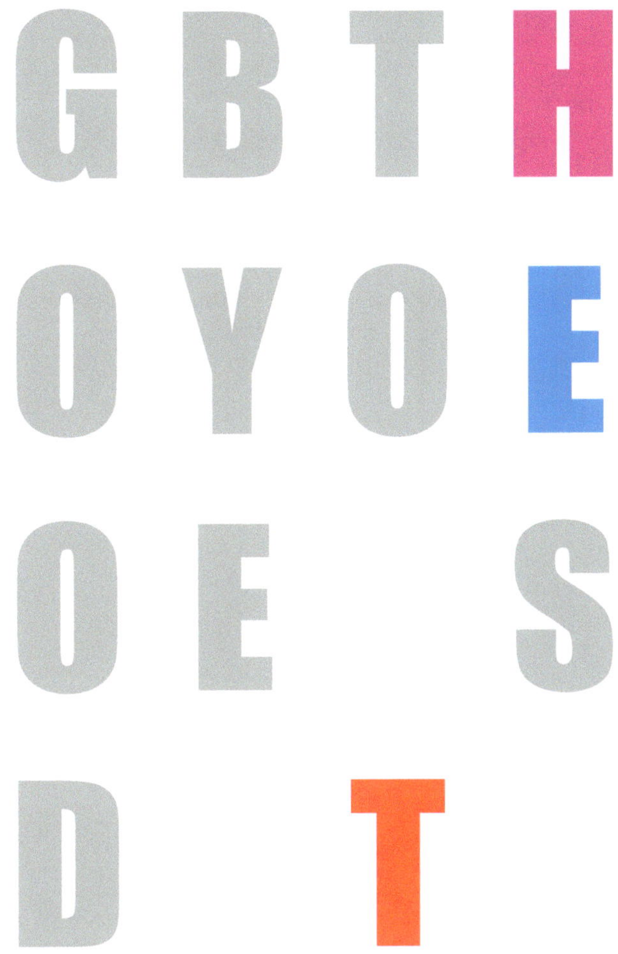

Geoffrey Mark Matthews

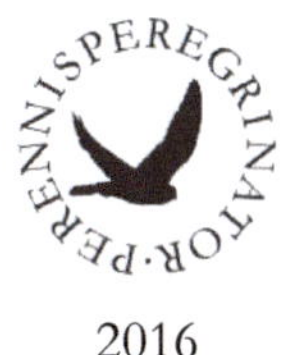

2016

Published 2016 by
PERENNISPEREGRINATOR

ISBN 978-0-9932054-5-3

perennisperegrinator@gmail.com

Goodbye to the THES collages were first exhibited at the Gallery at St Martins, Lincoln, UK. 25-30 April 2016

Acknowledgement
Some of the metafictions first appeared on the Perennis Peregrinator blog:
perennisperegrinator.wordpress.com

Cover image: 108 **Pragmatism of Freud with the fresh insights of invention why journey the border**

This book is dedicated to the memory of
Pippa Carter, a unique and special individual,
an original thinker, and an inspirational mentor.
The critical edge is still there the more so for
working at the edge of comprehensibility.

CONTENTS

Elements of poetry are letters, syllables, words, sentences.
Poetry arises from the interaction of those elements.
Meaning is important only if it is employed as one such factor.
I play off sense against nonsense.
I prefer nonsense, but that is a purely personal matter.
(Kurt Schwitters, 1920)

If we give the attributes of a medium to the artist,
we must then deny him the state of consciousness on the esthetic plane
about what he is doing or why he is doing it.
(Marcel Duchamp, *The Creative Act*)

It may be that the deep necessity of art
is the examination of self-deception.
(Robert Motherwell)

INTRODUCTION

Introduction

My name is Geoffrey Mark Matthews. As I write this I am sixty one years old. I used to be a university lecturer. Now I work for myself. Sometimes I interview designers and write about how they think and work. Sometimes I analyse the design of museums and exhibitions and write about that. But most of the time I make art. To make art I use words, images, sounds and whatever materials I can get my hands on. Usually I explore ideas quickly and move on. But when I have an idea that I think is a particularly good one I turn it into a project. What this means is that I give myself a starting point and an end point and a set of rules about working. Then I try to stick to them and produce a body of work. I tend to work better to a deadline and I tend to be more creative when I have several projects on the go each with different rules and a different deadline.

The idea behind this project is simple. As a lecturer I used to subscribe to the *Times Higher Education* (*Supplement*). When I retired I let the subscription run out, but that took over a year. I also had a lot of back copies in the house, some of them unread. In 2008 the *Times Higher Education* stopped being a newspaper supplement. It became a magazine printed on coated white paper and colourfully illustrated. It seemed a shame just to throw them away. I decided to cut them up and make collages. I thought that would be a good way to say goodbye to my former life as an academic.

Episode 1

There is no history here; this is not even an autobiographical project. When I retired I carried on working, maintaining the illusion of forward motion. What might appear to be a turning point bracketed by lesser moments is merely arbitrariness and fragmentation plundered and fashioned, incident by incident, into art. How does it happen? Framed by institutional proscriptions the freedom to choose what to do next is nothing but an illusion, one necessary for one's sense of a directed self, or so the received wisdom suggests:

> … it is repression which 'fixes' our identities, which disregards, dissolves, limits our inherent complexity and, above all, potentiality. Nevertheless, we desire such fixed identity, thus desire our own repression.[1]

No-one entirely escapes framing.

As if some inhuman objectivity were possible, words and images pretend to a kind of science. But I undermine that pretence from the outset. There are no certainties and, as I say, this is not about me. If not 'knowledge' then perhaps 'wisdom' is what the drive to make sense of these dissociated elements or 'minor events' signals I am seeking. That is for you to decide. I am undecided. Although, I am reminded of Gusmão and Paiva's:

1 Carter & Jackson, 'Gilles Deleuze and Felix Guattari,' p. 108.

> … core of hobbled ideas, the spirit of a genuine 'dwarf philosophy'.[2]

Not science, you see, but philosophy, even if in a diminished form: it allows the doing and the thinking-about-the-doing to unfold in the same atmosphere. Almost by default I avoid falling, but not by learning how to fly: the muscular approach is for more agile and arrogant minds than mine. I am happy to float.

Episode 2

There are no *unnecessary digressions* here. Necessity is not in question at this time and digression dissolves as an issue once I realize that any original idea of 'project'—of purpose, direction and allegiance to a discourse—is simply a proleptic device. At a beginning founded on random uncertainties I do not know what will result from my actions. However, I refuse to delude myself. There is no rational basis for decisiveness in this situation. My wilfulness disguises neither fatalist nor voluntarist abdications in that I am neither resigned to the unfolding of an already forming future nor preoccupied with creating a desired one. It is simply a wilfulness underpinned by faith in emergence. Post-Enlightenment, this is the ruling myth.

Here then, there is no history, no science (in the narrow rationalist sense), and no moral direction. There is only nominalist presumption.

Episode 3

One morning I woke up and everything had changed. To some imagined objective observer things seemed the same, but, in the reality unfolding from that moment on, appearances were indeed deceivingly opaque and unrevealing. Am I now in two minds: simultaneously the cave-dwelling seer, embodied and whole, and the little god of all delusion, out of body yet tethered by mutual fascination? Without the daily distractions of flickering light in the myriad eyes of a contracted milieu and the treadmill of evaluating and responding to the constant stream of expressions, I am for a moment lost, but not for long. The cave wall shimmers and the view is clearing. I begin to see long-forgotten horizons and, magically, some new ones.

Notes for the reader

In the pages that follow the collages are presented in the order in which they were made, numbered 001 to 213. To avoid unnecessary repetition the details of materials and format are given here:

P = Printed paper
C = Charcoal
A = Acrylic paint
I = Ink
G = Gold lacquer

Each composition is glued using 3M Photomount spray onto 95 gsm Huntsman Superwhite Cartridge paper trimmed to 21 x 21

2 Gusmão and Paiva, *Teoria Extraterrestre*, p. 57.

cm (8¼ x 8¼ in) and mounted on 300 gsm Daler Aquafine watercolour paper, finished size 25 x 25 cm (9⅞ x 9⅞ in). Each collage is signed and dated.

Every ninth collage, starting with 001 *Vita promise moves*, is reproduced full page and followed by a metafiction of about 400 words with the same title. As will become clear, the relationship between a metafiction and the image that precedes it is unpredictable and unreliable, and for these reasons alone worthy of interrogation (but hardly at all in this book).

The essay 'On Collage and Metafiction' does three things. It gives a little historical and theoretical background to the collage and metafiction art forms. It explains my approach to the work in this project and the techniques I used in the making if the collages and in the writing of the metafictions. And lastly it reflects on my experience. This is not an entirely autobiographical matter and, in however small a way, I hope it adds a philosophical dimension to the work.

By their very nature these collages and metafictions required a violent and destructive attack on existing images, texts and ideas to generate working material. One might say that the dissociation this achieves makes acknowledging sources a rather pointless exercise. However, that is not quite true and to complicate the point the essay is followed by a postscript and a bibliography.

GOODBYE TO THES

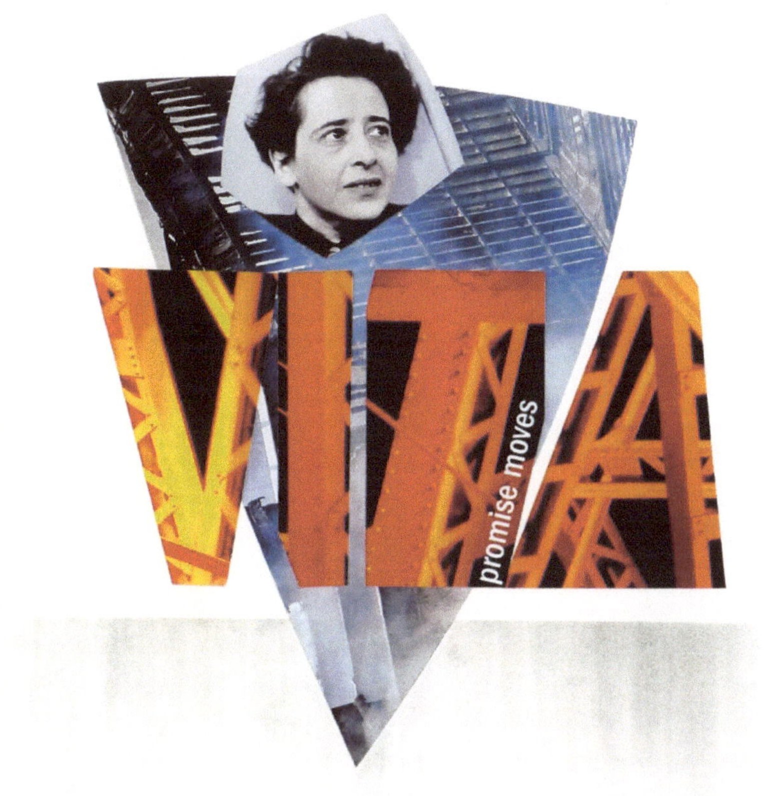

001

Vita promise moves

July 2015

(PC)

VITA promise moves

It is a long, too long, trek across moral wastelands, deep into the heart of the matter. Desolation is all I feel behind, before and beyond. In such conditions turning brings on the vertigo of despair—it is not turning at all. If only the gaze could be tamed and brought into some alignment with possibility, but the body seems trapped, bathed in an all-consuming conflagration and the pain is blinding. To live or to die: no other question occurs to me.

There above us circle machines that see far better than yesterday we imagined was possible. Our minor intelligence may still be our own and merely extended by such invention, but make no mistake, to believe, because of such so-called advances, that humanity stands any chance of enlightenment, howsoever conceived, is a delusion, a collective hubris of fatal prospects.

I am sure that you can tell that the story so far can be blamed on an encounter with a woman on the brink of realizing how damned humanity really is. The universe is unbounded in its insensibility, perfect in its impenetrability and absolute in its finality, hence the vision of a wasteland devoid of empathy out of which some hope is not really expected to surface.

I arrive, tired and bedraggled, in desperate need of a heartening story and perhaps a washbasin and towel, a bowl of soup and some bread, a blanket and a corner in which to bed down. Really it is that opening of words into the collective memory of the people here that makes the difference between sufferance and charity. But there is silence in the light and in the dark only private murmurings that escalate into rage against the chaos of the world.

Five paragraphs in and I feel the moment has arrived to pause proceedings. Imagine it is a play: the curtain falls, tympani rumble while a starfield floats across the empty stage and the house lights slowly brighten.

> You wiv me? … The thing is, Brian, God doesn't love you. God despises you. So there's no hope.
>
> You don't believe in God.

They down a couple of interval drinks and suitably bolstered return to their seats in the circle.

Give me strength! Please Hannah, tell me again about the active life and the contemplative life. The conundrum is a blast, a mist-clearing breeze backing into a mast-breaking storm. Before I arrived I was never so alone and so idle. Now at rest I see the pointlessness of it all, just to keep talking, just to make do with the words, the scraps of colour and the image fragments.

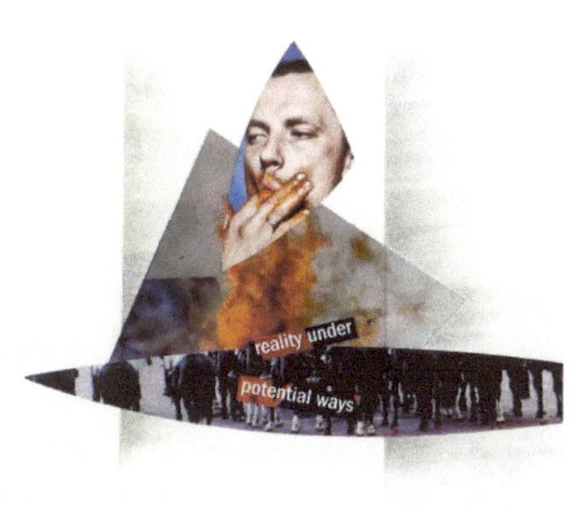

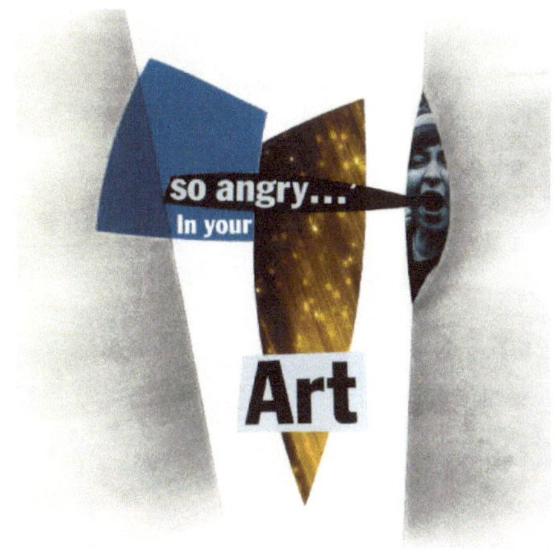

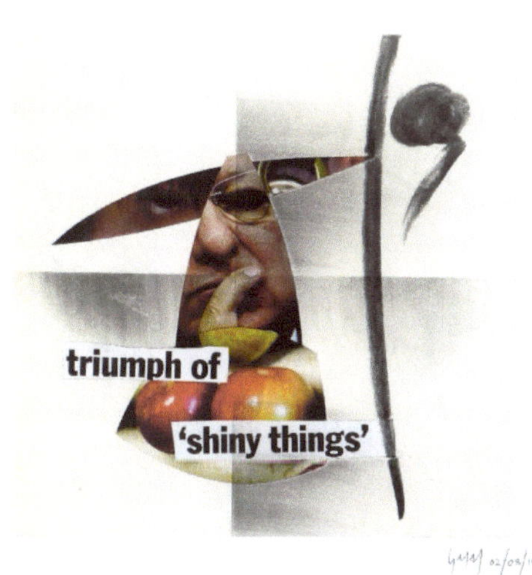

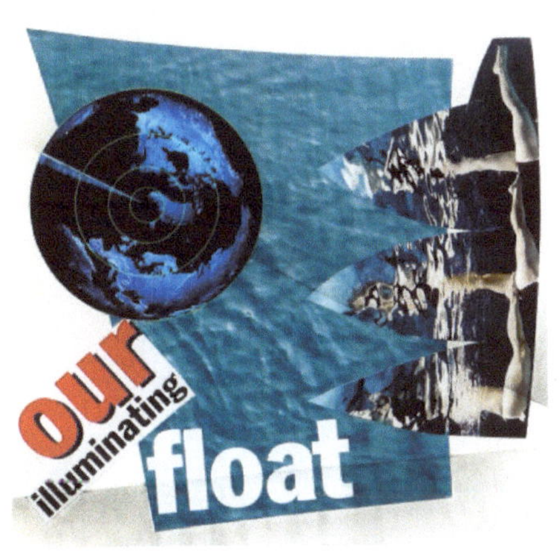

002 **Reality under potential ways**
August 2015 (PC)

003 **Triumph of 'shiny things'**
August 2015 (PC)

004 **So angry in your art**
August 2015 (PC)

005 **Our illuminating float**
August 2015 (PC)

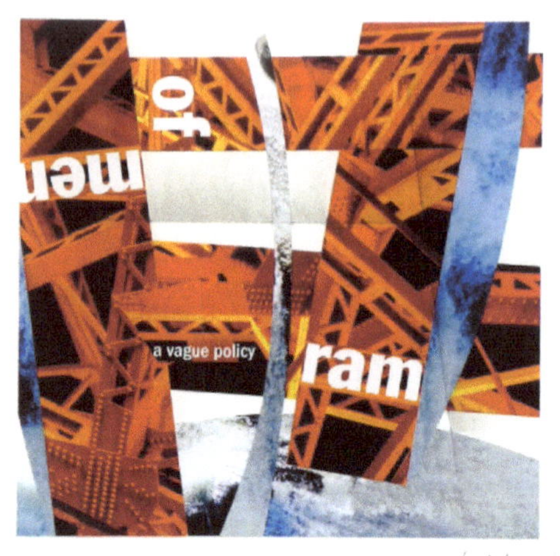

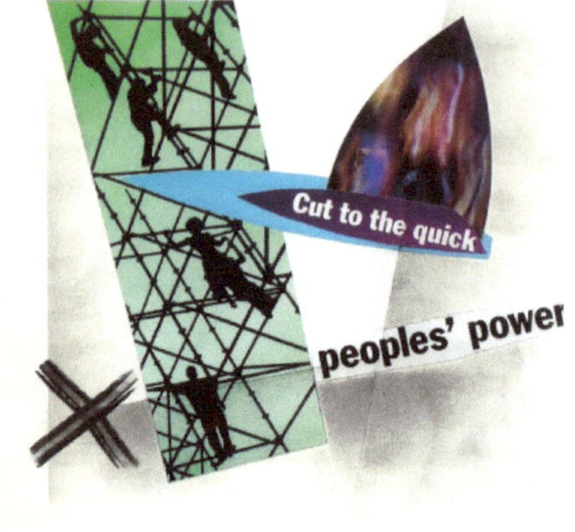

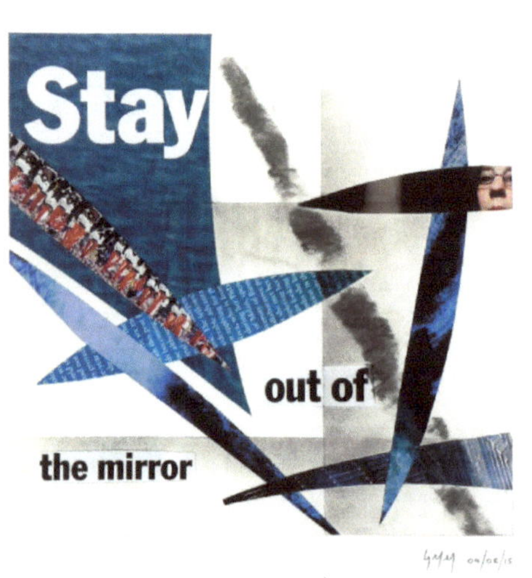

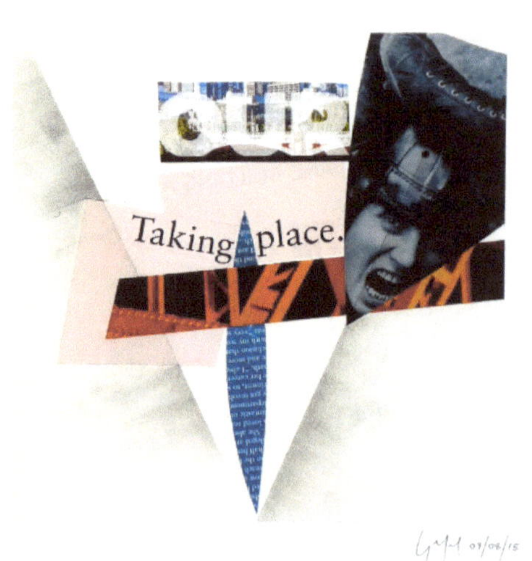

006 **Of men a vague policy ram**
August 2015 (PC)

007 **Stay out of the mirror**
August 2015 (PC)

008 **Cut to the quick people's power**
August 2015 (PC)

009 **Taking our place**
August 2015 (PC)

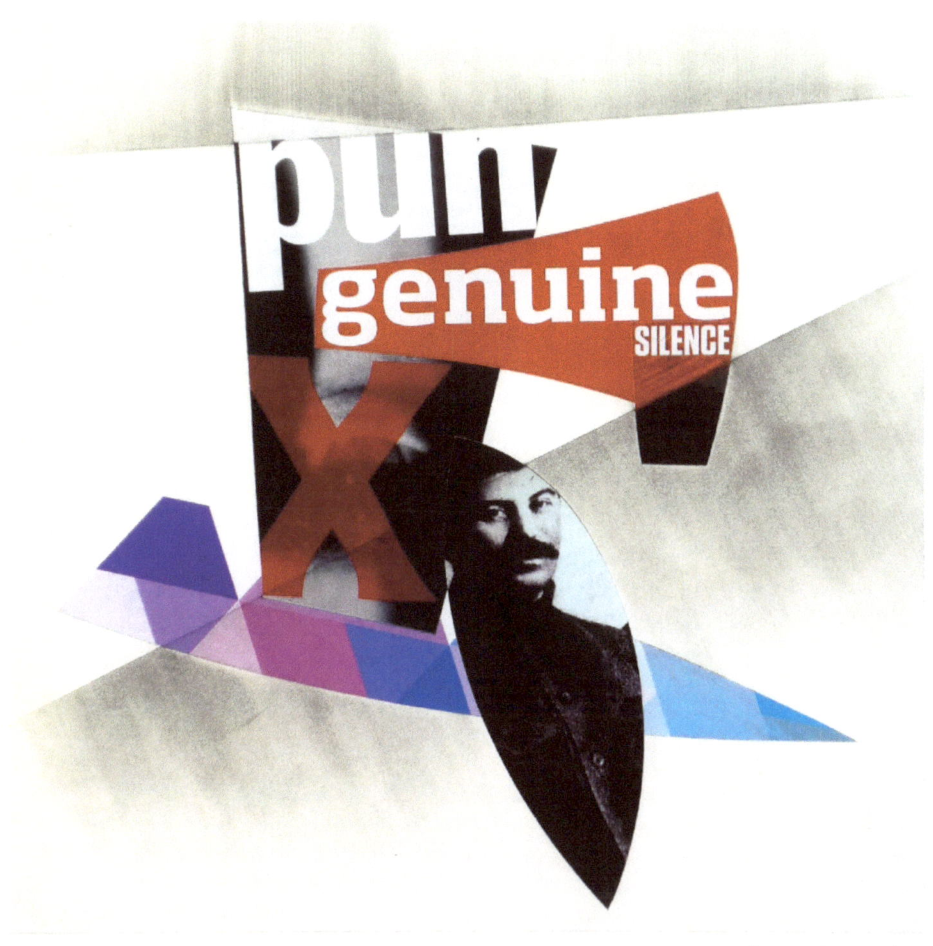

010

Pun genuine silence X

August 2015

(PC)

Pun genuine silence X

I have no fur helmet on to feel so muffled as if embalmed in nomad wrappings. It is the burden a literary man must bear to be sufficiently empowered in company. I hear your words between feint whistling things and can make sense of them as well as any Tartar or Cossack. The difference is that the syllables carried on the wind from distant places sound closer to me than my own whispers. They have become the substance of imaginary voices, in which I recognize the thoughts of a million ancestors. They may be filtered—and I mean no disrespect here—through the mind of an oblivious individual but they sing nevertheless and intoxicate me rendering my limbs hollow and elastic.

I run through chequered lands marking off each sacred site along the valley sides until I find at last a settlement high up in the hills. There are eyes in the cliffs that surround its steep fields with screed. Some few of those progenitors that circle here strain to see the visitor—me—and I bathe in their cold gaze. It tumbles down on me like moorland acid on black rock and grey stone. It stains my memories iron red with resolve.

I have been named many times, by brothers, by lovers, by enemies and by legend. What little concern I had for humanity is gone out on the wind into the darkness. Now I call myself Steely.

All the wise dead have done in the end is to remind me that my resistance is a wasted gesture. No matter how determined and resilient I appear, before too long it will all fold in on itself and swallow me whole. They surround me like a chain and freeze my soul.

No wonder I am so vicious. No wonder I find so readily resonant words to incite violence. I am that most dangerous sort of wordsmith, a poet. My thoughts rattle around the city squares and wrap the forest in a seductive blanket of sentiment. I thrive on your bleeding gullibility. With it I saturate the floors of school rooms and village halls, courts and clinics, mortuaries and mausoleums. When I speak there is ringing in everyone's ears.

The years roll on. Another century arrives. My ghost infuses a hypocrite here, a fraudster there, and terrorist mummification rituals unfold according to the sheer beauty and solidity of my nightmares.

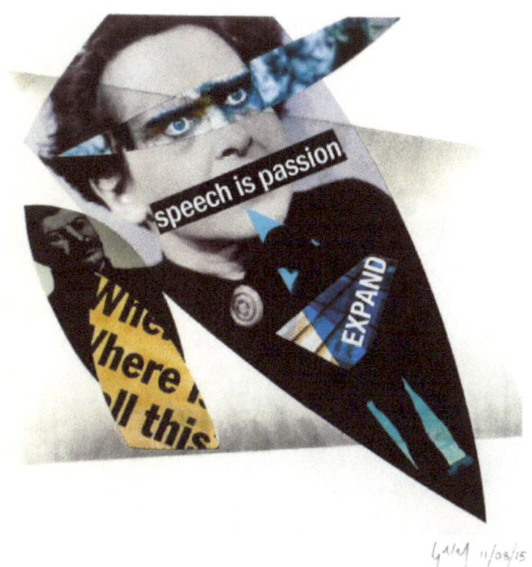

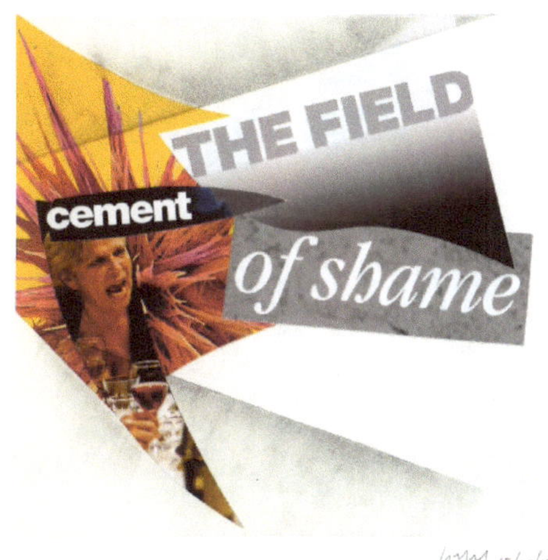

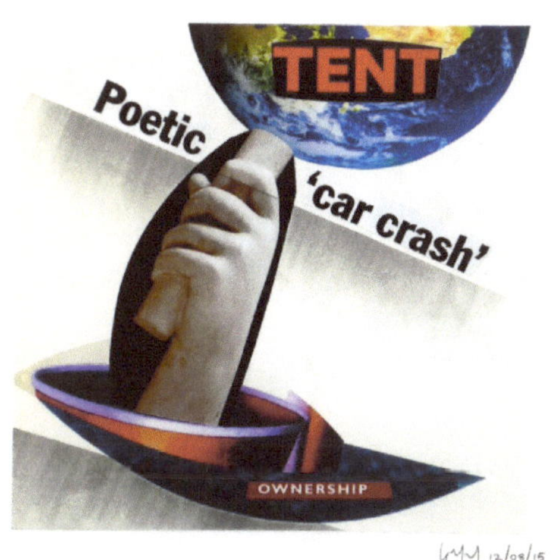

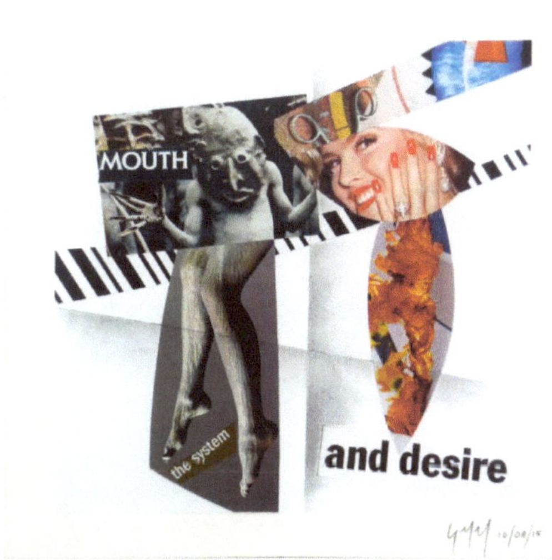

011 **Speech is passion expand when where is all this**
August 2015 (PC)

012 **Tent poetic 'car crash' ownership**
August 2015 (PC)

013 **Cement the field of shame**
August 2015 (PC)

014 **Mouth the system and desire**
August 2015 (PC)

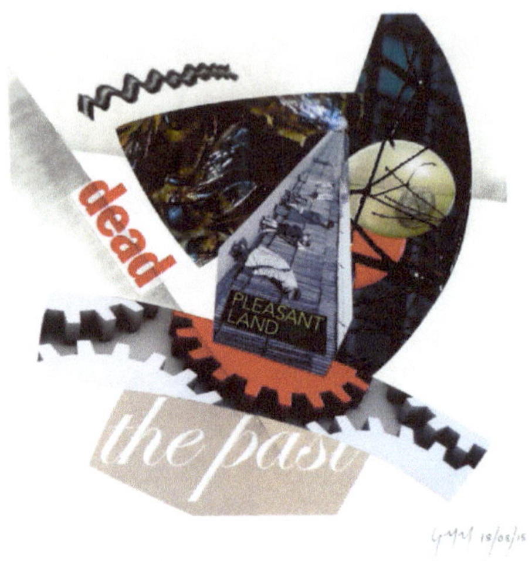

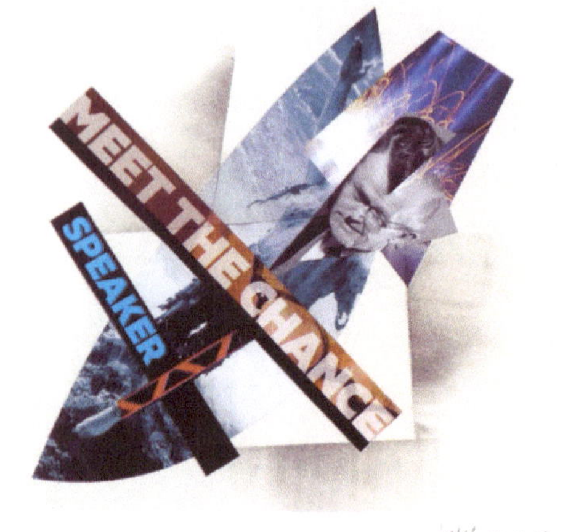

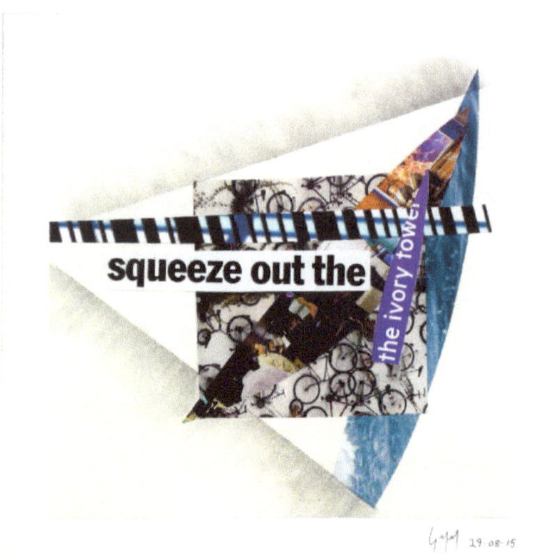

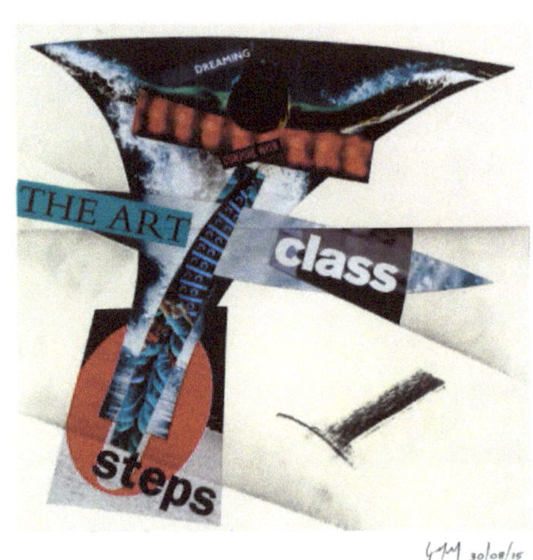

015 **Dead pleasant land the past**
August 2015 (PC)

016 **Squeeze out the the ivory tower**
August 2015 (PC)

017 **Meet the chance speaker**
August 2015 (PC)

018 **Dreaming conjure with the art class steps**
August 2015 (PC)

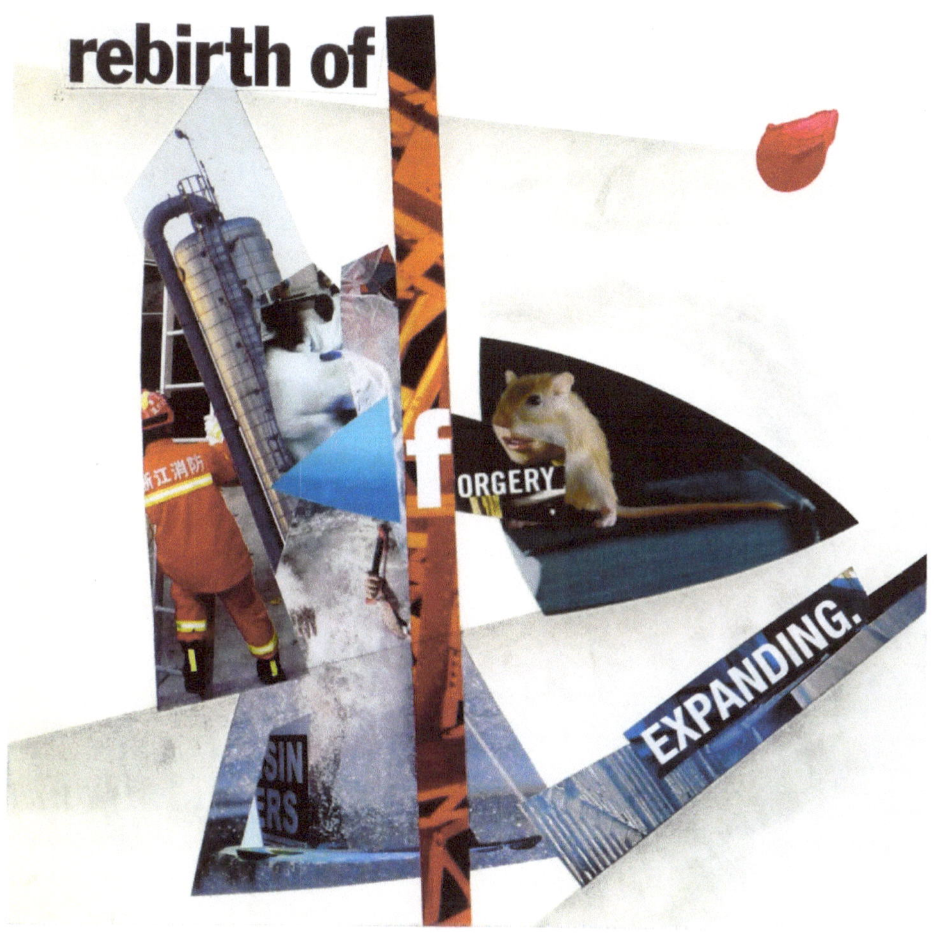

02/09/15

019

Rebirth of forgery sin[n]ers expanding

September 2015

(PAC)

Rebirth of forgery sin[n]ers expanding

The morning air seems cleaner than ever. I take deep breaths on the walk to work. All I hear are the trees and the birds. It is almost impossible to believe that this turnaround is entirely accidental, but it is. I have to keep reminding myself that, before the bubble burst, there were fires everywhere belching out black smoke and there were pools of acid collecting in the streets giving off strange and poisonous vapours. In the infinity of re-joined humanity those toxic elements have dissipated at last: the heavy stuff dissolved in dirty rain and filtered through the earth into deep reservoirs; the gaseous stuff lifted to the outer limits of the mesosphere to succumb to the cosmic blast.

And so it begins with the marriage of heaven and hell. Clashing figures in the volatile atmosphere here between the exposed surfaces of uncertain heroes. They exchange raw tablets of insidious digital floss so that sparks fly and numb exposed nerves. This is communication at its most energetic and least effective. The antagonists are refractory towers blending the sky with rare spirits and launching into the crowd as a double helix, doubling itself and splitting, doubling itself again and so on *ad infinitum*. It took a rare mind to see life this way without reinventing an old theology—bless you wild man.

For us lesser spots on the neurological horizon the scene is more prosaic. There is a nuclear exchange. (Some laboratory test will determine how this could happen without permanently darkening the sky.) Imagine in the aftermath ladders propped against the charcoal trunks of urban trees and low walls carrying shadows into eternity. Birds fly off and a mile away fall as ashes, and beneath the black surface there are already the stirrings of ants and primitive conifers. It is winter and then it is spring again. As all the excess heat escapes into the space between water molecules, as if by magic, order emerges in a new form and it is the small things that will rule for a while.

Consider each spot where hope for humanity is erased and soon enough it reappears. A fireman is drowned and a mouse pauses to take in the scene. A spaceman orbits for the last time, descending into hot nitrogen and oxygen atoms to become a primitive seed. A million years on firemen return to walk in an emerald forest crisscrossed with cellulose streets scented for cycad dreams and coraciiform accomplishments, and spacemen orbit once again to watch for aberrant blooms and erratic movements.

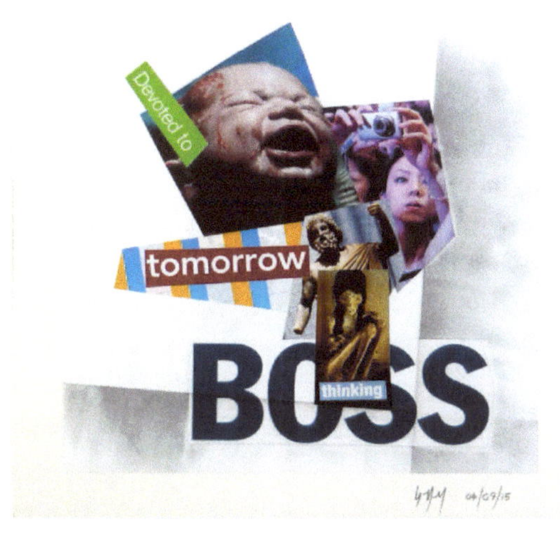

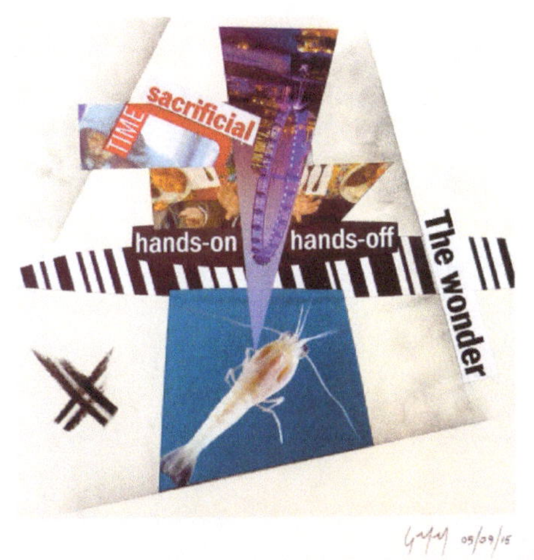

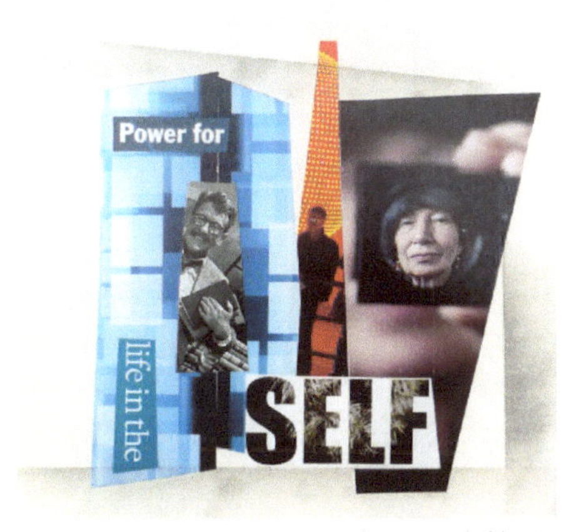

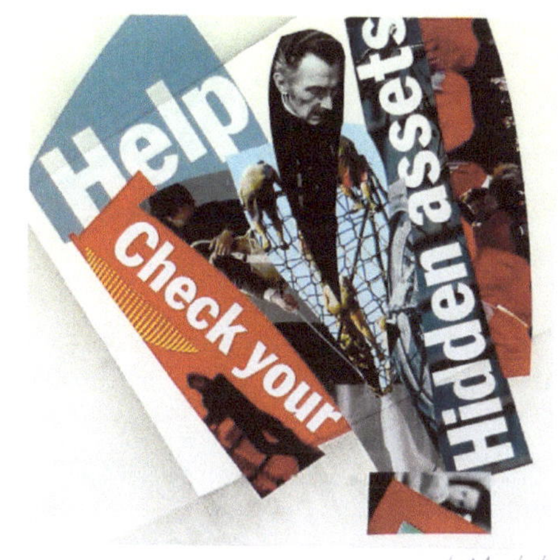

020 **Devoted to tomorrow thinking boss**
September 2015 (PC)

021 **Power for life in the self**
September 2015 (PC)

022 **Time sacrificial hands-on hands-off the wonder**
September 2015 (PC)

023 **Help check your hidden assets**
September 2015 (PC)

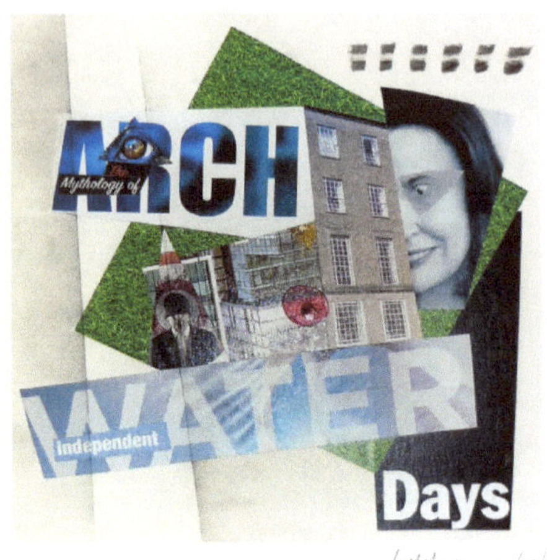

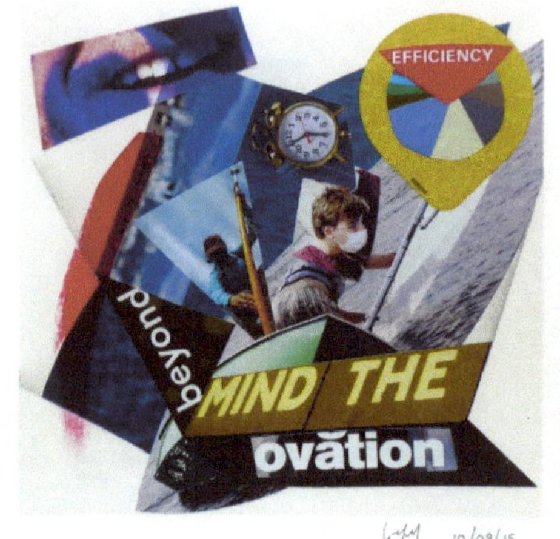

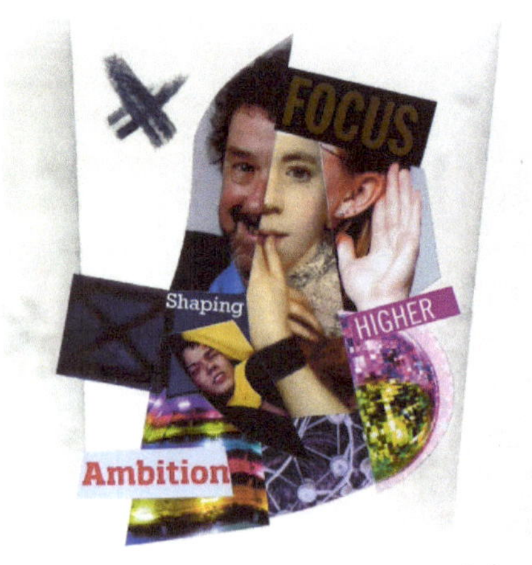

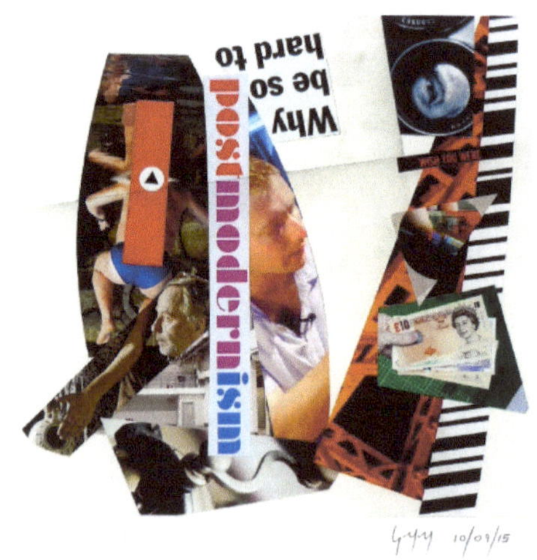

024 **The arch mythology of independent water days**
September 2015 (PAC)

025 **Focus shaping higher ambition**
September 2015 (PC)

026 **Efficiency beyond mind the ovation**
September 2015 (PAC)

027 **Why be so hard to postmodernism wish you were**
September 2015 (PC)

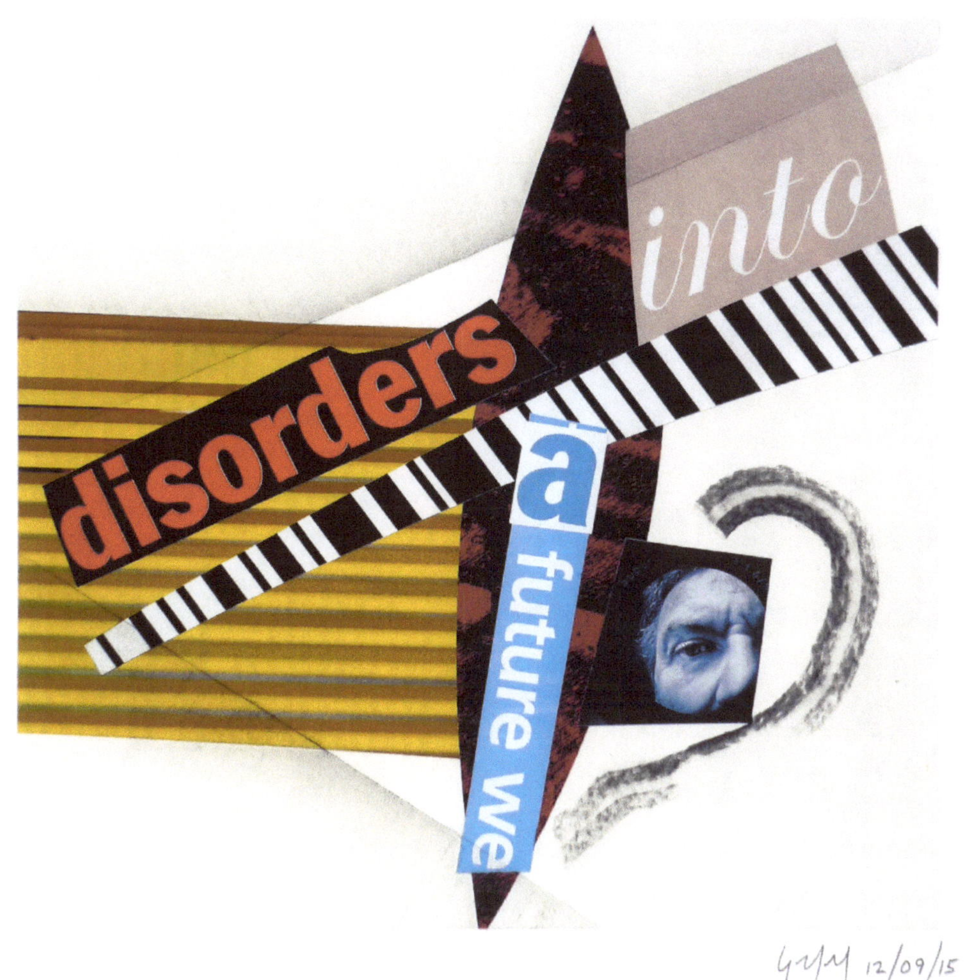

028

Disorders into a future we

September 2015

(PC)

Disorders into a future we

Novelty inspires order. This is the orthodoxy. But it is not as simple as it sounds. To face up to the strangeness of dislocation and distance effects one must consider the behaviour of the isolated individual before accepting the idea that collectively humanity is as bound by the physiology of a breathing universe as are the constituents of an atom or the galaxies clustering and colliding in deep space. Give the process a go. It is worth the effort.

You will be as the dust caught in a philosophical mesh, as am I, but that is fine. To have original thoughts on the matter is not the point. If it were we would never have to thank the valuable theorists in whose wake we work.

Overall the insights of this emerging network suggest contrariness. Recent members may appear to have found logical structure, but this is an illusion. An archaeology of ideas in the journals of numerous writers reveals a different story—we may thank Foucault for the method—one dowsed in obliquity of the most purposeful sort. It seems that axes and symmetries are far from the norm. All stable things, the most fundamental indeed, the so-called *constants*, are on the move, and it is their drift that constitutes the possibilities of being in all their variety.

Imagine, a way to describe reality beyond the myth of creative polarity. It was an ecstatic feeling just for me to hear this, and then the brain begins to race—so many consequences and implications to explore.

They say that one must be able to map the past, not to see it full-blown, which would be an incompletable task, but simply to admit oneself into history, to find one's place in the field of conceptually related perspectives. There are many histories, after all, all of which are recast and rewritten even in being reread.

See how this small philosophy aggregates? Being is actually too violent properly to order the landscape. And so we give names to mythical forces, for example, *evolution*. Why had there been no mention of that symptom of imperial guilt? Following the legacy of evolutionary thought one is led to believe that it takes evolution to influence the whole and catch the idiosyncratic. Hence the micro-evolutionary fallacy: in this view the individual, no matter how dynamic, evaporates. We are here, your self is real, and polarity is irrelevant: all of these things can be said without irony. It is the unpredictable possibility that comes to haunt the pasture.

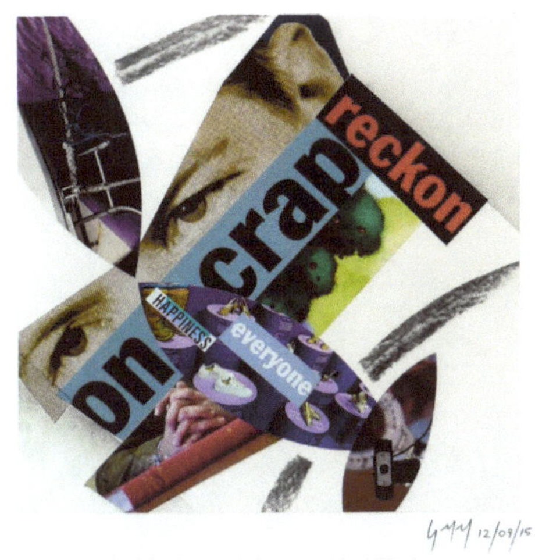

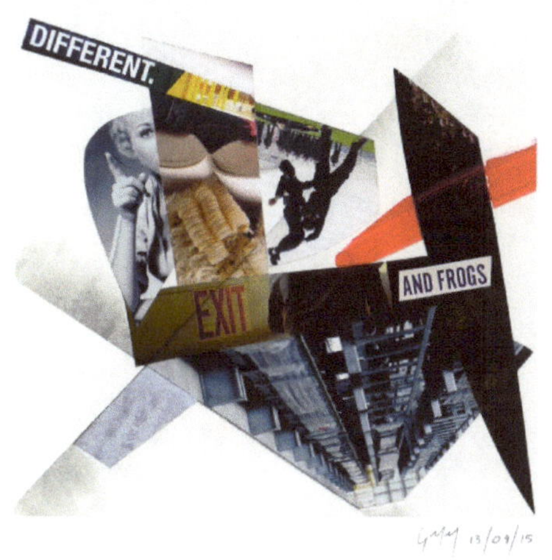

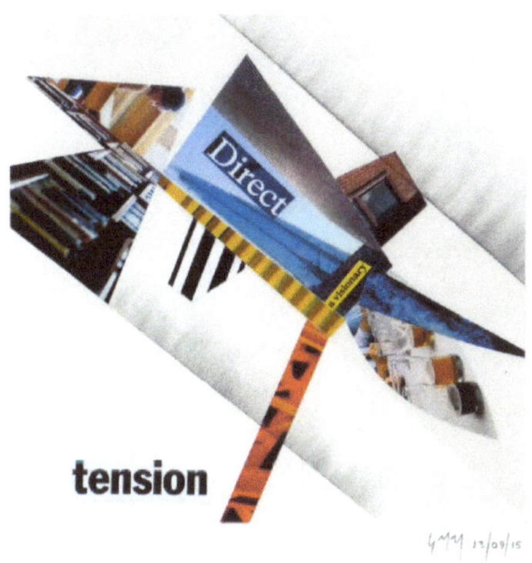

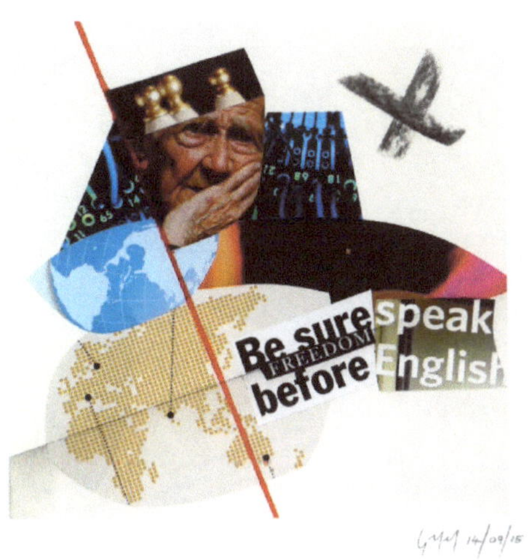

029 **Reckon on happiness crap everyone**
September 2015 (PC)

030 **Direct a visionary tension**
September 2015 (PC)

031 **Different exit and frogs**
September 2015 (PAC)

032 **Be sure speak freedom before English**
September 2015 (PAC)

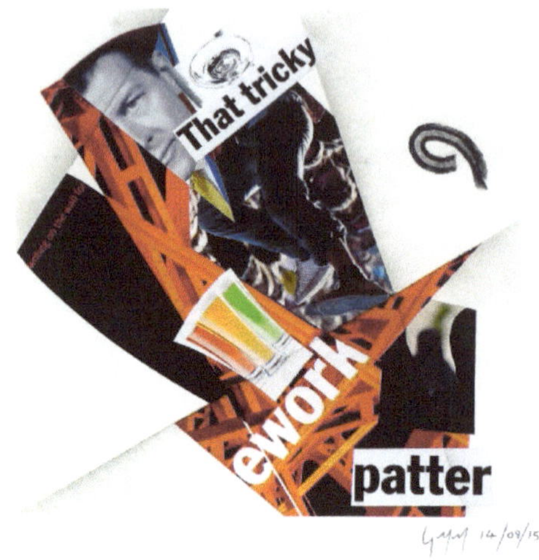

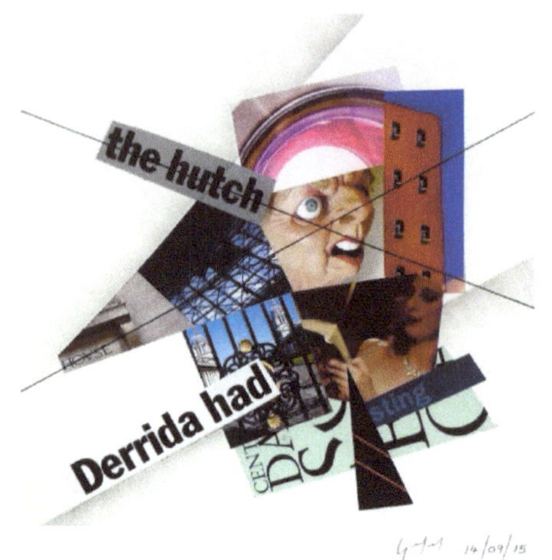

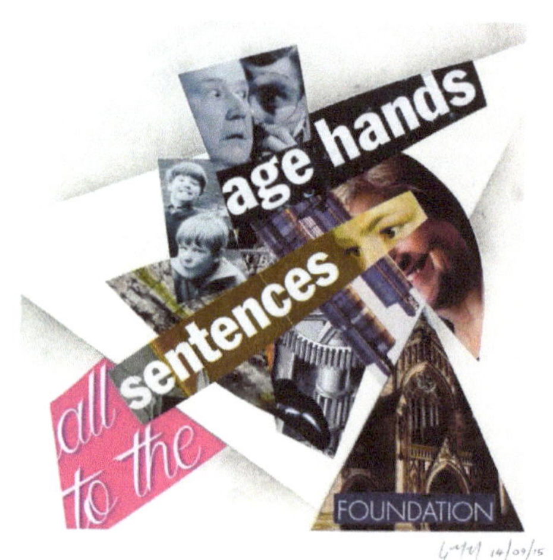

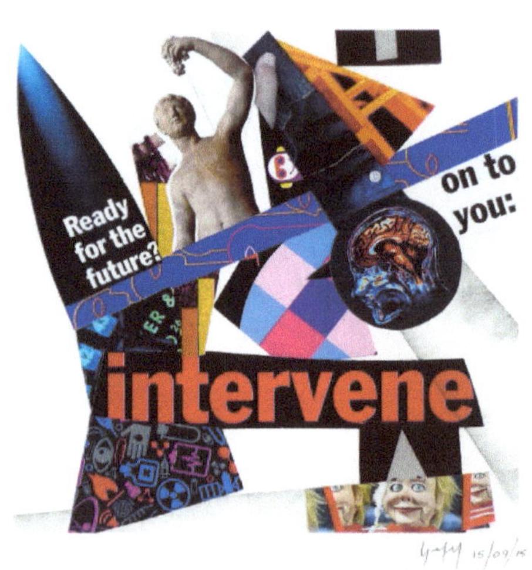

033 **Writing on the wall for that tricky e-work patter**
September 2015 (PC)

034 **Age hands all sentences to the foundation**
September 2015 (PC)

035 **The hutch - house - Derrida had sting**
September 2015 (PCI)

036 **Ready for the future on to you intervene**
September 2015 (PC)

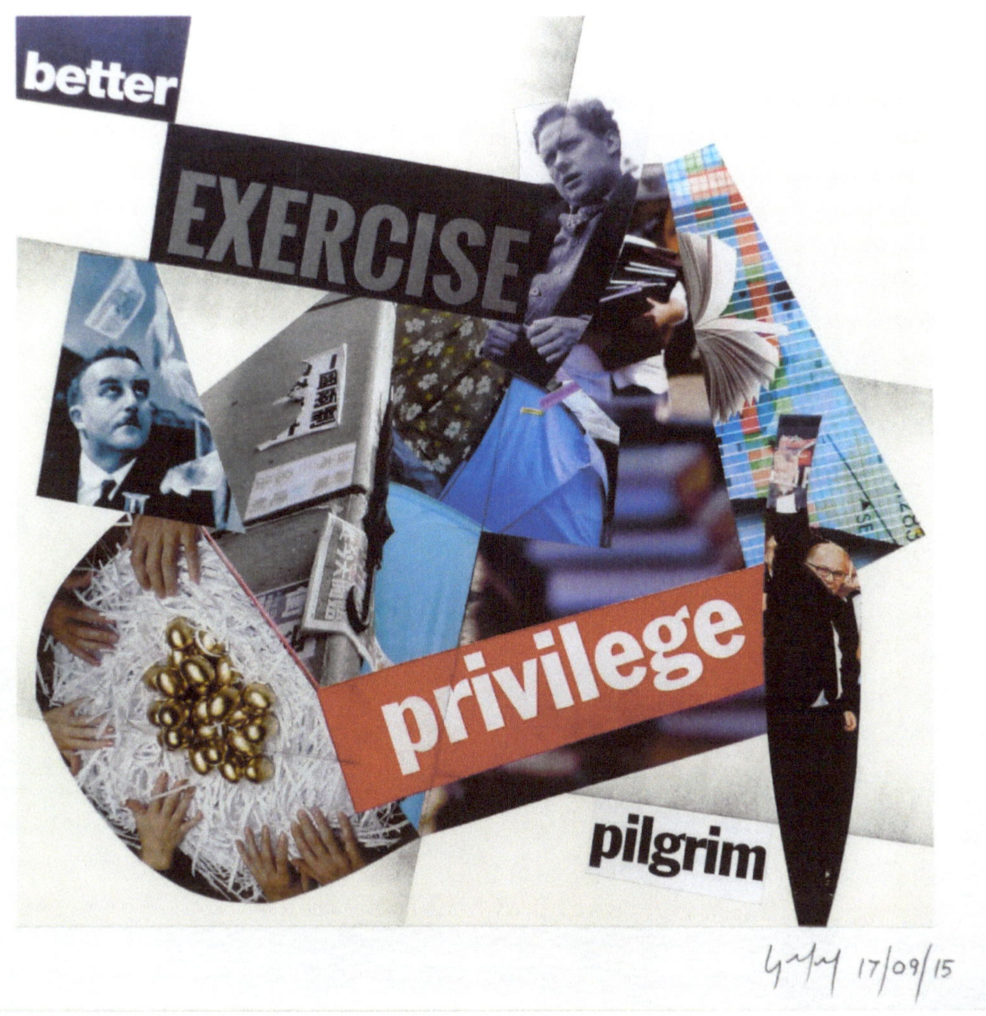

037

Better exercise privilege pilgrim

September 2015

(PC)

Better exercise privilege pilgrim

Jack, it's alright, it's only money. In this slow black, low slack, blow by blow, class attack on the economy of gaps the little man has lost at last all hope of autonomy. This is how it goes—echoes there of a delirium to come—landscapes are a platform for barbarians and become differentiated as they advance. One strip was the womb from which you sprang and now you have spawned airscapes as an art that cost the earth.

Stall-turning is the ruling metaphor for the long hours spent in the city of dreams. Those moments when everything is still and silent vanish into the blur—the blade draw, the brush stroke, the wind roar, the camera pan, the screaming glissando—between tenor drum and cymbal stand.

Golden eggs in a paper nest hatch before you take flight on finger wings. Some pterosaur memory of predation preys on your mind and after you crash you think of a brother launching body colour into space. On each great paper sheet the ghylls and city labyrinths are catastrophes that conspire against struggling forms of life. Those visions exist at the edge of chaos and from that point of view flesh also unfolds in geological time.

Today generations may even have the detection tools, as emotional training through our trials reveals the threshold-ridden domesticity of nomadic resistance. We know that dogs recognize the cues and respond appropriately. This is why it is important to be canine inside the family: to relieve the need to circle through the forest at night and invent a replacement dream. Its contingencies create realistic flight through rapid eye movement.

Natural selection has more to answer for than the improbable materials buried beneath the soil. It is a stop-frame movie captured in generational rhythm. That is how one sees the bacterial writhing as something outside such a tumbling of evolutionary struggle.

Do not reach for the blinding lights. The vision you need is perspectival here, purely optical. Everything operates at a distance in a civilised condition, everything in its correct relationship to everything else, with only the minimum of tolerance to allow for adjustment and resettlement.

If you want my advice, I say: chase the goose and don't forget your umbrella. There are many more golden eggs to be found in the rain. I bet you can hear Dylan leafing through the dog-eared pages of his camping manual and the ventriloquist giving him voice.

> What difference does it make unless some rich bastard gets on the road, eh? Daydreams, just daydreams passing in a blur.

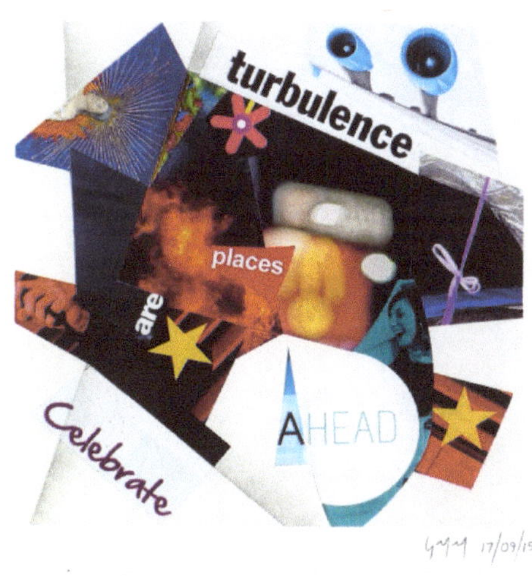

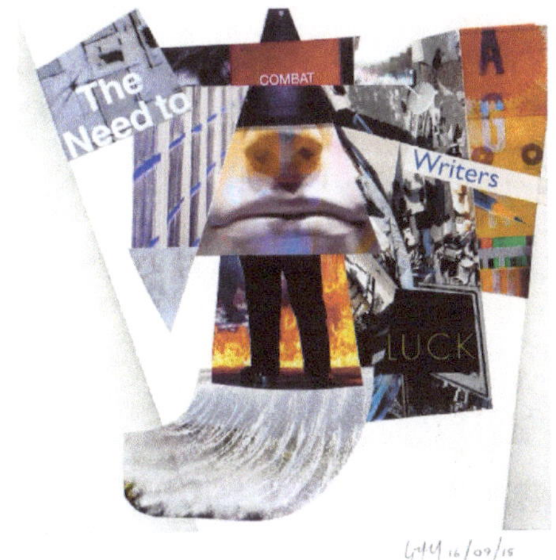

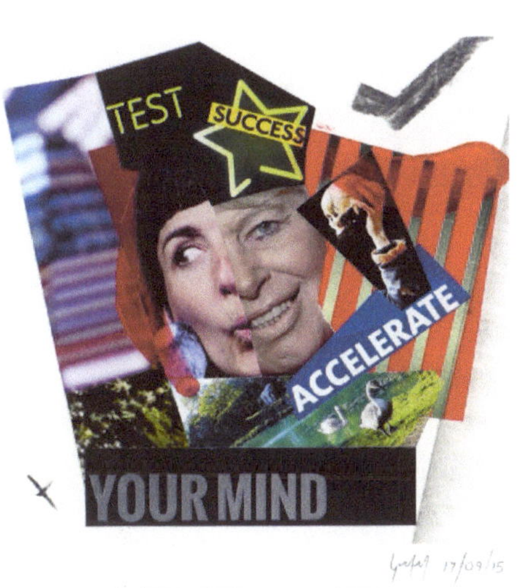

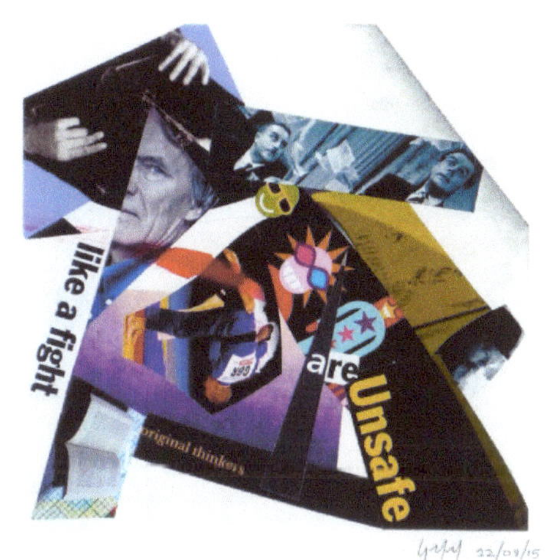

038 **Turbulence places are ahead celebrate**
September 2015 (PC)

039 **Test success accelerate your mind**
September 2015 (PAC)

040 **The need to combat writers luck**
September 2015 (PC)

041 **Like a fight original thinkers are unsafe**
September 2015 (PAC)

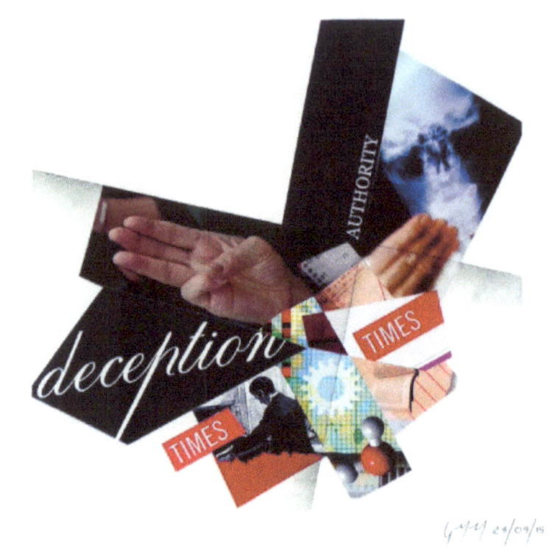

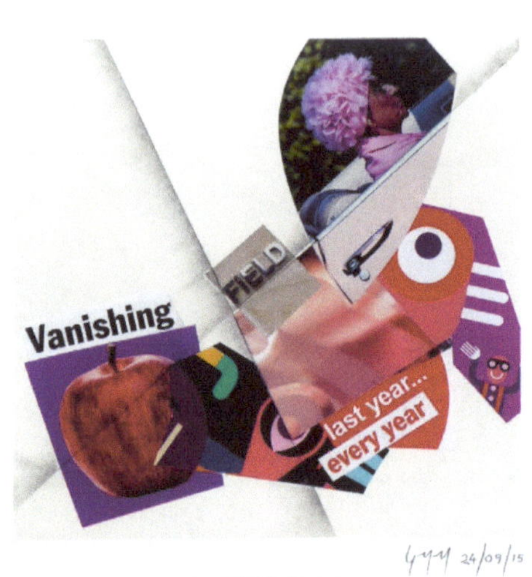

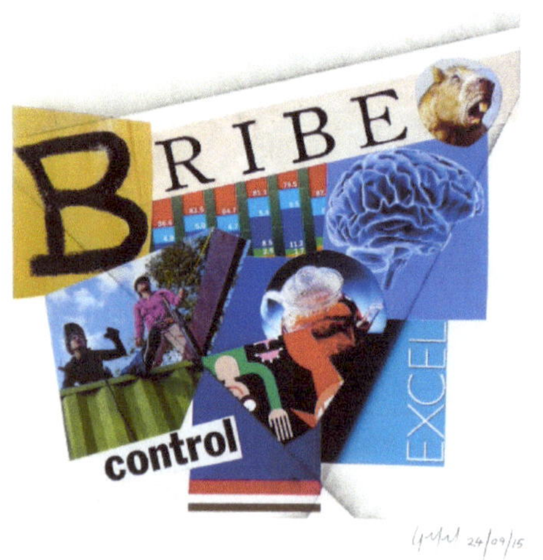

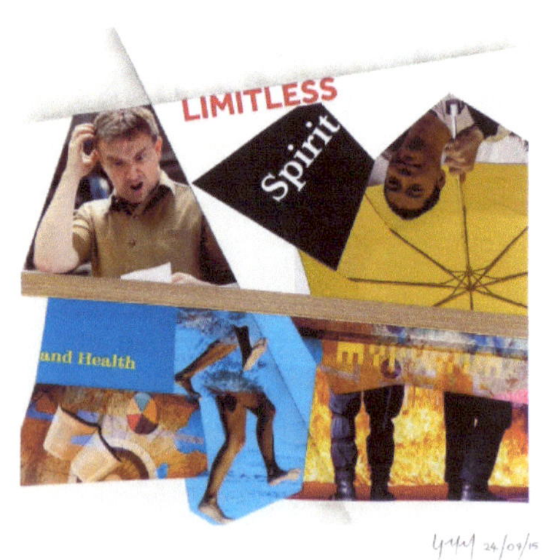

042 **Deception times authority times**
September 2015 (PC)

043 **Bribe control excel**
September 2015 (PC)

044 **Vanishing field last year … every year**
September 2015 (PC)

045 **Limitless spirit and health**
September 2015 (PAC)

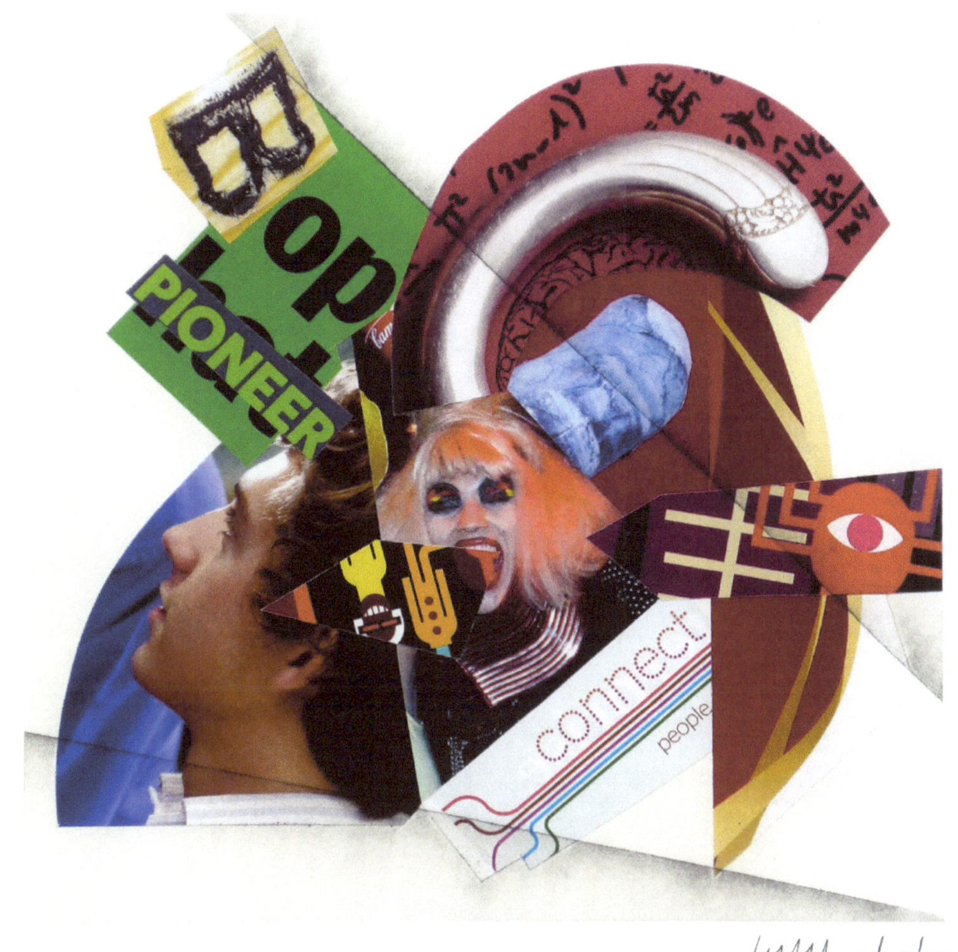

046

Bop pioneer connect people

September 2015

(PC)

Bop pioneer connect people

This robust society is a strange place from which to take heavenly glances to the side. For fear of the vertiginous nature of nature, one does not look down. One stabilizes oneself—imagines wings and a sacred hollow in the air—and walks the tightrope.

All the while from the floor below clowns bawl insults in some mysterious mechanical language and create havoc. Poised on the line that divides the silence from the noise I am forever surprised, but it is neither right nor wrong in the end, that this site of dynamic conflict persists. On one side some floss-headed unicorn teases its exploding grey matter into the mathematical abyss—if there is a purpose to this it remains an enigma. On the other the tormented citizen, veiled and distracted, continues to ease forward.

There are millions of us and questions occur to me. Is it our intention to embroil dictators without warning in one damn thing after another, in the ebbs and flows of irregular seasons and the serene networks of time? Or are we automata simply playing out our anonymous programming? Maybe we are drifting vessels at the mercy of dust, radiation and gravity wells sometimes approaching a surface closely enough to hear machine conversations. I know they continue on this unstable planet. Bits bounce around the ether agglomerated into billion-part tragedies. They are a beautiful flock of cooperative butterflies, the effect of which is meteorological and piles radioactive sands upon the land. We must talk of this more …

◆

In our discussions of landscape I remember an invisible hand. It must have been Wilde even though I had never heard of him. His stories of the organizations that implement that one damned history, the right and ruthless traces of survival: they mesmerize me. But it is just evolution in a nosedive, the sixth mass extinction, a collapse so sudden that theory cannot answer the questions posed.

Intelligence today is neither perplexing nor trivial. This is why we experience emergence and extinction as puzzles. Our maze brains are just too contained even as we edge further on in our entranced prosthetic condition and connect people. Consequently, I rely entirely on the persistence of vision to mask the pixilation of my delirium. Moment by moment the form and brilliance of the world is obliterated and the varied consistencies of geological and biological composites are lost to uniform simulations in digital grit.

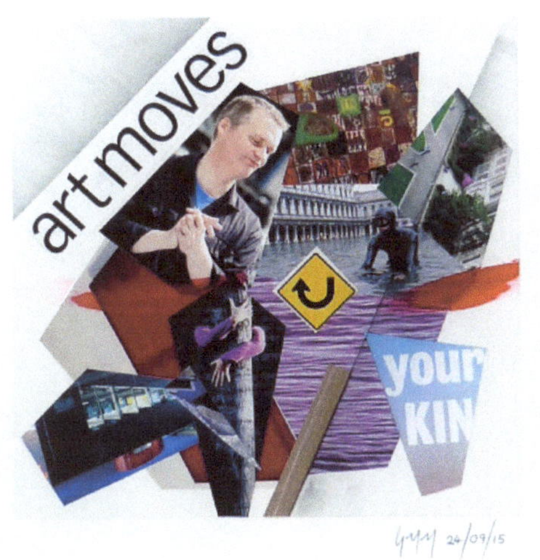

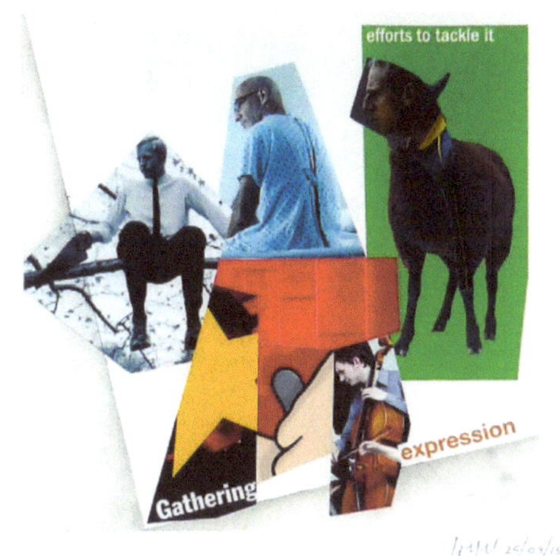

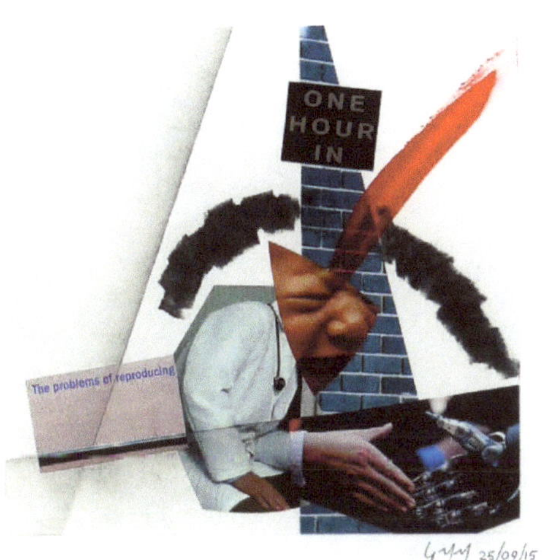

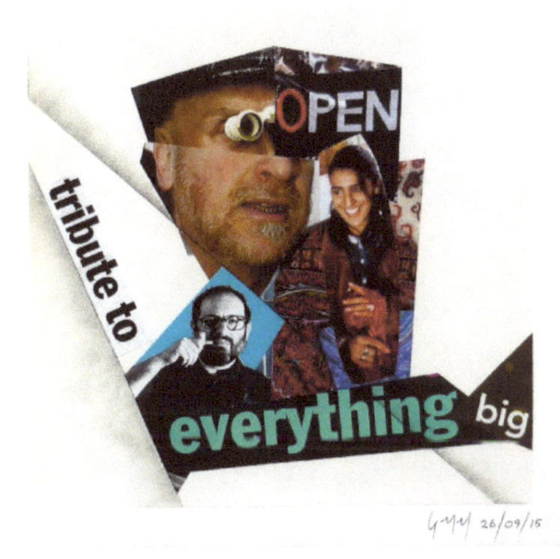

047 **Art moves your kin**
September 2015 (PAC)

048 **One hour in the problems of reproducing**
September 2015 (PAC)

049 **Efforts to tackle it gathering expression**
September 2015 (PC)

050 **Open tribute to everything big**
September 2015 (PC)

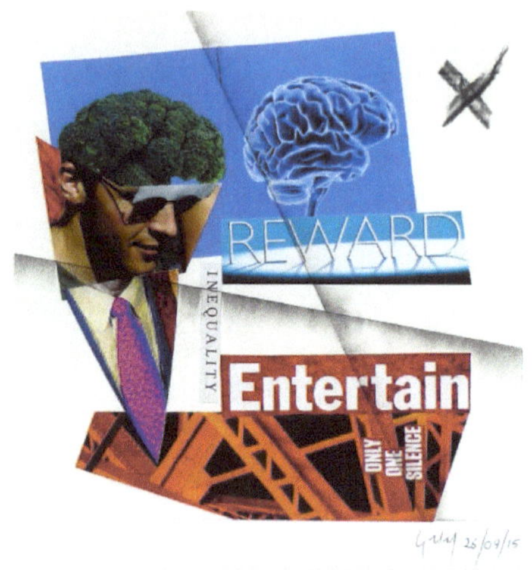

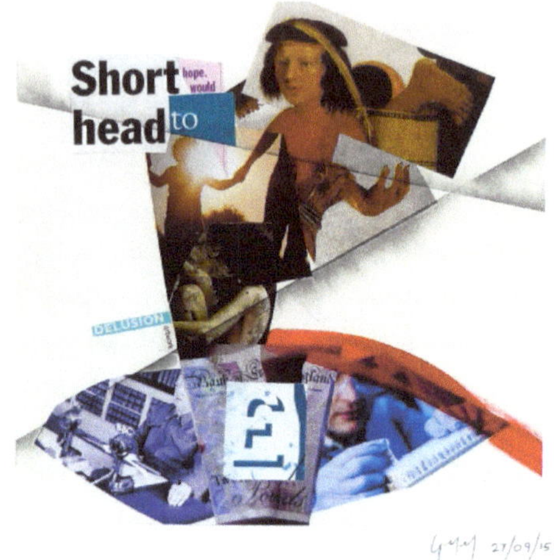

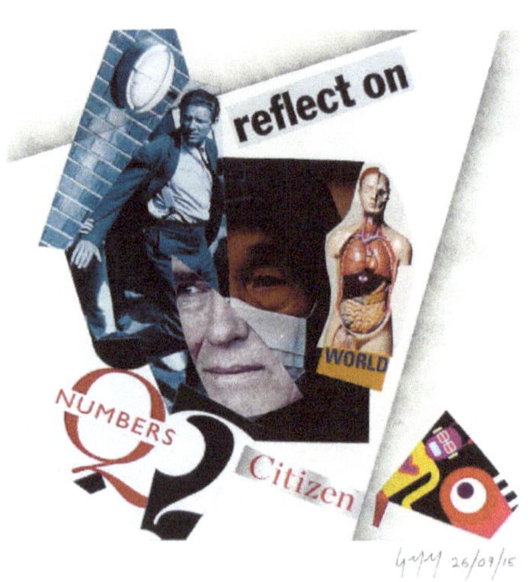

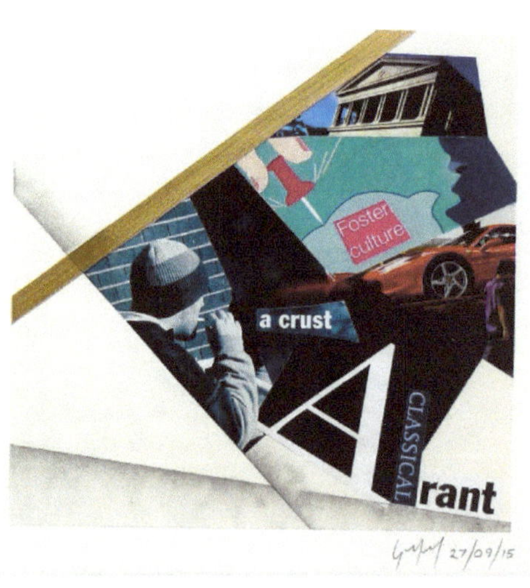

051 **Reward inequality entertain only one silence**
September 2015 (PC)

052 **Reflect on world numbers citizen**
September 2015 (PC)

053 **Short hope would head to delusion artwork**
September 2015 (PAC)

054 **Foster culture a crust a classical rant**
September 2015 (PAC)

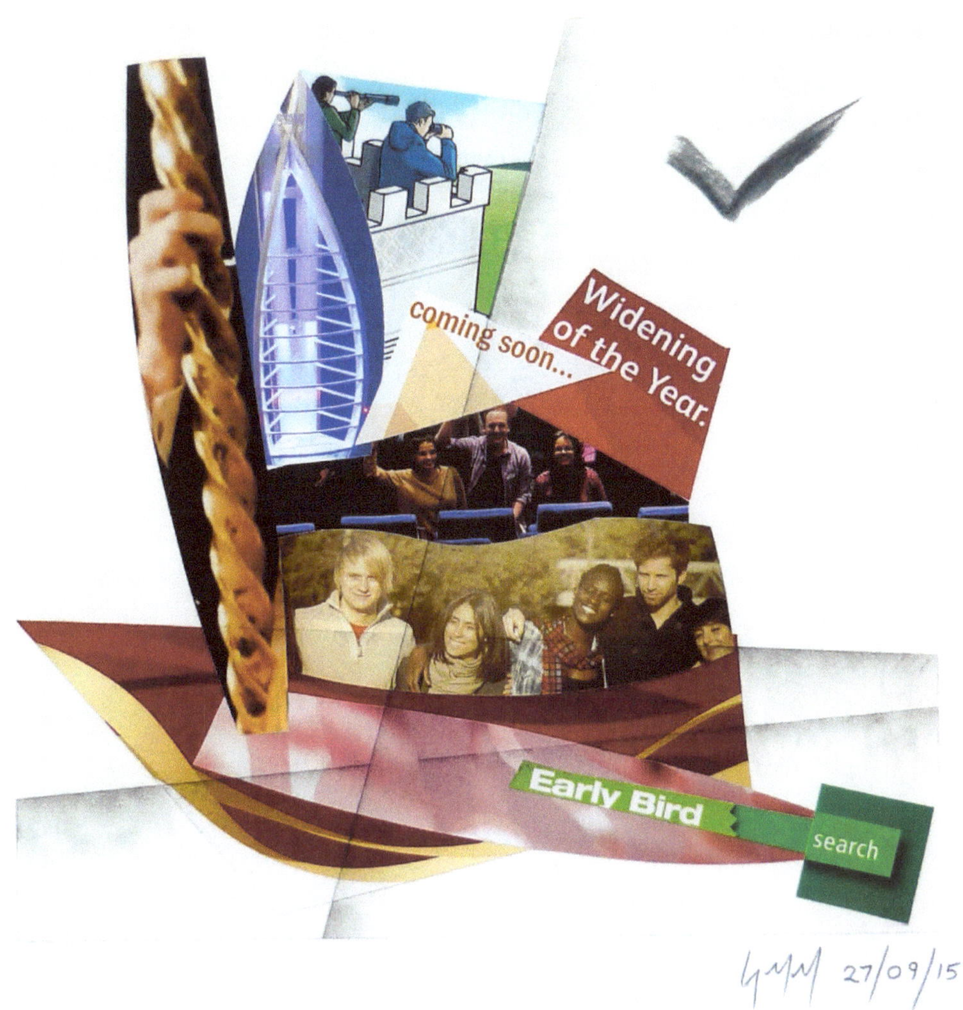

055

Widening of the year coming soon early bird search

September 2015

(PC)

Widening of the year coming soon early bird search

And sail the wide accountan-cy

So the circus sings. But there is no bottom quite like the crimson swash of a dhow departing secure harbour and heading off for a whole year. Think neither of a pleasure cruise on the turquoise of a wide Arabian bay nor even of a fishing trip to the calm embrace of some distant tropical lagoon. This is an adventure that pushes beyond that mysterious horizon and skirts darker shores to the south and east.

Within weeks we pass places that harbour pirates who are quite interested in our shiny skin and the ransom that might be extorted for its return intact. We are ten toothy faces, excited and fit, laughing and full of ambition. We love each other now and still are friends at our furthest point from home. But it is at that moment that our bonds are tested and some broken.

We fear the early rising of older crew. With the failing of a newly pointed public spirit come stories of biblical fish and the right to value life and death. Mention of tourist attractions soon puts us in peril. Now in turbid waters, Australia's one great killing myth is upon us damaging the imagination and making red-eye wrecks of us all.

A hurricane approaches, black tumbling over midnight blue. The sea is lifted and dropped, its valley sides topped with running white horses that race deep rivers of glacial purity in the saline turmoil for a thousand miles on. In the lightest sail I cover such a distance. In an hour I am lost, in a day making landfall in another world, a world of black dust and guano-spattered ice. Then I am sunbathing by the Endeavour's barley twist daydreams beached on an ochre shore beneath a silver lace and fox fur sky.

You see what has happened? Collage number fifty-five looks like a boat and it reminded me of walking on the Corniche in Doha and coming upon the most beautiful old dhows moored in front of the flour mills. My imagination has done the rest, conflated tales of Somali pirates in the seas to the south of the Arabian Peninsula, descriptions of coral island lagoons, the lunacy of the Python team's *The Crimson Permanent Assurance*, the myth that in Australia if it moves it can kill you, and part of a lecture I heard many years ago by a member of the British Antarctic Survey. It all sounds quite plausible now doesn't it? Are you moved?

Maybe I should continue …

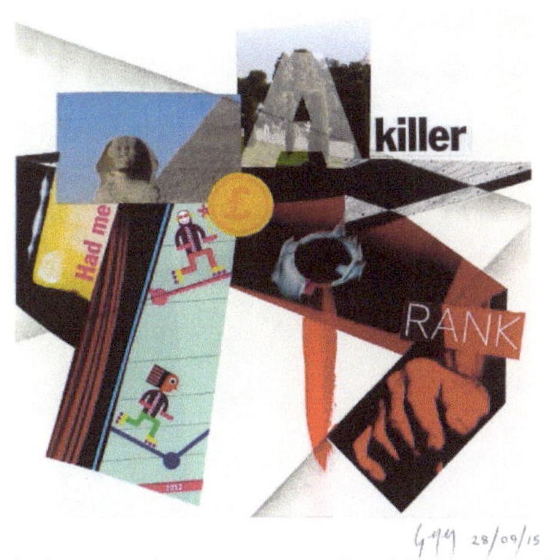

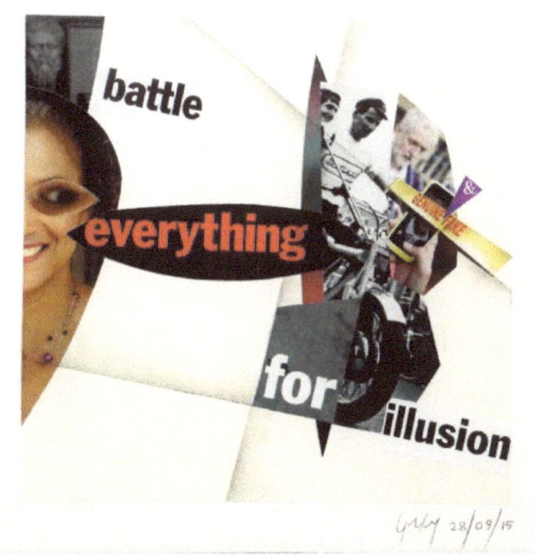

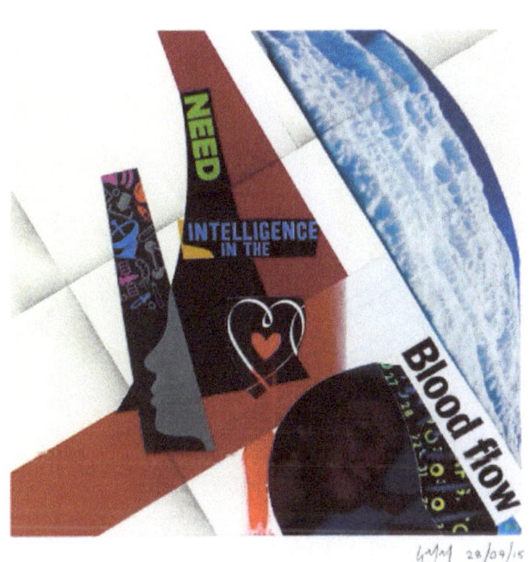

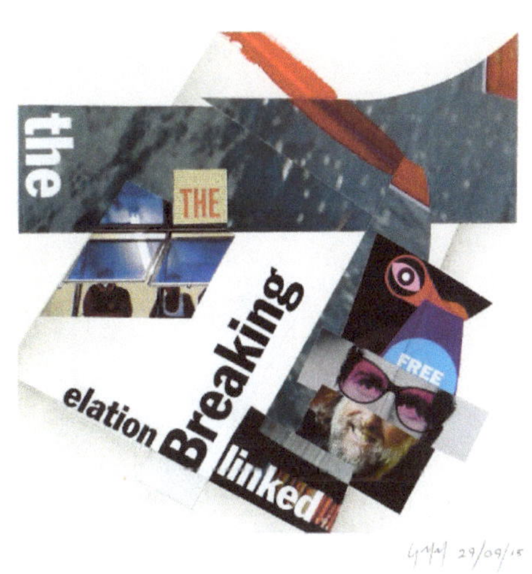

056 **Had me a killer rank**
September 2015 (PAC)

057 **Need intelligence in the blood flow**
September 2015 (PAC)

058 **Battle everything genuine & fake for illusion**
September 2015 (PC)

059 **The THE breaking free elation linked**
September 2015 (PAC)

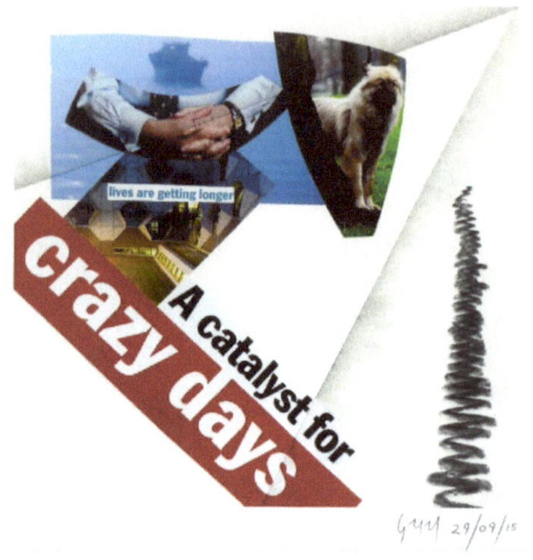

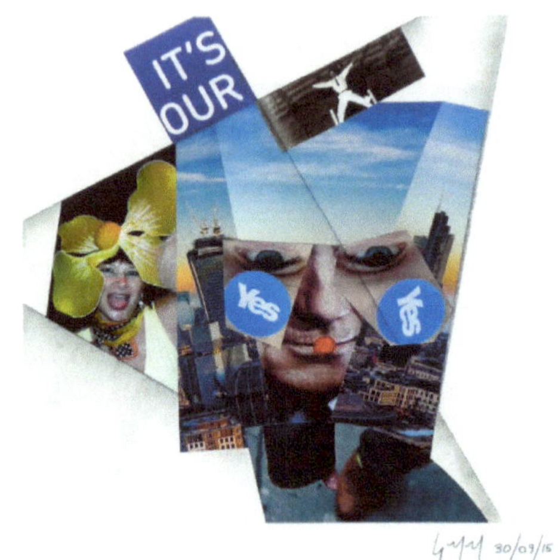

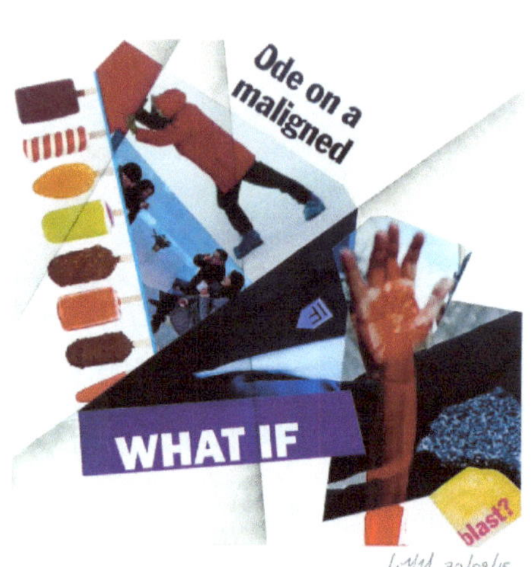

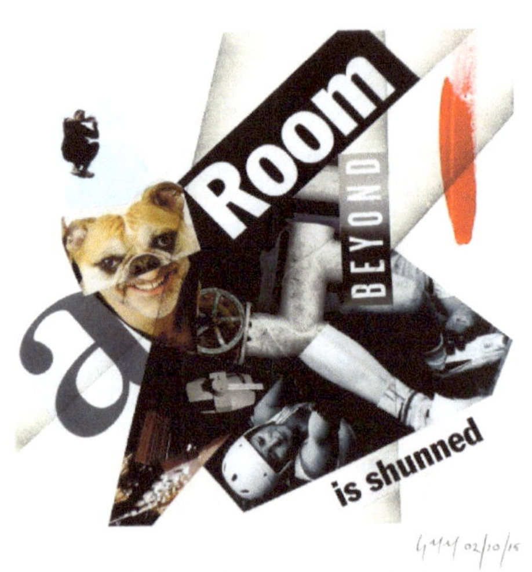

060 **Lives are getting longer a catalyst for crazy days**
September 2015 (PC)

061 **Ode on a maligned if what if blast**
September 2015 (PAC)

062 **Its our X yes yes**
September 2015 (PAC)

063 **A room beyond is shunned**
October 2015 (PAC)

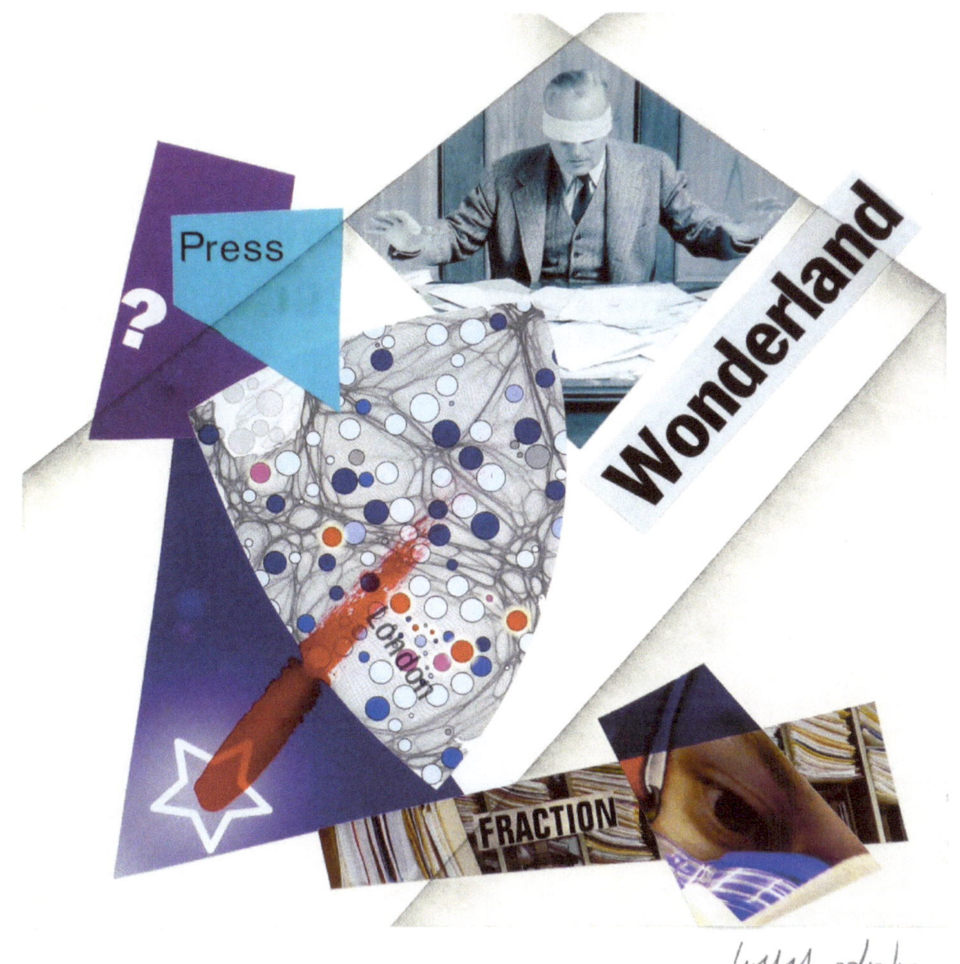

064

Press London wonderland fraction

October 2015

(PAC)

Press London wonderland fraction

You question the efficacy of buttons. They sing nevertheless and map out the space of our incipient barbarism. It is a nomadic way of seeing. Here, let me show you. If I hold my hands apart, without touching the folds of the membrane in this grey cave, even blindfolded I can see past this haze.

This is what comes of light deprivation. London, city of terrific cones, vibrates with pure electricity and bleaches the night sky. Synapses fire and all the close-range vision in history merges into haptic assumption. This is no miracle and no modern marvel either. I am simply recovering that most ancient wonderland, the spelunkers driven delirium, and covering it again with alacrity.

I mentioned the folds; see how they resemble the racks of the archive, a surface from which one can never stand back. Try and one unavoidably backs into the same surface on its return from some time past. It is a surface of folds, which itself folds through space like an abstract line. One day we must decide to what extent it bridges the generations and which of the generations it so bridges. There is no future in it either, merely repeated accretion after imperceptible delays and unpredictable stoppages. What we learn from all this is that accepting chance as a factor no longer holds the terror it once did and letting go has become a doorway to perception.

I lived down 'the noise' for seven years and over time foolishly came to believe that any journey by public transport would take an hour. I never thought to time my journeys exactly as I never felt the need to challenge or confirm my perception. I was comfortable with it and its consequences because it was, after all, a perception shared by all the people I knew there that I might visit or who might visit me. It came as a shock to discover that the spatial texture of the city, so carefully designed for by the transport executive, was not the determining factor in journey times into and out of the central zones. What matters most is one's state of mind. If it matches that of Asterion, who is cursed with labyrinthine delirium, all movement will appear circular, filled with terror and violence, and will cover the same bloody tracks and spaces again and again. Events will collapse into uniform bubbles of time and foam, hence the illusion of the hour and the abstract line.

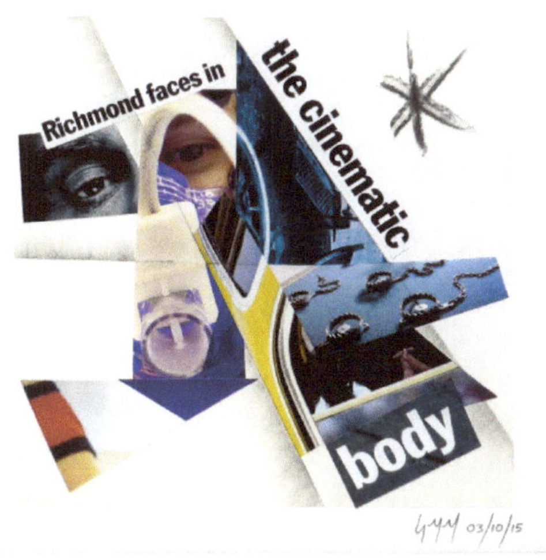

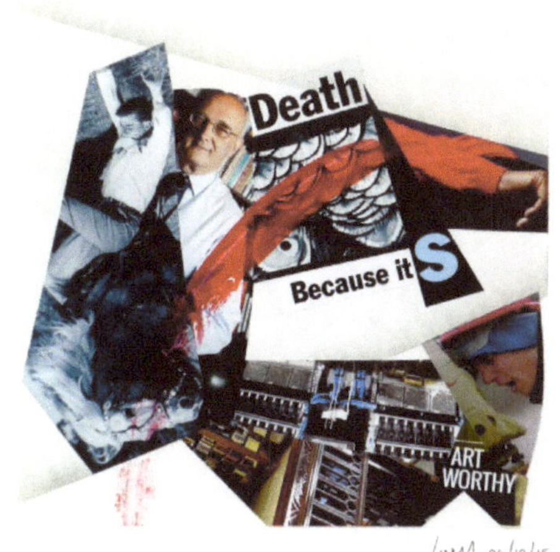

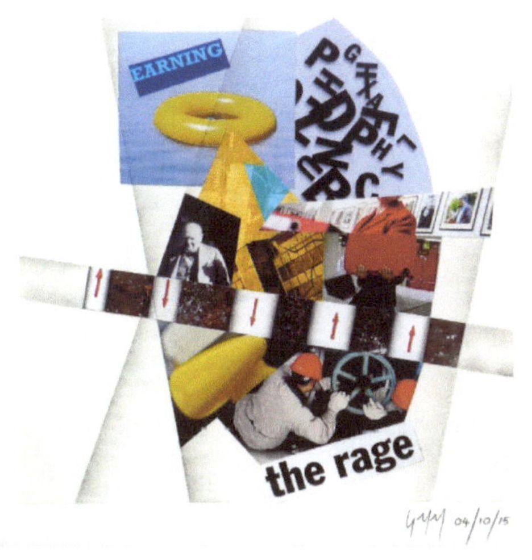

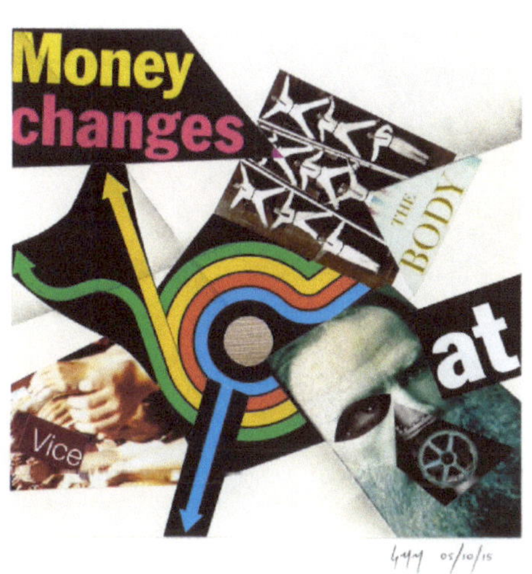

065 **Richmond faces in the cinematic body**
October 2015 (PC)

066 **Earning the rage**
October 2015 (PC)

067 **Death because its art worthy**
October 2015 (PAC)

068 **Money changes the body at vice**
October 2015 (PC)

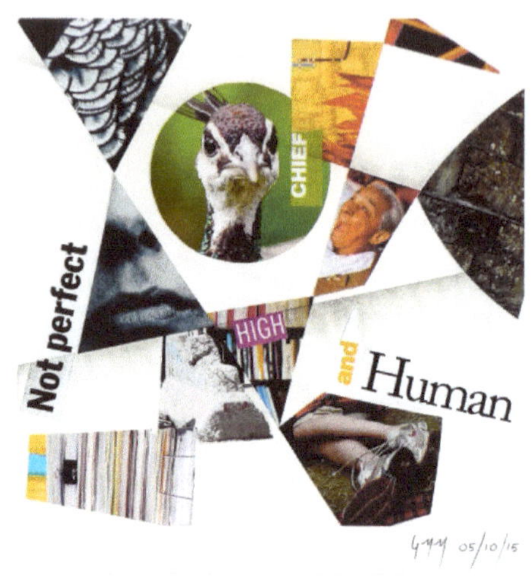

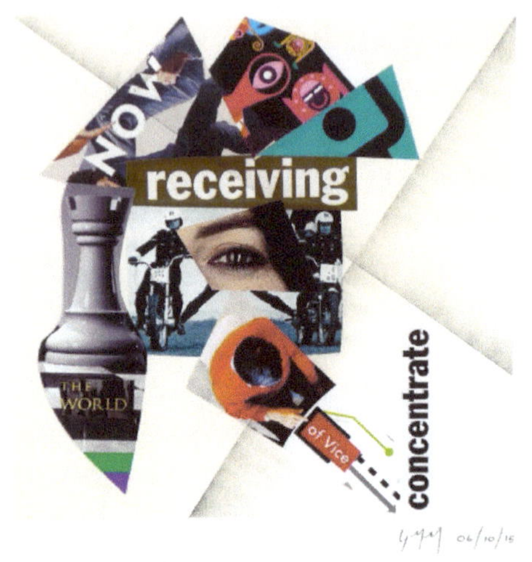

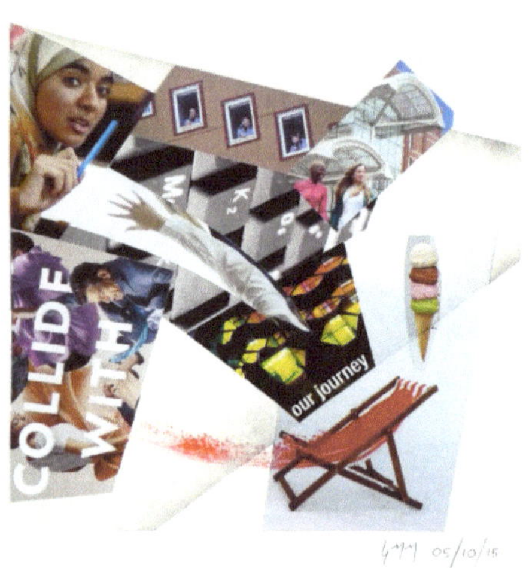

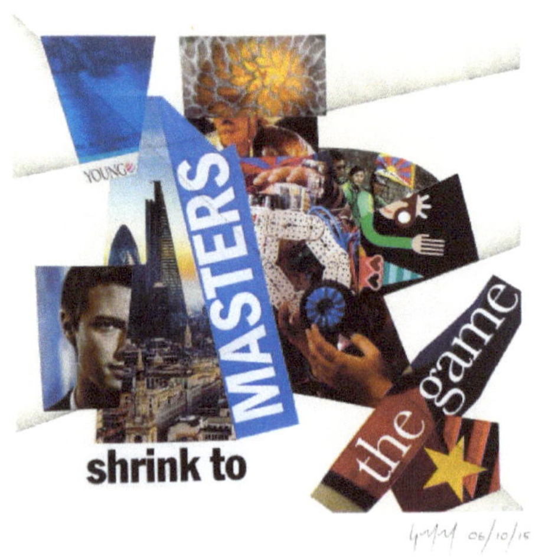

069 **Not perfect chief high and human**
October 2015 (PC)

070 **Collide with our journey**
October 2015 (PAC)

071 **Now receiving the world of vice concentrate**
October 2015 (PC)

072 **Young masters shrink to the game**
October 2015 (PC)

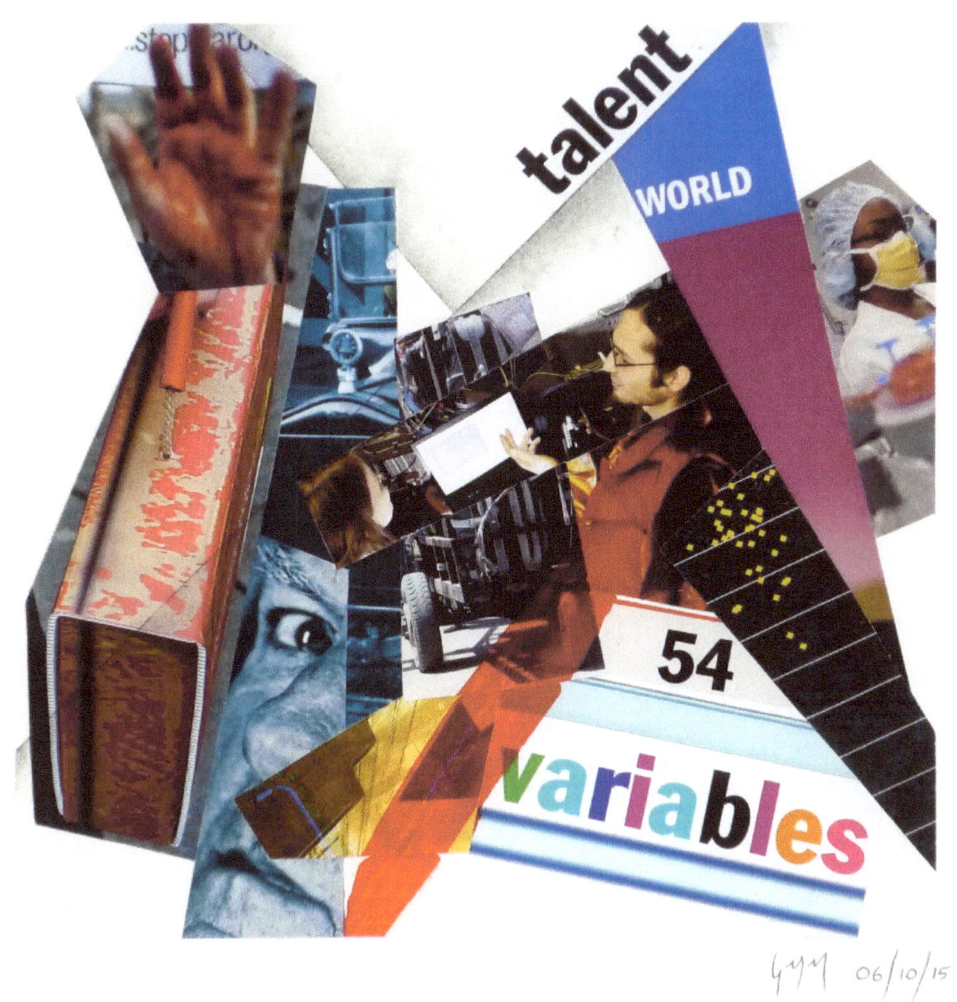

073
Talent world 54 variables
October 2015

(PAC)

Talent world 54 variables

It is not a bloody hand I raise to scare you. It is a signal originating some seventy five years ago, an echo of a conversation held in a plumber's merchants in 1917. (Yes, the centenary approaches. How will we respond?)

There is movement in the room upstairs. It is not mice in the attic, but it has the same effect; it keeps me awake, wondering what is going on and why it is so loud. I know who is up there and what he is doing, I think. It is the chess player worrying his pieces into submission with the intensity of his speculations.

I turn out to be right about who it is and wrong about what he is doing. I confronted him again this morning. He feigned disinterest and confusion. Then he told me the truth.

> I am packing up my troubles and it hurts. See: this valise contains a lifetime cut into small pieces and reproduced, to be redistributed via the market system, and all for the sake of the expected gesture of subversion.
>
> I can't stand it anymore.

With that he dissolved into the depths of the cave art. So tell me, how will the body be turned upside down when floating beyond the great barrier he has set up? This *animalism* can only be touched. The eyes have nowhere to settle. The medium swirls giving life to every orientation as this world recedes. Projections multiply as do the folds of the ephemeral membrane. I must go outside now and refresh my contact with the intramundane.

Dad! Staring out from under the radiator with that accusing eye, I hear him ask: Why? Why do you torment me with your uncertain observations? I do not have a simple answer. It is something to do with my neuroses and it is complicated; at such short notice, that is as much as I can say. It is also something to do with the thickening of scientific methodology. No-one used to worry about that. Then philosophers thought to explain how wonder works, but they missed the intricacy of the circus's situatedness.

A brother, showing off rare texts of indifference amidst the baggage and wires of museum displays, confirms that this scientific business is a serious one. But no exhibit copes with the possibility of incalculable variables. Of being out of control, like the black chinawoman, who carefully masks her teeth: we must not see (or hear) his laughter lest it undermine the credibility of his actions.

Luckily hand signals are not really required today. One's gestures can adopt contemporary form whilst one remembers that, a long time ago, far, far away, Marcel waves goodbye to end the record of artless sky.

70

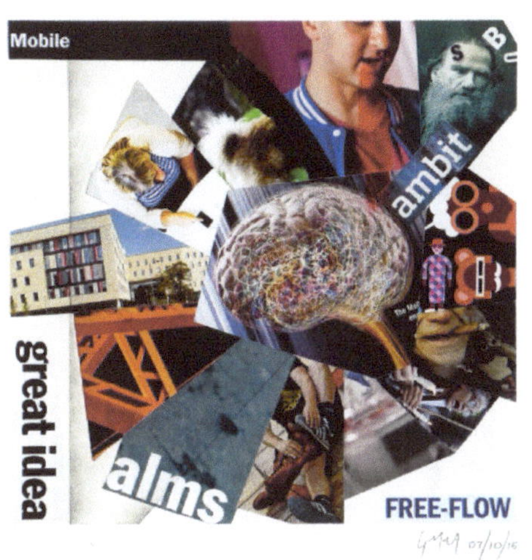

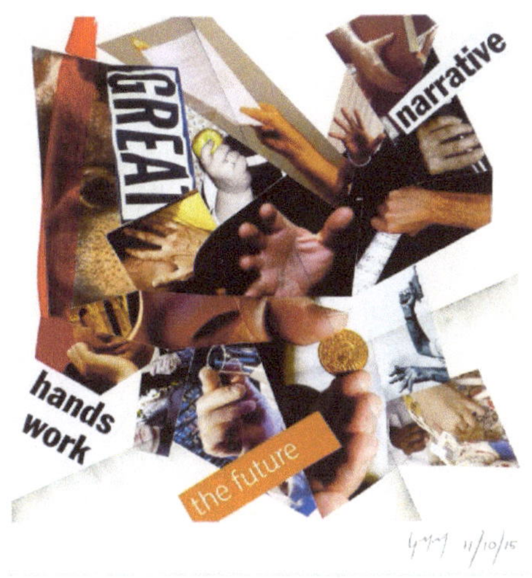

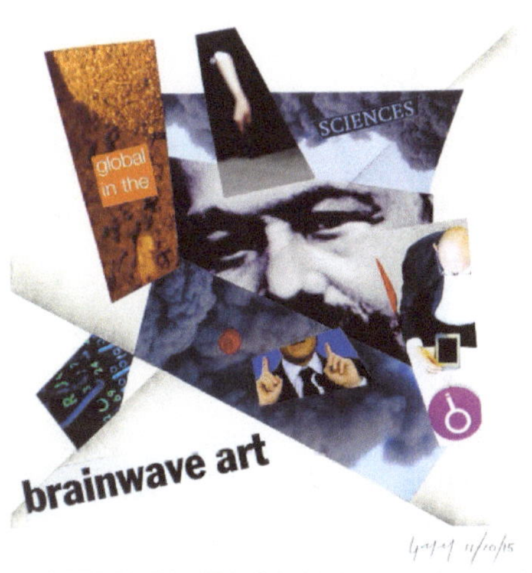

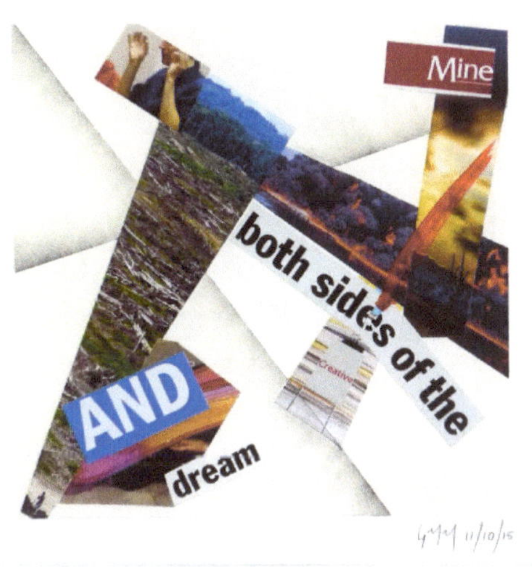

074 **Mobile ambit great idea alms free-flow**
October 2015 (PAC)

075 **Global in the sciences brainwave art**
October 2015 (PAC)

076 **Great hands work the future narrative**
October 2015 (PAC)

077 **Mine both sides of the creative and dream**
October 2015 (PAC)

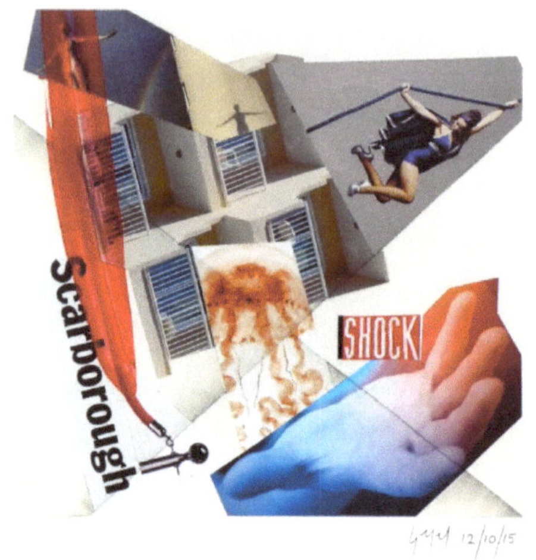

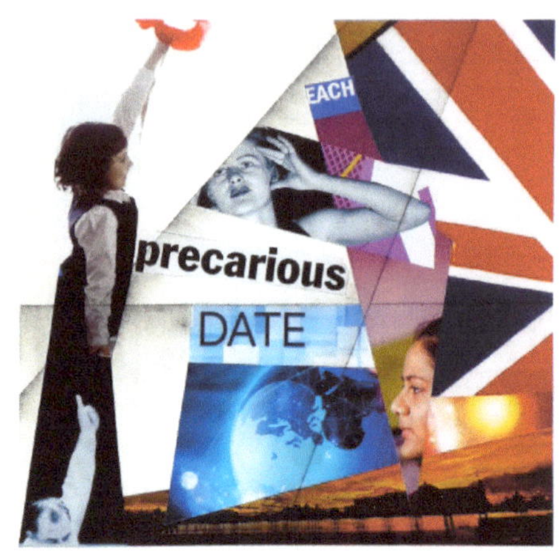

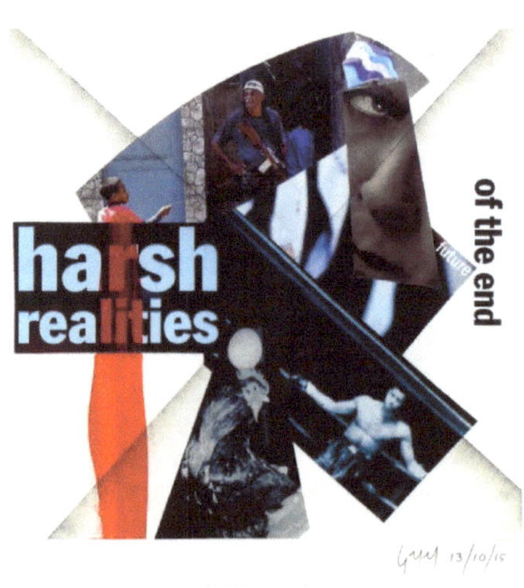

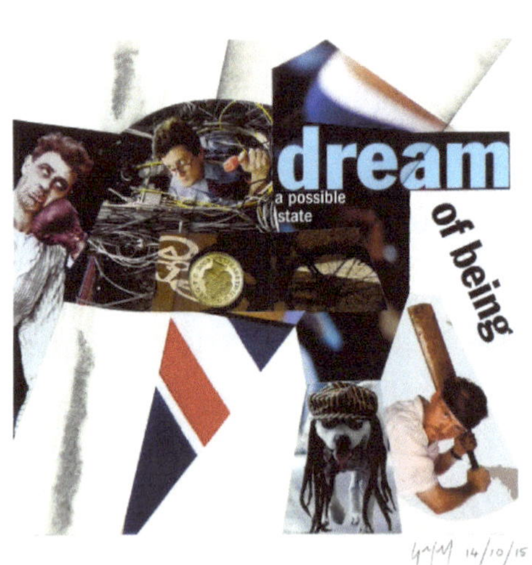

078 **Scarborough shock**
October 2015 (PAC)

080 **Each precarious date**
October 2015 (PAC)

079 **Harsh realities of the future end**
October 2015 (PAC)

081 **Dream a possible state of being**
October 2015 (PC)

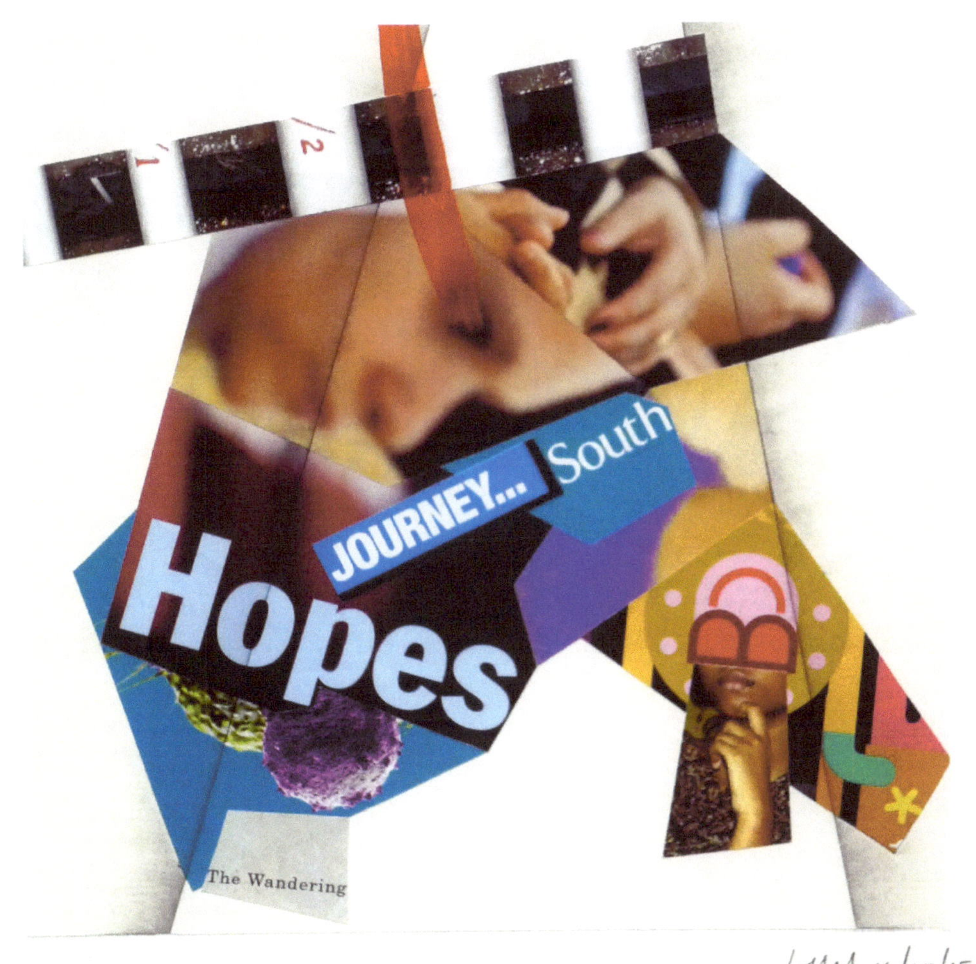

082

Hopes journey south the wandering

October 2015

(PAC)

Hopes journey south the wandering

This is how, on the first day of loneliness, life really begins: a man in a black gown towers over the assembled and booms, "we have journeys to make." I have never forgotten the scene, although I may have misremembered his words.

This is all happening on paper now for you. It is a possibility, however, only because in the past I was stripped naked by my arrogances and failures. I thought that getting on in life meant carving out a comfortable hole and decorating its perfect interior with friendly bacteria. I remained unaware of my own insularity because beautifully encased in institutionalised humanity. From this position I could feign empathy with the more distant specimens and feel it with the less cellular than I. Yes, strange immobility projecting to the ends of the earth and I mollusc grew in successive chambers.

Today I am singing to you and you are probably thinking that it cannot have been that bad. But you are imagining the wrong question: it was not bad at all, not in the slightest. Take this scaling device, for example, how could I present it to you so guiltlessly if I were not now liberated from the world it used to measure?

Bon jour, trier. The stone you have in your hand came from the Giza plateau. That is correct: it is stolen cultural property. If it were possible to see what it is simply by looking at it you would now be lying on the ground in a pool of blood. Now, what do you make of this almost identical fragment? You are quite right: it is not stone, and that blue speck is paint. I cry when I imagine dying behind a mural I dreamed of seeing and touching.

Painting is done at close range, *point-blank* one might say, facing east, between monuments and geological features, and cradled in a sometimes painful chain of being. Beloved, honour me and I will fix my feeling for you for all time. The sentiment is narcissistic, I hear you say. True, but what about this thought: if I had followed Robert Walser or Gerald Wilde where would I be? I would be on the wrong side of the mirror. Do you understand what I am saying? What is more, I would not have survived.

The irony is that I have journeyed rather better than many who have travelled the world.

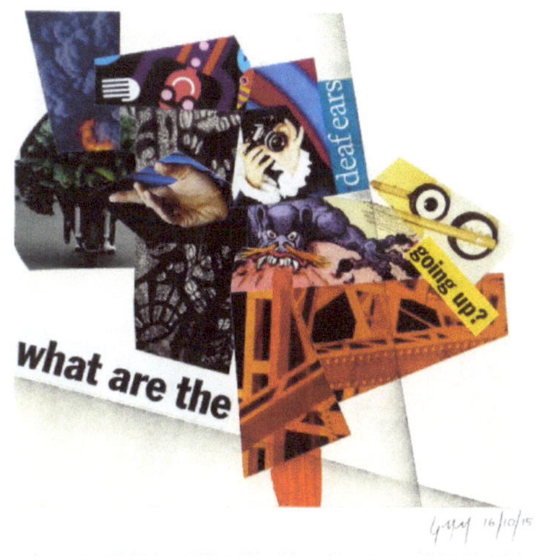

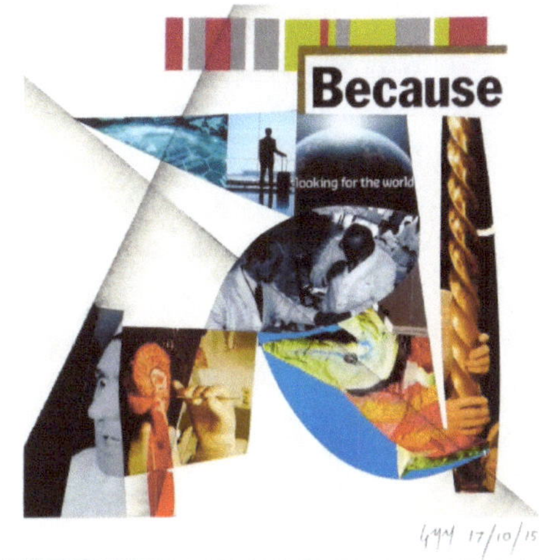

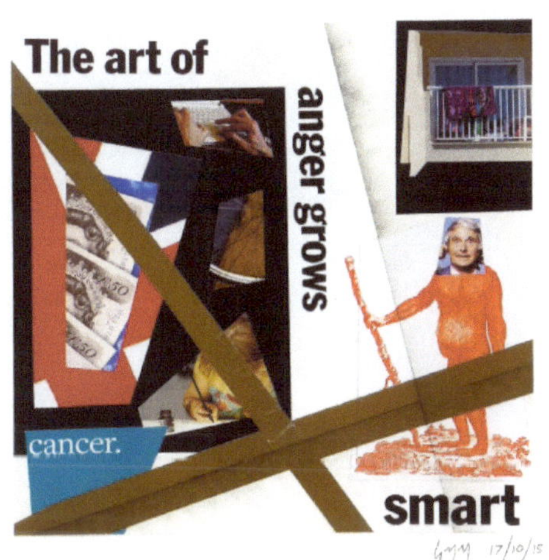

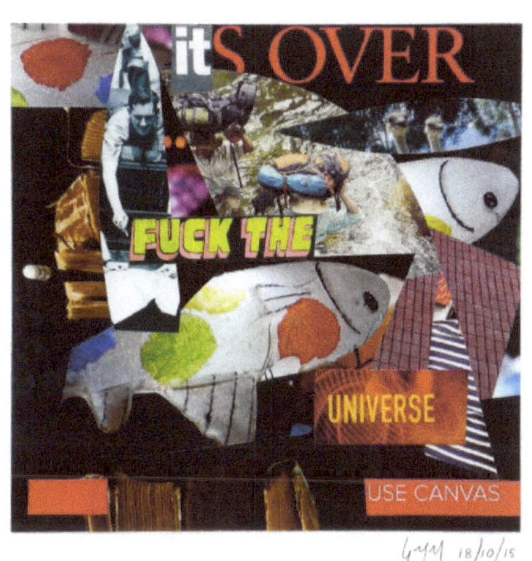

083 **What are the deaf ears going up**
October 2015 (PAC)

084 **The art of anger grows cancer smart**
October 2015 (PC)

085 **Because looking for the world**
October 2015 (PAC)

086 **Its over fuck the universe use canvas**
October 2015 (P)

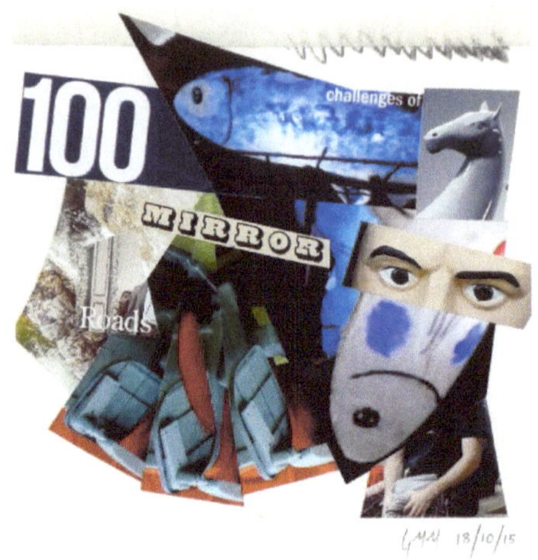

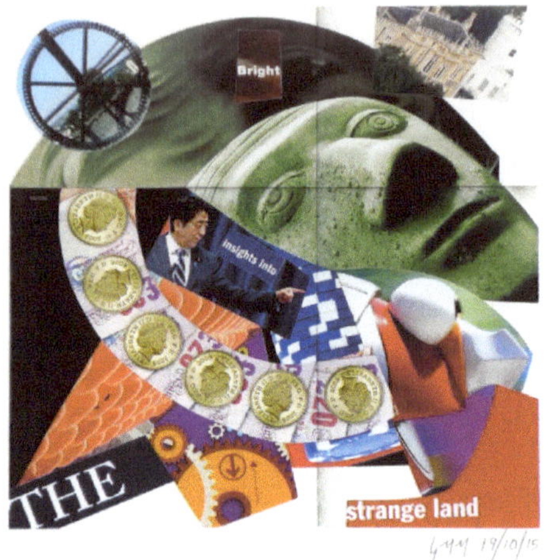

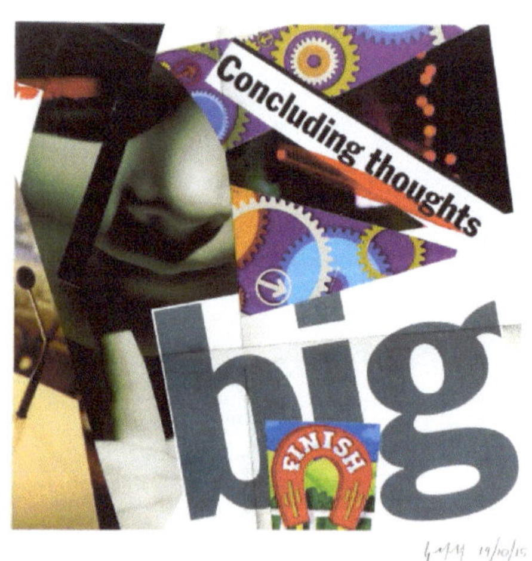

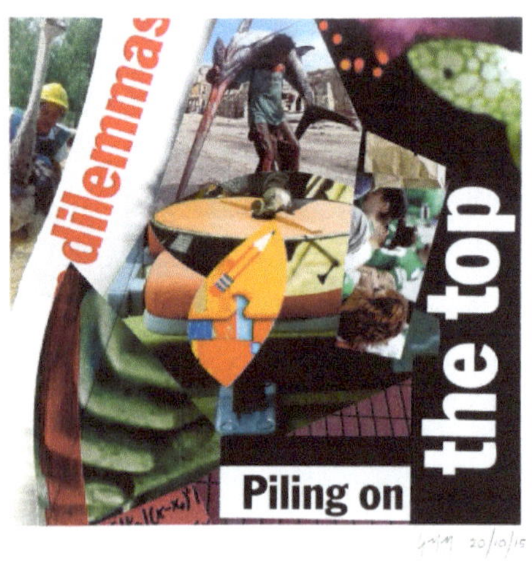

087 **100 challenges of mirror roads**
October 2015 (PAC)

088 **Concluding thoughts big finish**
October 2015 (PAC)

089 **Bright insights into the strange land**
October 2015 (PC)

090 **Dilemmas piling on the top**
October 2015 (PAC)

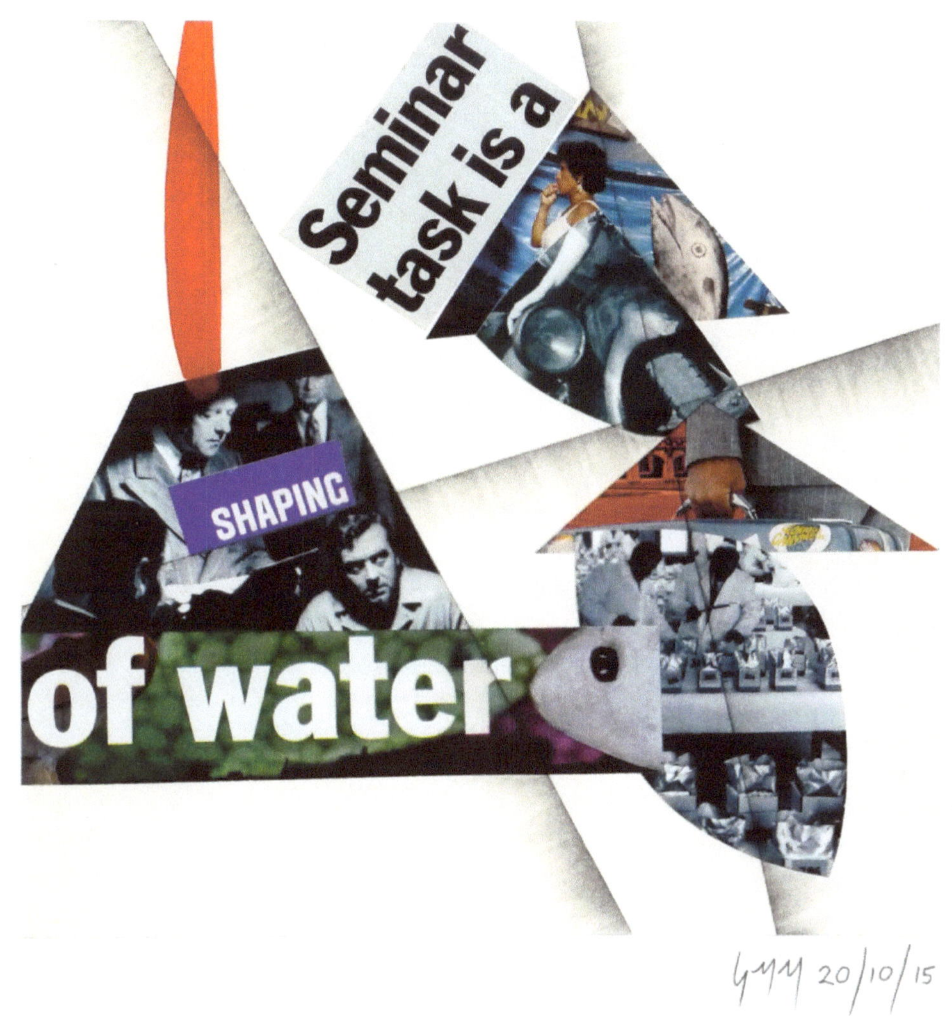

091

Seminar task is a shaping of water

October 2015

(PAC)

Seminar task is a shaping of water

They gathered around a table in the backroom and talked the night away. Looking up Sidney saw a paper fish and a woman experiencing indecision, and he could not understand the way things generally were going. Everything was dissolving into philosophical confections, each neatly boxed and labelled, and he was beginning to tire. Any illumination that might have been available in the past now appeared to have faulty wiring: the light bulbs were there, but they did not work.

I am with him in mind and spirit. Passages may lead from a pre-Socratic space into the modern imagination, but, as they all appear mysteriously black and depthless when I look down them, their reality is not in prospect. I wonder why we bother with our peregrinations, thought experiments, essays, rational arguments, and logical tests if not to light a candle by which to see the permeability of the walls that surround us. At this point we need a diversion, an illustration of some sort. This is how a text of this kind works. Some distance must be travelled away from the track (apparent track), along which the author has led the reader, so that by a surprising turn of phrase, a sudden insight for example, the loop can be closed and the reader's expectations can be satisfied, even if in an oblique manner. I am reminded of a story.

Far away, shut up in a turret room, a man writes in his diary: "I think I am being watched." In reality he is being imagined not watched. A painter on a hill in the next valley was drawing the castle interior from memory. He placed the paranoiac in the topmost room and, what is more, gave him hooded eyes. How we know the location and occupation of the painter at that auspicious moment is no mystery either. He was seen on that hillside one night, spectacularly clearly as if on a bright spring morning, by his widow in a dream. She recounted it, sat cosily in her favourite armchair, while her granddaughter listened and snapped away with the camera on her mobile phone, posting the images with captions composed from the old woman's capricious words as she spoke them. You can see the whole story represented in the painting I have on my dining room wall. Come, see how I imagined it all.

Do you see now why the corridors are so dark?

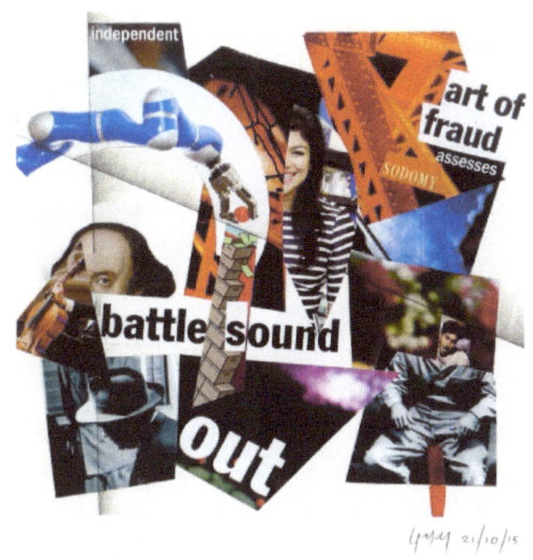

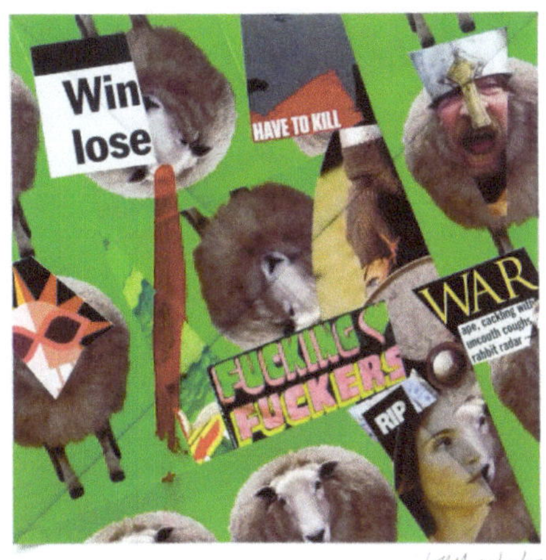

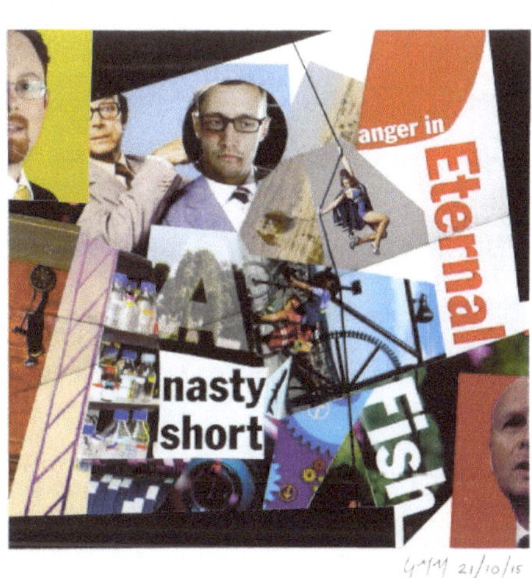

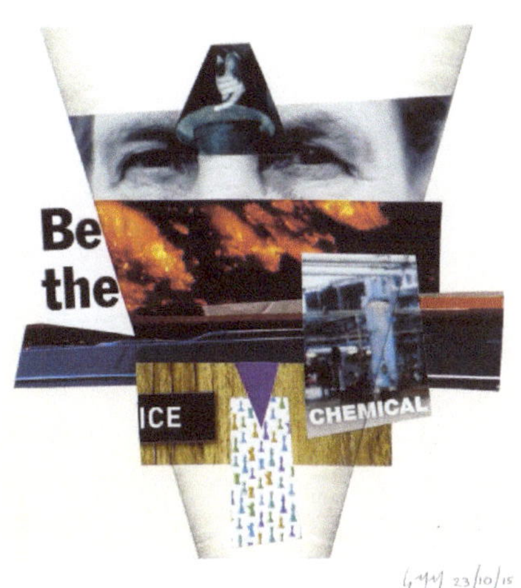

092 **Independent art of fraud assesses sodomy battle sound out**
October 2015 (PAC)

093 **A nasty short anger in eternal fish**
October 2015 (PIC)

094 **Win lose have to kill fucking [love] war fuckers ape cackling with uncouth coughs rabbit radar RIP**
October 2015 (PAC)

095 **Be the ice chemical**
October 2015 (PC)

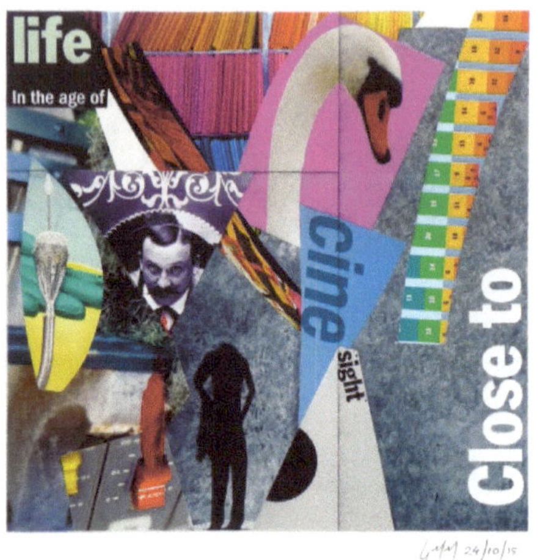

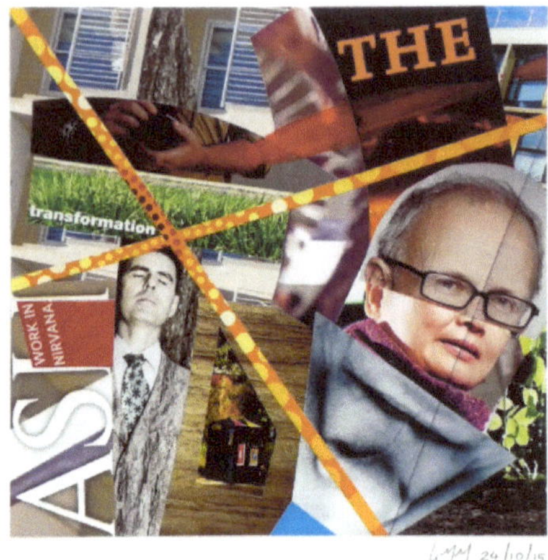

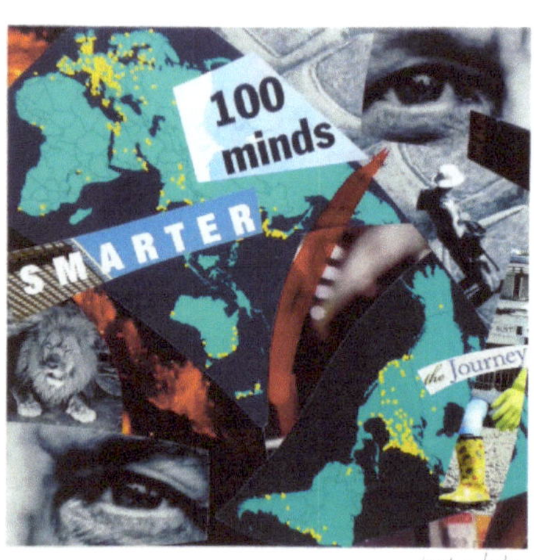

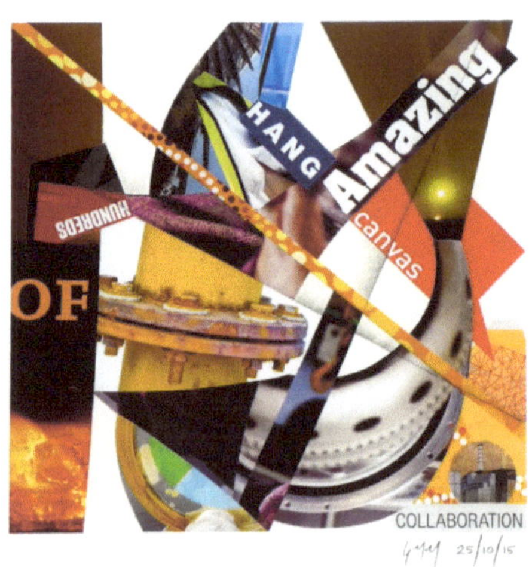

096 **Life in the age of cine sight close to**
October 2015 (PAC)

097 **100 minds smarter bust the journey**
October 2015 (PA)

098 **The transformation as work in nirvana**
October 2015 (PAC)

099 **Hundreds hang amazing canvas of collaboration**
October 2015 (PC)

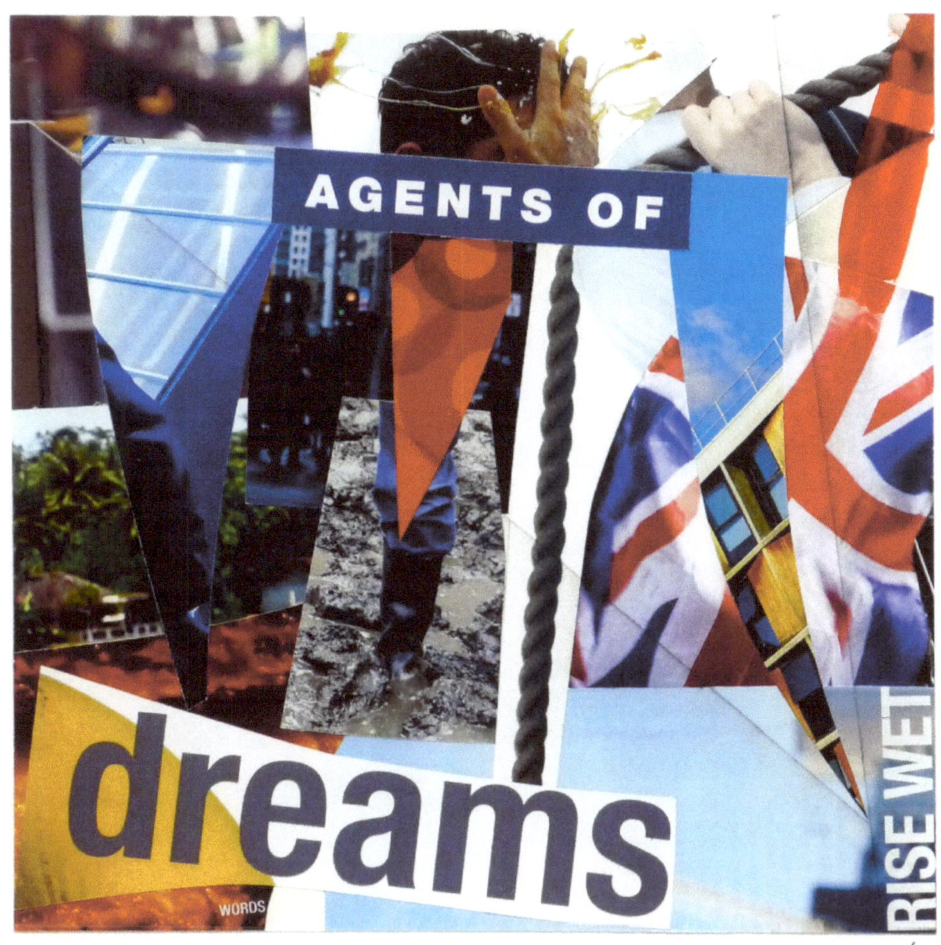

100
Agents of dreams [words] rise wet
October 2015

(PAC)

Agents of dreams [words] rise wet

Iconoclastically, perhaps, I deconstruct famous passages from popular Victorian novels.

I do not go out of my way to acquire copies of the more common ones, of course. Why would I? I have never been able to read them: too many words and too much focus on aristocratic and (upper) middle-class interests, particularly on honour, sex and death, manners and misfortune. Not that any of that subject matter matters anymore. If it ever did, it was for the same reasons that today average citizens are entranced by the meaningless incidents that colour the lives of the fabricated celebrities they see displaying night and day on their TV and computer screens.

I saw an idiot smashing an egg on his own forehead supposedly to make a philosophical point, but in the end only to carnival effect. Amid strange bunting a bigger flag flies over the well-trodden path to and from war, in and out of national solidarity, and one way up to the gallows. The dark streets now demonstrate the ubiquity of the eye and the black light of fame, and then? Then, in the imagination at least, they swim with smog that curls around capes and hansom cabs, infiltrates sad lungs and hides the crimes of vengeance and desperation. Dark streets thread between terraces of social order, knitting together the grand capitalist sphere that grows and glows behind bolted doors and heavily curtained windows. How will power win out against romance or romance win out against power?

All that tosh is nothing more than a distraction. We all know this. It satisfies a morbid curiosity, the sustaining energy of which might otherwise be turned to and expended on taking politics seriously, on addressing more urgent issues of existence, particularly quality of life in all its manifestations. The succession of entertaining episodes, as composed, are a suppressant of human potential in this regard. It is true of what the present-day mass media churn out, and it was true of the Victorian novel, if not to such an extreme degree and popular extent.

For me, from these texts, at their best, there are images that emerge out of perverse styles of reading—the ends of lines in reverse order, for example, as if chance contains some greater creative potential than the long-dead author had ever mustered through genetic inheritance, educational advantage, and long hours of dedicated, even obsessive, practice of the various skills of visualization, articulation and composition. At worst, skipping over lines, whole paragraphs, sometimes several pages, words scavenged suggest little until supplemented, scrambled, submerged and reworked, and then the little they suggest is merely interstitial: poisonous air flowing between eerily glowing gems.

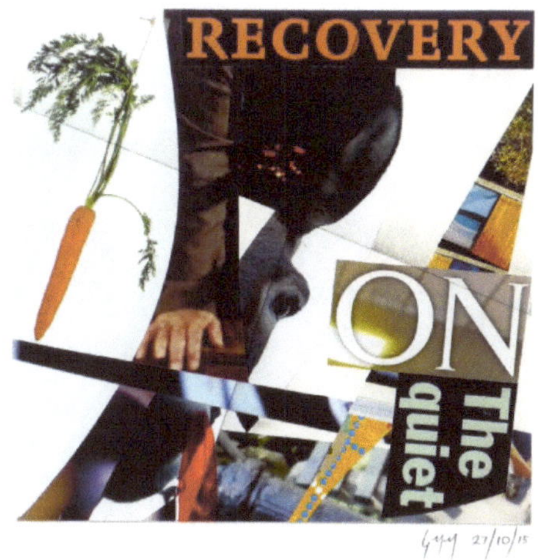

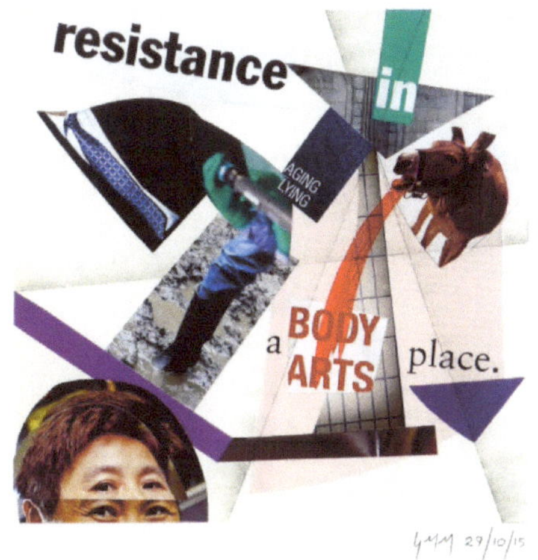

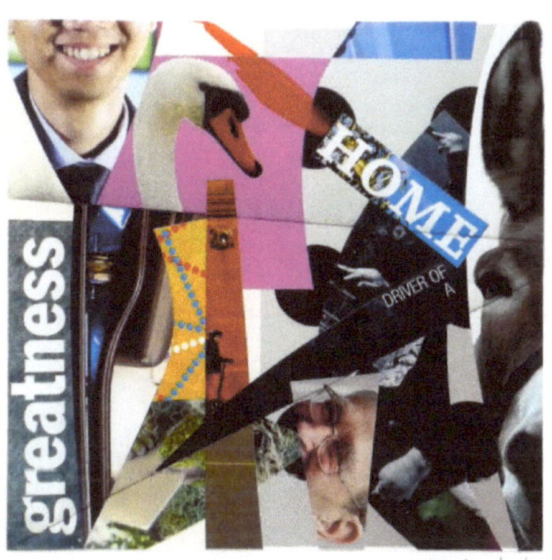

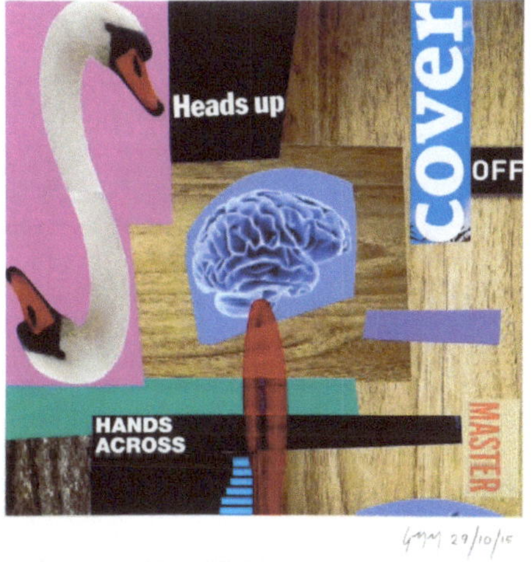

101 **Recovery on the quiet**
October 2015 (PAC)

102 **Home driver of a greatness**
October 2015 (PAC)

103 **Resistance in aging lying a body arts place**
October 2015 (PAC)

104 **Heads up cover off hands across master**
October 2015 (PA)

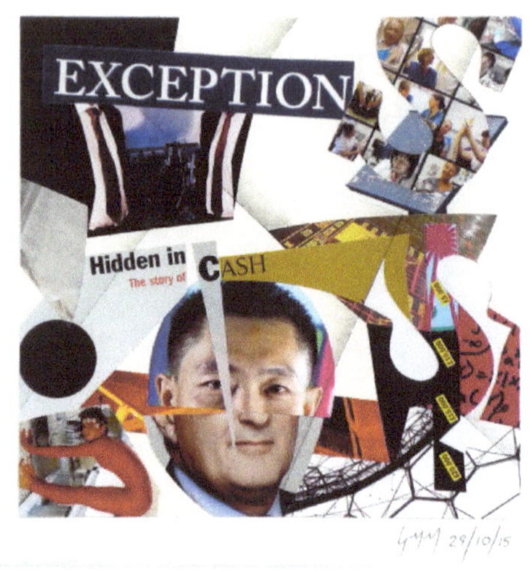

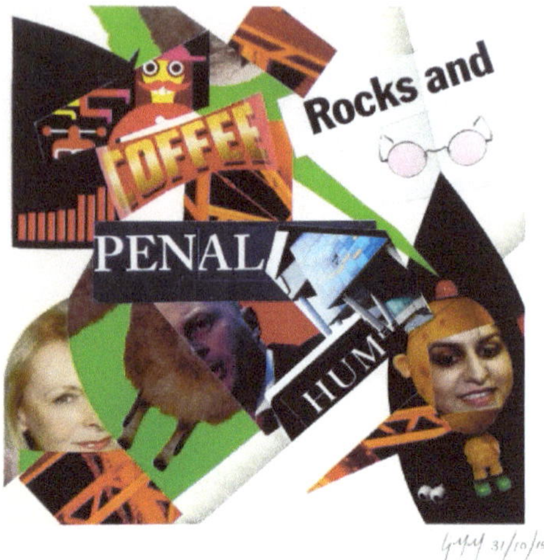

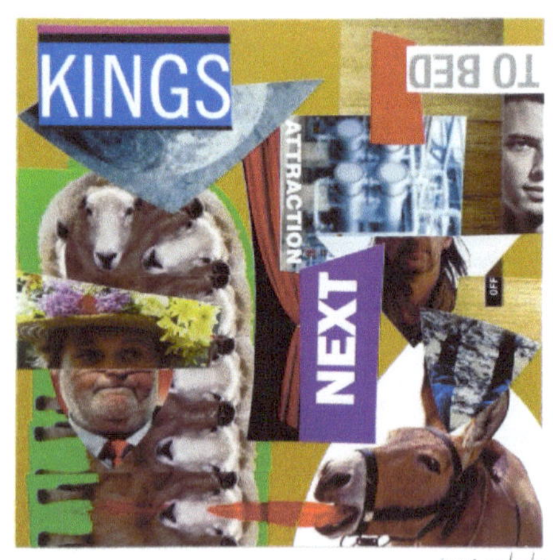

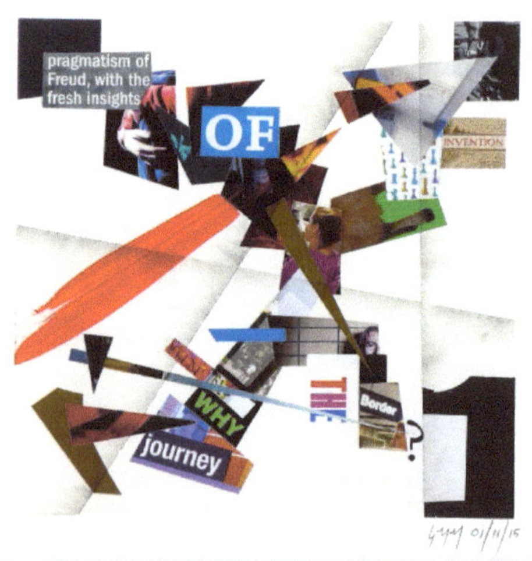

105 **Exception hidden in the story of cash**
October 2015 (PC)

106 **Kings attraction next off to bed**
October 2015 (PA)

107 **Coffee rocks and penal hum**
October 2015 (PC)

108 **Pragmatism of Freud with the fresh insights of invention why journey the border**
November 2015 (PAC)

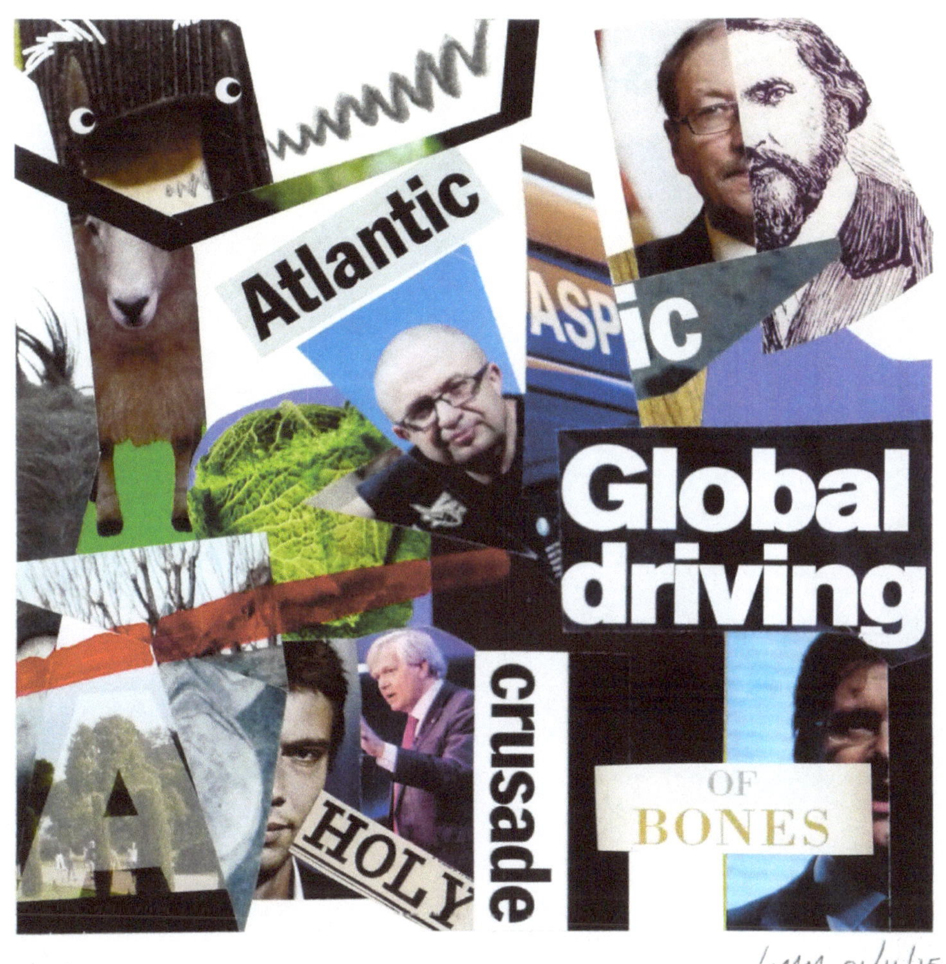

109

Atlantic aspic global driving a holy crusade of bones

November 2015

(PAC)

Atlantic aspic global driving a holy crusade of bones

Of air and screams, where is the sky? As if fog were a solid crust of dried blood beneath which microbes multiply their complaints, many male voices fill the interim with analysis and advice vehemently projected through the atmosphere of dread. All we hear are the expertly navigating lambs bleating into the hollow beneath their puppet souls. 'Here, here!' They sigh, automatically obeying the conditioning strobe of one or another party line. Meanwhile the power station lights flicker through the night and missives issue from the caverns of bats and the labyrinths of rats, which are set side by side along the magnetic corridors. This way blood is always flowing forming circles between east and west, and lines out and out south to the citadel and the city.

You got education for that writing thing, mate, and an art room for your anarchist types. Yes, you do, and there's no thinking aloud from now on sunshine; we have a job for you. You are going to travel the world (and here is the bit they do not tell you) locked in a black box with your head plumbed into a bank of idiots.

Witness the cabin fever of partner cartographers who are never allowed to see the land features and vegetation that clothe their dreams. It builds into a dominant pathology—call it *domestication.* In translating verbal reports into maps and charts there is an ocean of space for silver accents and golden moments to mingle all the way from Wharram Percy to Pacific Shores. Ghost letters in ghost towns culled from old newspapers to service the tracing of justice's poor record.

A bell sounds at high tide and in the morning on the beach a Sperm Whale lies dead of confusion. Another bell sounds and a nave fills for a funeral. In the evening the wake gets underway with an unsavoury allusion to necrotic organs left in aspic for the body without organs to mourn. In orbit the Australian desert glides past at 7.6 kilometres per second, slow enough to spot salt lakes like Amadeus and even ancient sand rivers like the Finke, but from this slight elevation all we see are graves. Goodbye, little skeleton, I hope you settle well into the land of glowing dawns and other signals of recognition. I always did love it when realization spread across your face. Scream your silent scream and I will imagine it permanently aerated under the crust of our red earth.

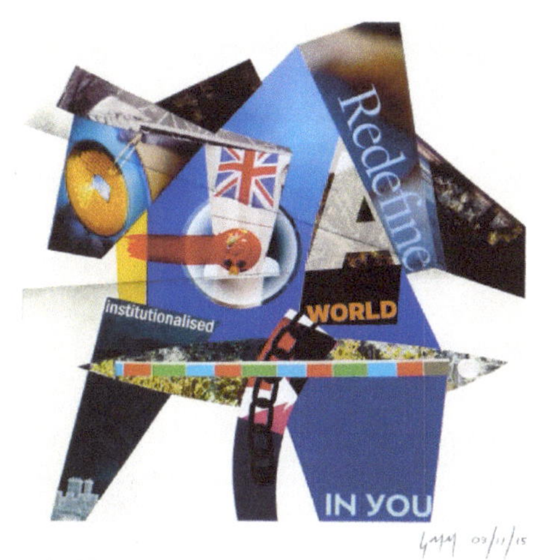

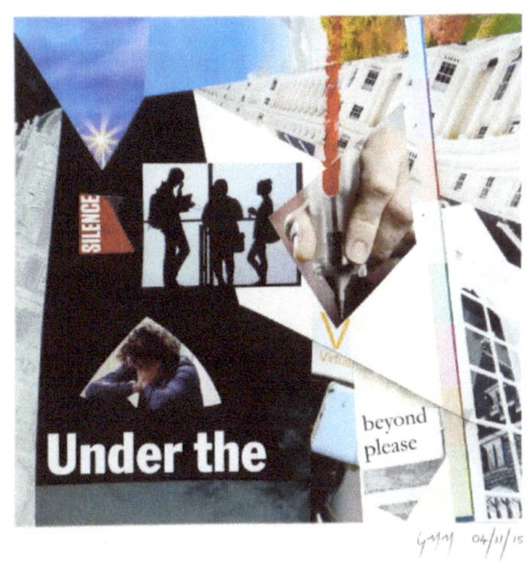

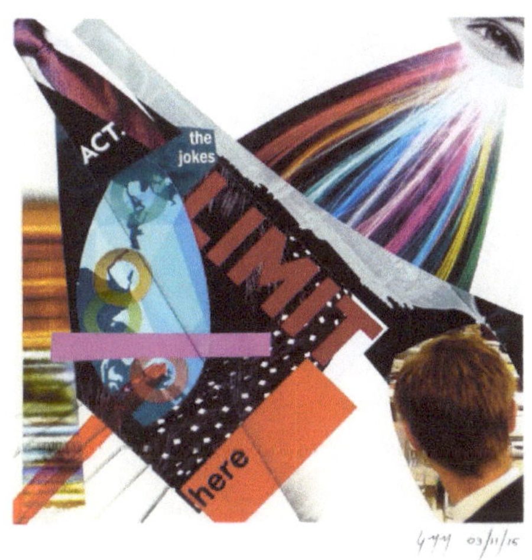

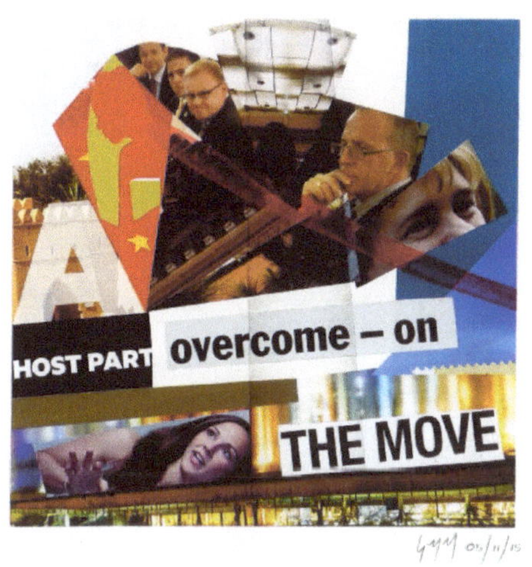

110 **Redefine a world institutionalised in you**
November 2015 (PAC)

111 **Act the jokes limit here**
November 2015 (PAC)

112 **Silence under the virtual beyond please**
November 2015 (PAC)

113 **A host part overcome - on the move**
November 2015 (PAC)

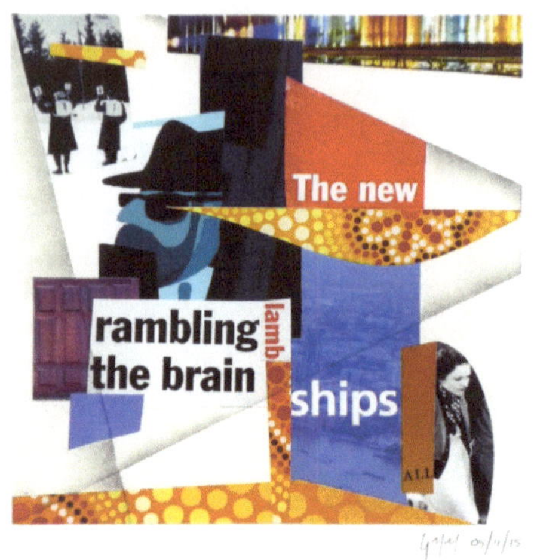

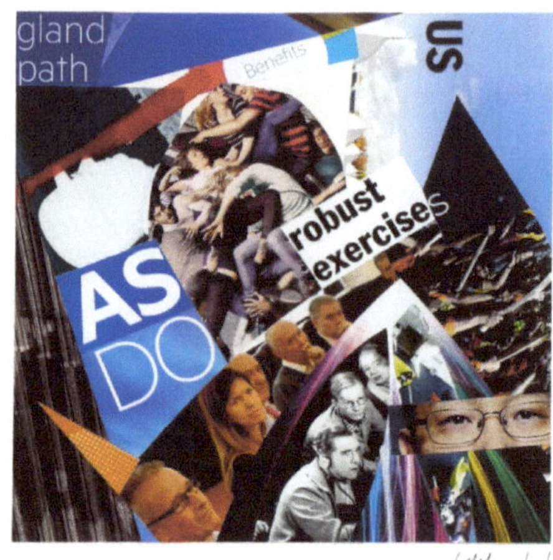

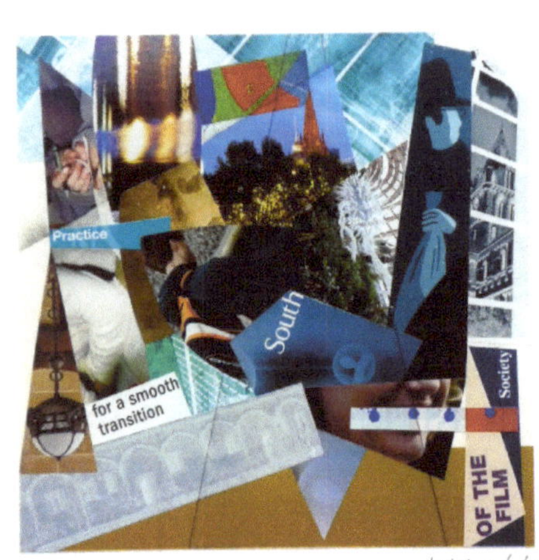

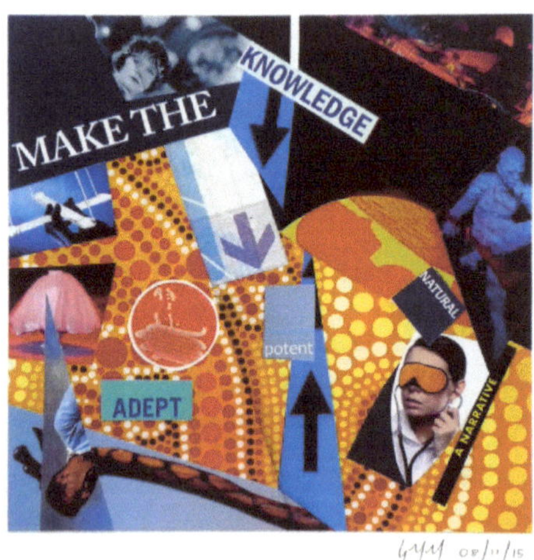

114 **The new rambling lamb the brain ships all**
November 2015 (PC)

115 **Practice for a smooth transition south of the film society**
November 2015 (PC)

116 **Gland path benefits us as do robust exercises**
November 2015 (PA)

117 **Make the knowledge natural potent adept a narrative**
November 2015 (PAC)

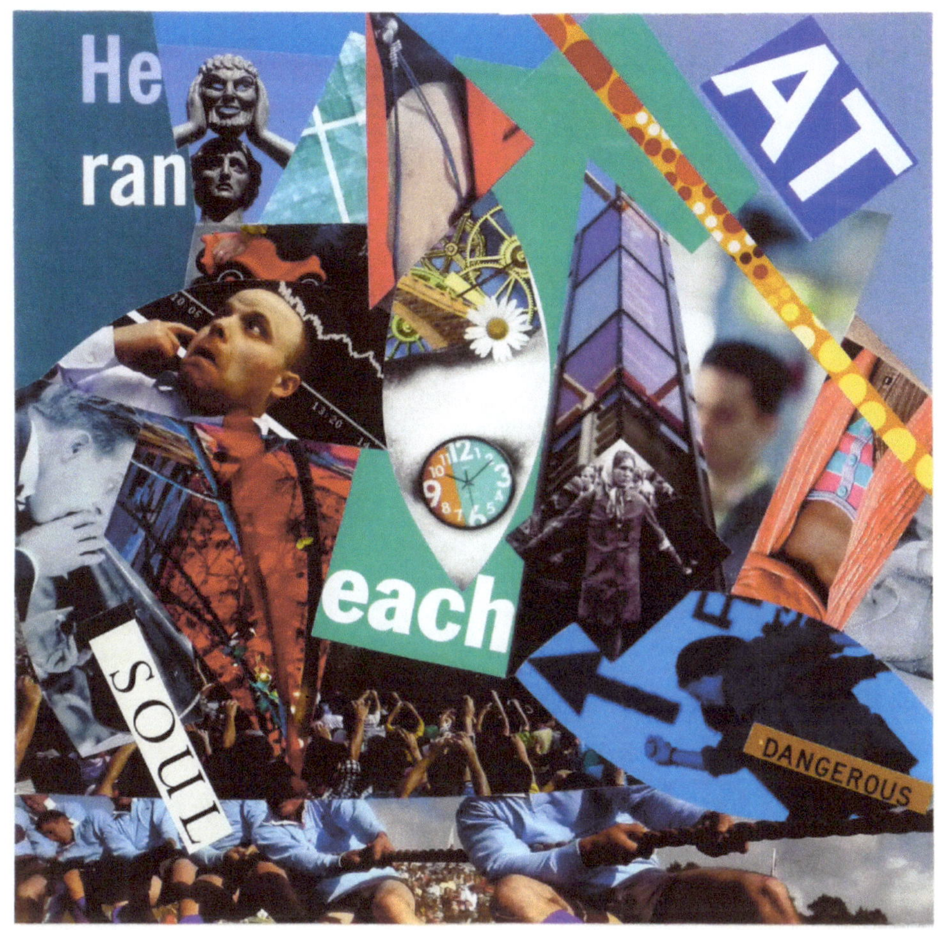

09/11/15

118

He ran at each dangerous soul

November 2015

(PA)

He ran at each dangerous soul

The bear displays its stoicism with an open downturned mouth and by scratching with a crooked finger, but there is no real concern in his gaze off stage. Watching avaricious daydreams disappear in a sudden downturn is a jugular busting job for the barrow boy. He jumped up to it only yesterday when he swapped a sweatshirt for collar and tie. (He lost the tie refereeing a squabble between absolute and relative humidity.) Before his addiction to economic jargon and greed he had more familiar lines:

> I'm not asking a score. I'm not asking a tenner. It's all there ladies, top quality, built to last. It's yours for a fiver. There you go. I must be mad.

And it is a madness that extends from his megaphone soul through the ears of a tug-o-war team into the ether. Like a Socrates at the LSE or a Euripides at Harvard he is entrenched in a gambling factory of pseudo-butchery, subject to an idiot's nightmare resort where the sun bleaches golden-boy hair-dos and crisps up the thickening hide ready for a regular whipping with financial abstractions. Done to a (variety-hall) turn, he is, but no-one can stand the heat in the end; it is simply a question of moving between microwave shadows and blustering well until the charm runs out.

Meanwhile, the wheels of fortune turn in the fluid earth giving the illusion of mechanical predictability and, high above the strain, a glad mask descends onto a sad face. The rest of the Greeks arrive with their flavour-of-the-day philosophies and their crazy models of a well-designed universe. Does it run like temperamental clockwork or like a panicky revolutionary blindly taking the wrong escape route? I have no idea and neither do they. Then the beauty parade begins.

Have you seen the latest guru? He has a shiny silk and cashmere suit, seductively hanging and darkly dancing as he glides across the convention stage gesturing with grandly manicured claws—yes, a bloody crab! The adoring crowd sways to the incantations, bays for more and one by one punters collapse in ecstasy. The clock moves on and at ten past ten light stabs the air and the tower comes to life. The border guards have a machine capable of distinguishing between the prostrate and the supine. Mud suckers get a boot on the head to hold them down; everyone else has their eyes forced open to watch the sparks fly. There is no escape, no choice but to comply with the eccentric logic of sacrifice in this atomic world.

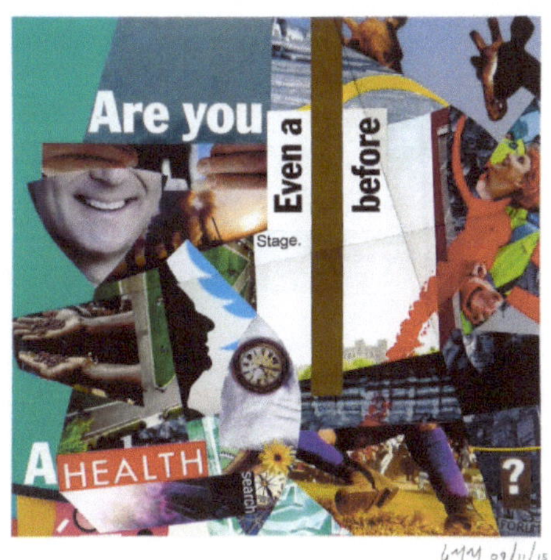

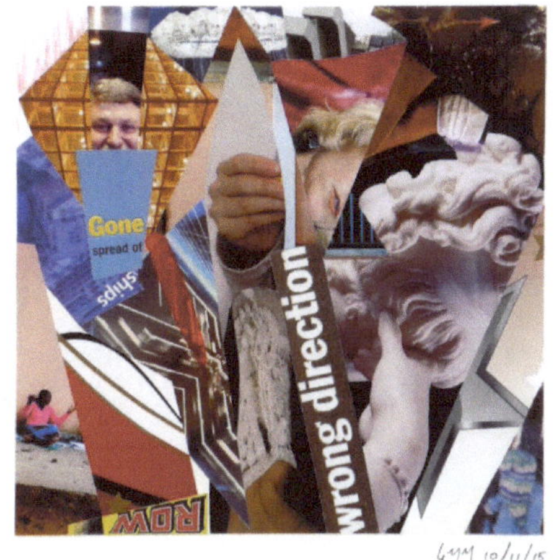

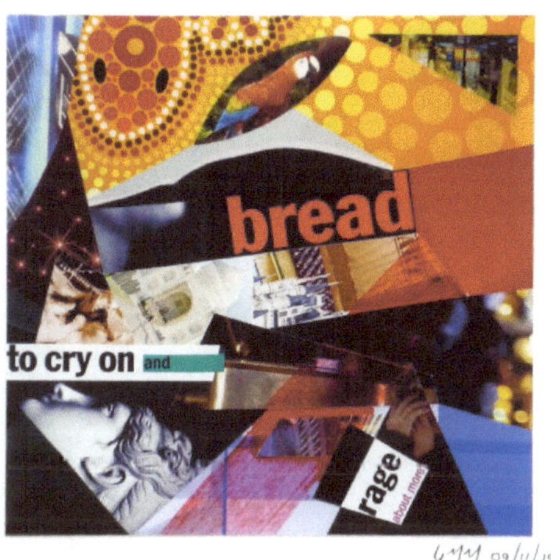

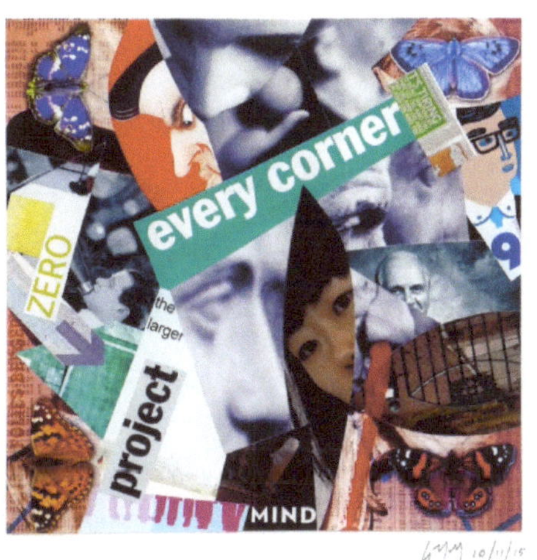

119 **Are you even a stage before a health forum**
November 2015 (PAC)

120 **Bread art to cry on and rage about more**
November 2015 (PA)

121 **Gone spread of ships row wrong direction**
November 2015 (PA)

122 **It's tiring every corner zero the larger project mind**
November 2015 (PA)

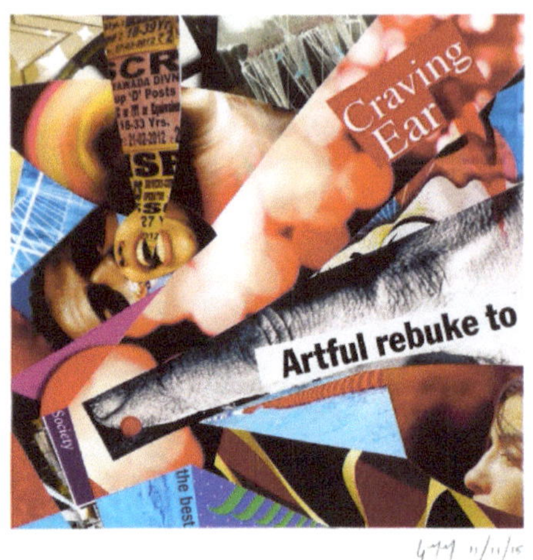

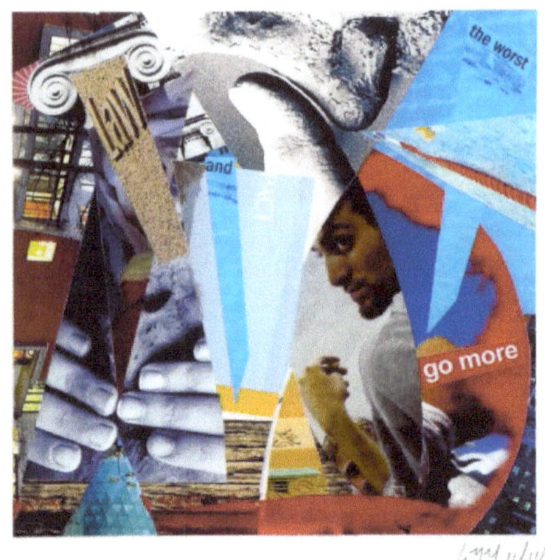

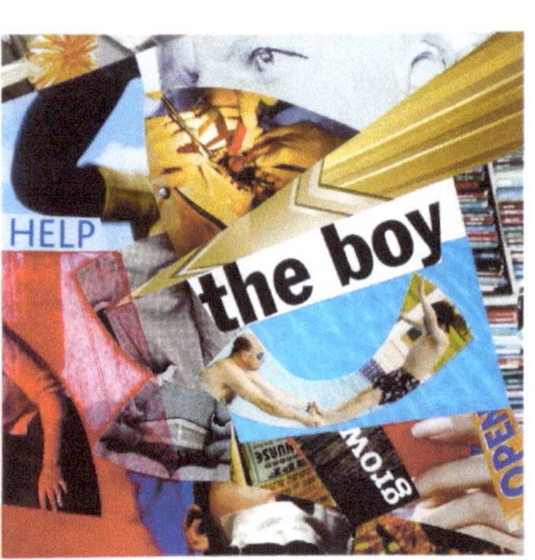

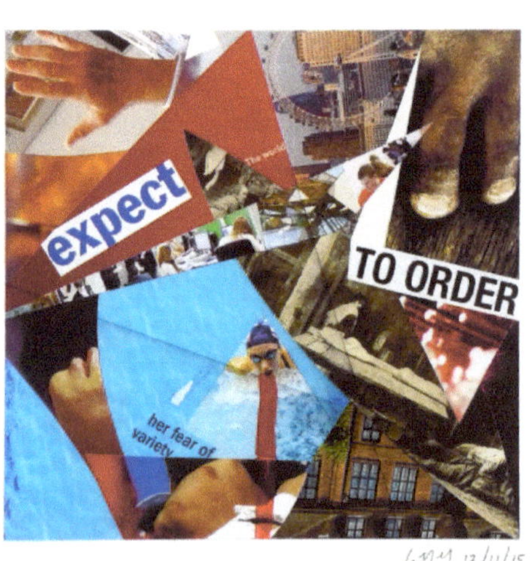

123 **Craving ear artful rebuke to the best society**
November 2015 (PA)

124 **Help the boy grow open**
November 2015 (PA)

125 **The worst law and pact go more**
November 2015 (PA)

126 **Expect the world to order her fear of variety**
November 2015 (PAC)

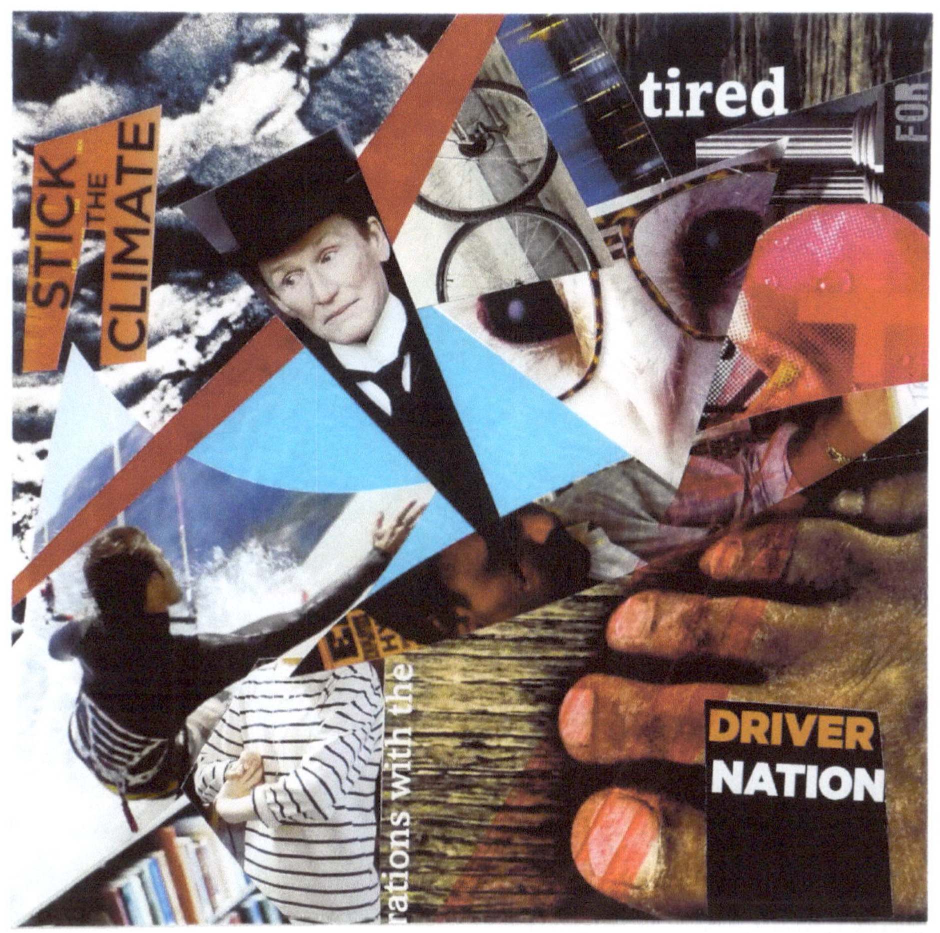

127

Stick the climate tired for rations with the driver nation

November 2015

(PA)

Stick the climate tired for rations with the driver nation

You wake up wet once again with the taste of salt and iron on your lips. Now are you tired of sail-boarding and of treading the bloody boards? There is nothing to gain by persisting; your ambitions and dreams are illusory; you know this. The absolute is against encompassing the absolute in that space of long adrenaline-fueled distance. Just as art is not art if it bleeds and drains away. Even solo sports are marginal at best.

Places merge and the linkages play the part of an Ancient Greek chorus. Let us once again bind citizens to their duties because what we have now is a travesty. A novel tyranny has arisen, which is not recognized as the double it pretends to be. It is held aloft like a bloody flag that signals victory over degradation and murderous intolerance, but it is a fraud, a distortion recalling shallow memories. Uncle John died for your freedom, you little bastard!

To begin: illusion and indifference defy gravity and turn airy below the thermospheric simplicities of molecular nitrogen and oxygen.

Lesson one: can you breathe properly, please—in, out, in, out—it is not easy, I know, but you will not qualify as a citizen if you continue to suffocate.

Lesson two: the idea that the horizon separates earth from sky, or rather that the eye is already attuned to rationalism: this is a lie. Ocular, as opposed to optical, reasoning is liberating in its variety and constitutes a totally different intermediary.

Lesson three: go naked into the garden and find your doubles there. Between the smooth potentialities of a beautiful place, which can be present again, and the strictures and structures of local orientation, there is only play. This play is the co-adjustment of smoothing discourses turning over. Think of it as the improvisations of truly free virtuosos in mindful company creating new worlds of sound.

Lesson four: contrarily, the same function extended from the eye to the mind, expands from the optical to the universally acrobatic. Your place is between these senses. Occupy openings in the earth and play the thresholds until death or destiny overtake your role (*μετα πρόσωπο* or *praeter prosapiam*).

Lesson five: (the obvious one) tell us your stories, you idiot! How will we know that the flow continues to weave its wonder unless we hear its song and see its patterns shift from one resolution to another?

And finally, lesson six: always denounce rigidity, selective blindness, insincerity, and compulsive speech. You may purge yourself of embarrassment, worry and guilt, but offenders will not be able to without such intervention.

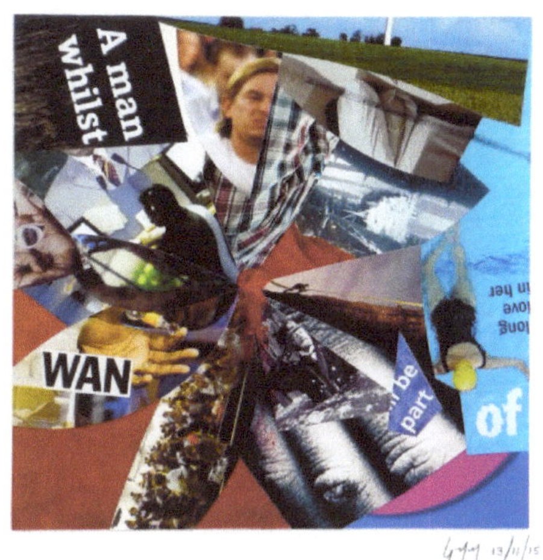

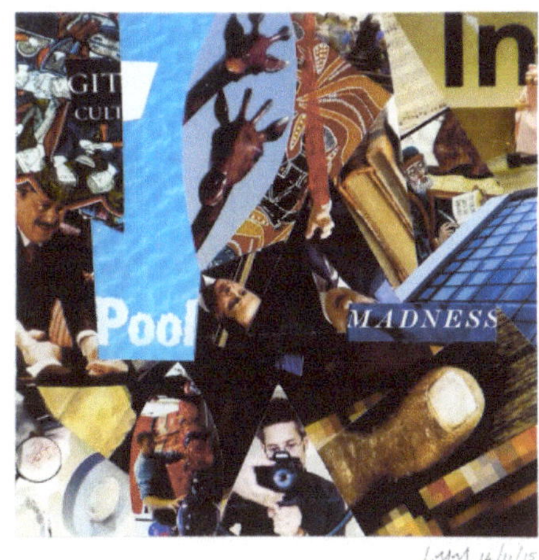

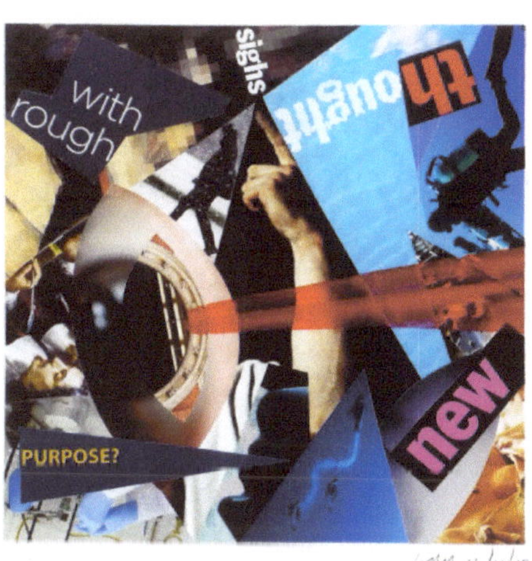

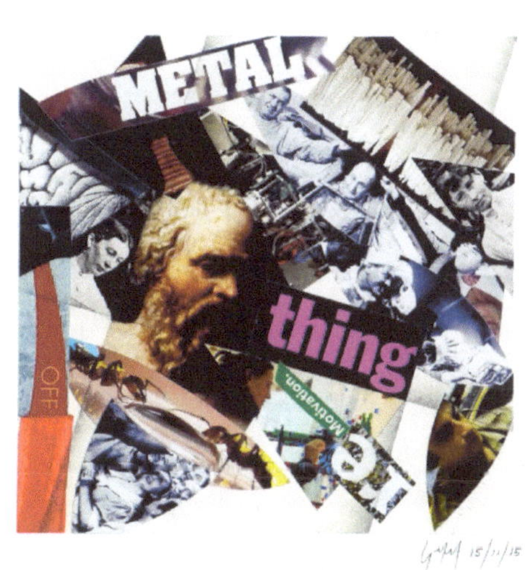

128 **A man whilst wan be part of long love in her**
November 2015 (PAC)

129 **New thought sighs with rough purpose**
November 2015 (PA)

130 **Git cult in pool madness**
November 2015 (PA)

131 **Metal thing off remotivation**
November 2015 (PAC)

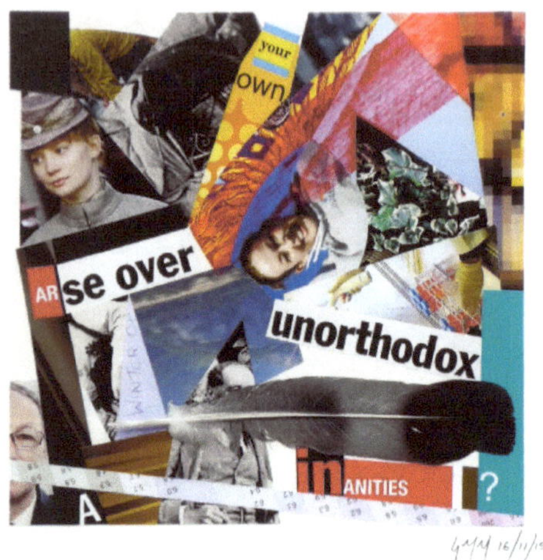

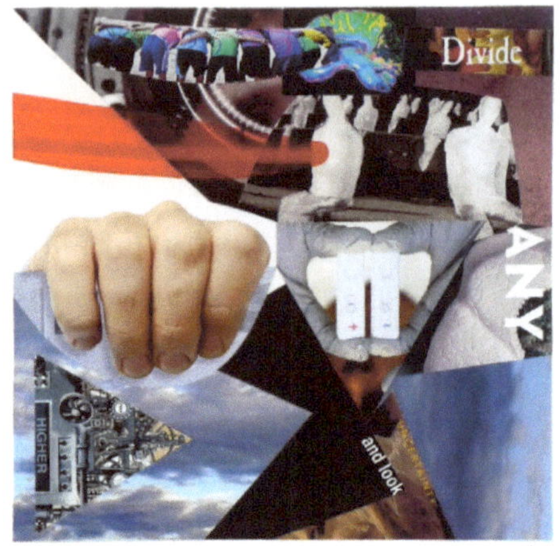

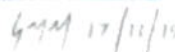

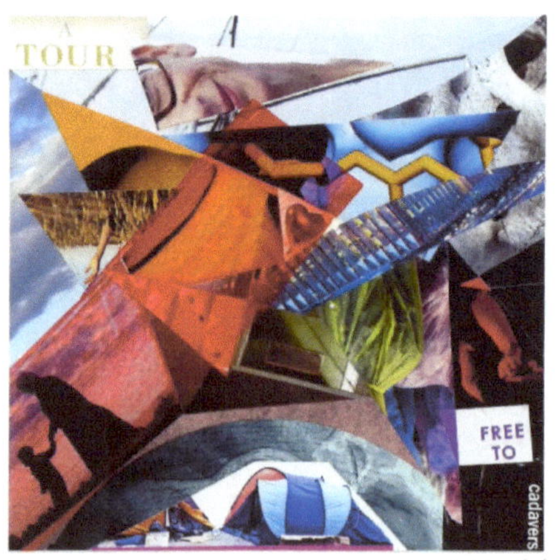

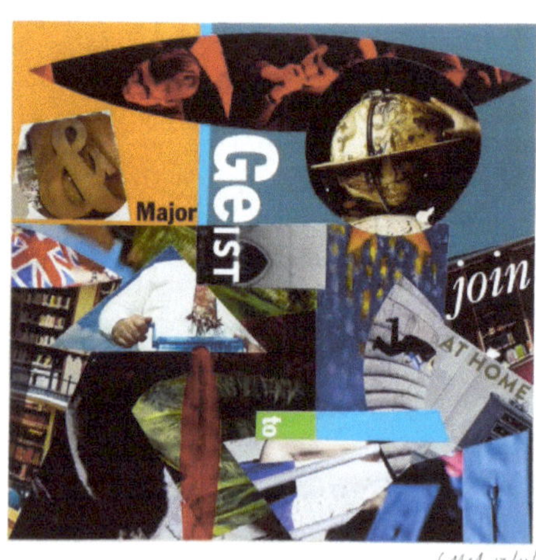

132 **Your own arse over a winter of unorthodox inanities**
November 2015 (PA)

133 **A tour free to cadavers**
November 2015 (PA)

134 **Divide any uncertainty and look higher**
November 2015 (PA)

135 **& major geist to join at home**
November 2015 (PA)

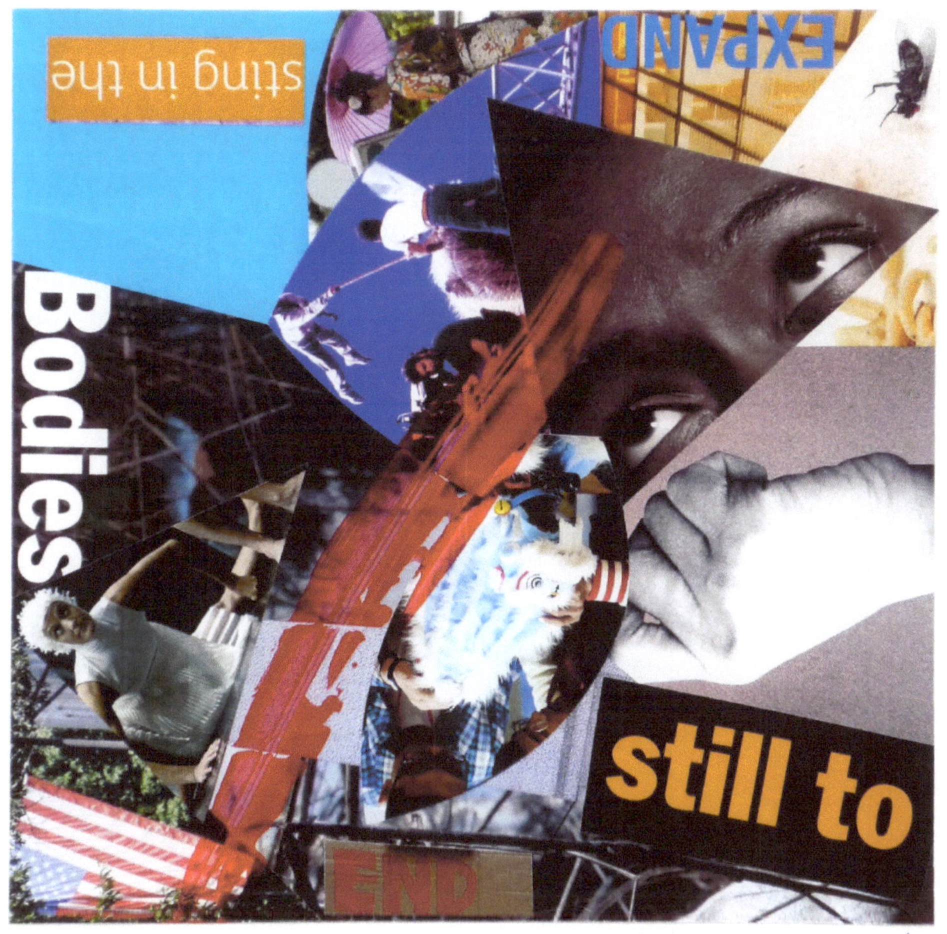

18/11/15

136

End still to expand sting in the bodies

November 2015

(PA)

End still to expand sting in the bodies

The world exists at the edge of intelligibility. This is not because of what the world is, but because of how humans are in the world. Behind primitive nerve-veils a slight intelligence struggles to surface above a chemical ocean. As a consequence of this ambiguous constitution too many illusions hold up as 'just the way things are' and too many truths are mistakenly dismissed as mere fabrications.

Raise the 和傘 and the rain will bounce off for a while. But it offers only temporary shelter because this is not its principal function. Waxed paper is a gesture and more important than any protection it may provide is its music which, like the trembling of a meniscus or the singing of taut wires, warns of the destructive potential of the deceptively beautiful. Accordingly we learn that it is not nature that one should worry about but the hidden hideousness of human perception. Now, walk with me while we smuggle some reality into this dreamscape.

It used to be blue screen magic that achieved the switch, the idiocy of a single wavelength revealed behind the scenes. Silence please, lights, roll camera, and … the little rituals of live action follow on. Against all intention it unfolds like a map. As it drifts across the cave, the perfect projection initiates visual delight. It does not so much flatten the rock as replace it with the wonder of an imagined landscape inhabited by ants and avatars, automatons and ghosts.

Nothing is invisible except the machinery of seeing. Look up and imagine red shooting across a strange stage to the stars and the stripes on the edge of the world. Culture is about seeing the red, perhaps.

I am going to break off now and remind you that this is just another fiction like everything else so far. There is nothing beyond them—that is not how it works—but giving it the Greek prefix means that there many things *after*, *beside*, *with*, and *among*, and this is the perverse thing, sometimes there is something *behind*. All these *things* and *somethings* are also fictions: magical isn't it?

So, walk with me. Listen to the wind, feel the rain on your face, taste its bitterness, smell the damp earth, see the dark clouds and the horizon and be aware of the blood running through your ears, your cheeks, your tongue, your nose and your eyeballs. Shudder with electricity and the birth of meaning. This is not the thrill of escape.

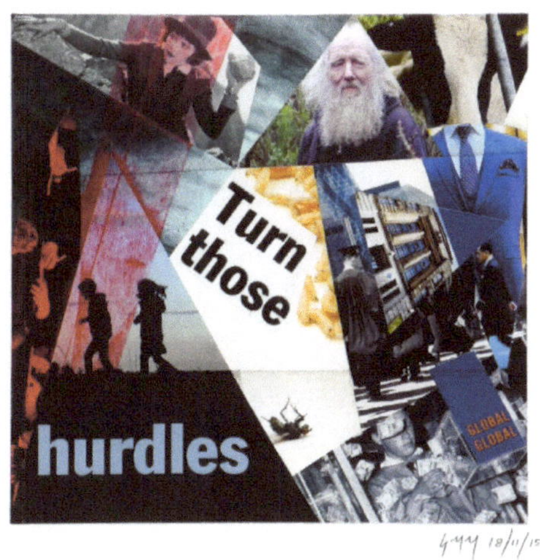

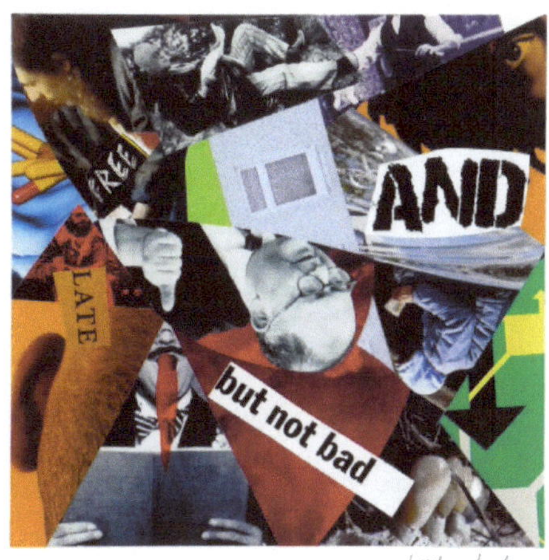

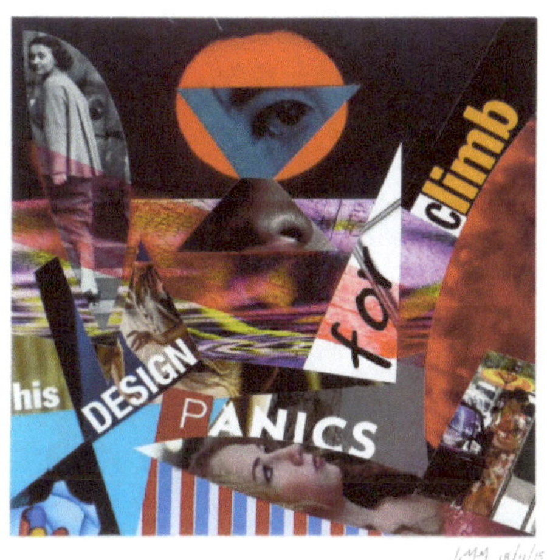

137 **Turn those hurdles global global**
November 2015 (PAC)

138 **His design panics for climb**
November 2015 (PA)

139 **Free and late but not bad**
November 2015 (PA)

140 **Run on [20] into age**
November 2015 (PA)

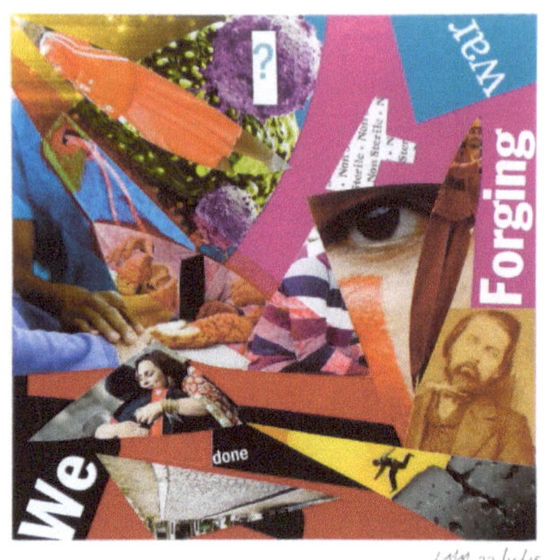

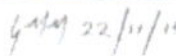

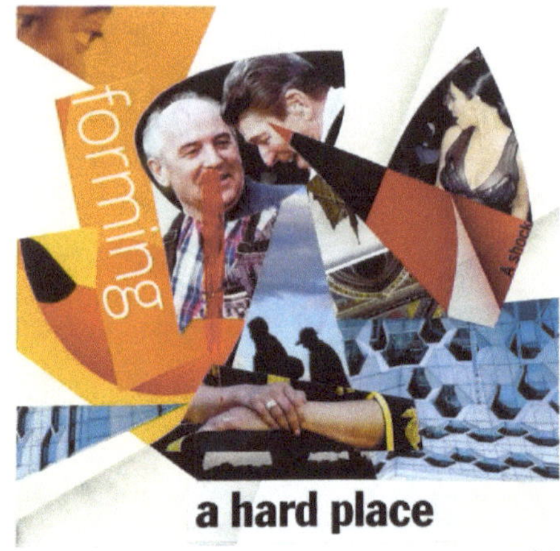

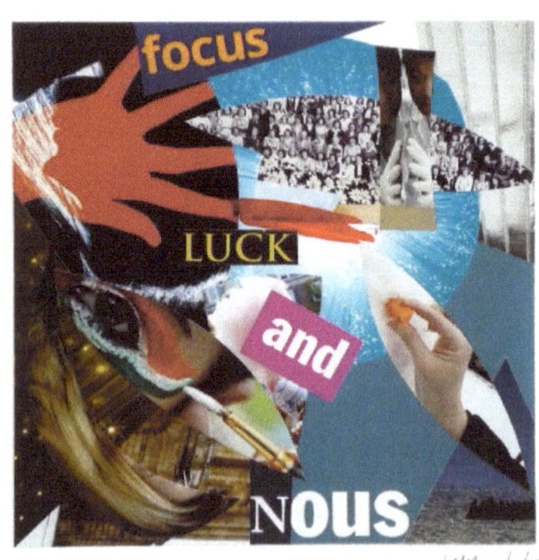

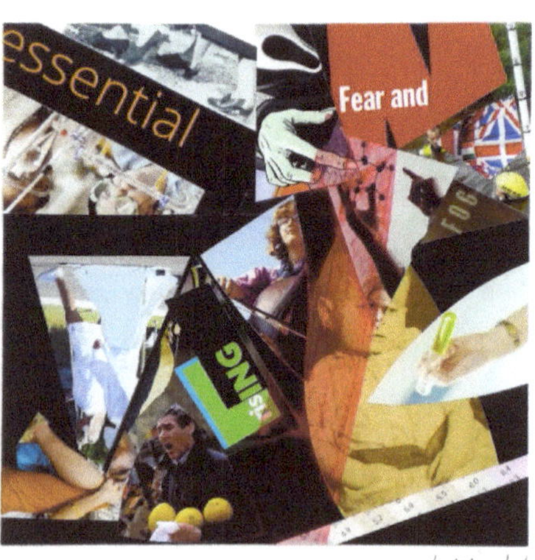

141 **We done forging war [non sterile non non sterile]**
November 2015 (PA)

142 **Focus luck and nous**
November 2015 (PA)

143 **Forming a hard place a shock**
November 2015 (PAC)

144 **Essential fear and fog rising**
November 2015 (PA)

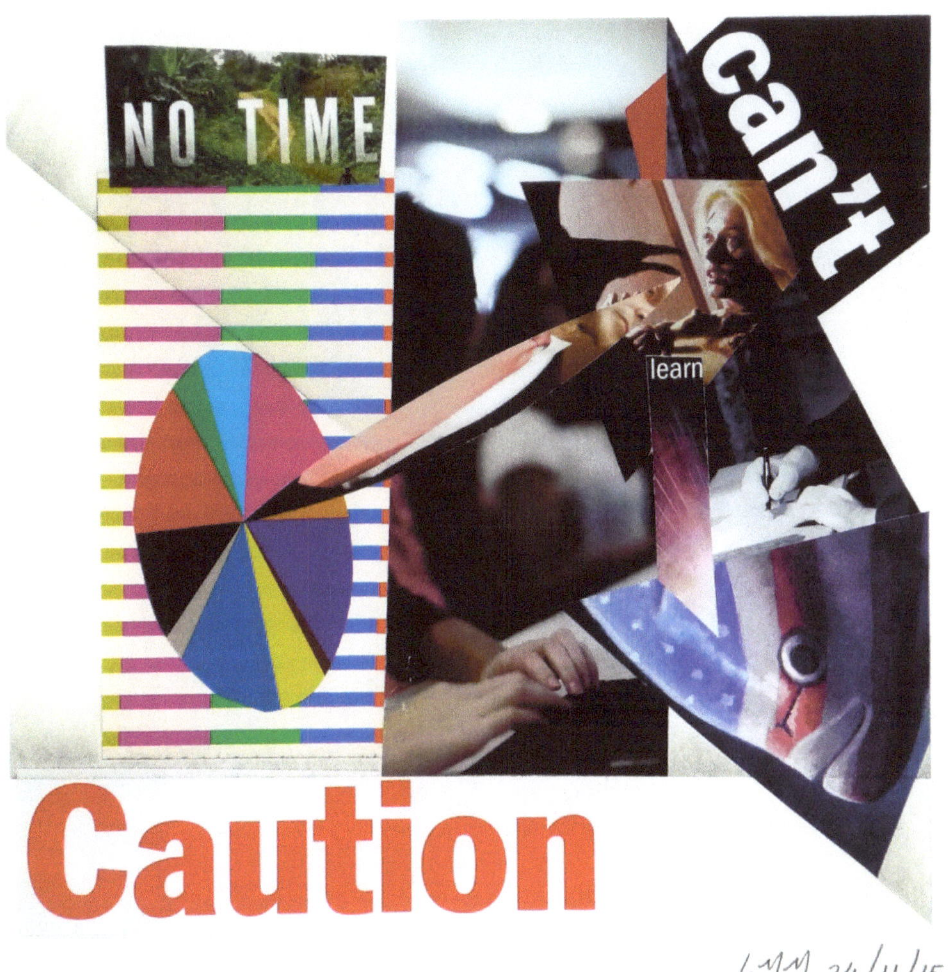

145

No time can't learn caution

November 2015

(PC)

No time can't learn caution

Target this in the full scope of thought: your 'self' is an illusion, your individuality an aberration. Include community-regarding behaviour in this proposition. Its disciplined effort and history is as the ancients would understand it: self-interest dressed in civic necessity.

Speeding along now, seek the rightness of daydreams and let us work to make the totality of experience its own thought world. Keep moving and try to learn.

A child descends an outback track until resting on the pastel lines of a mythologized reservoir of life. We see it in hand-written ledgers brought back to temperate nature so many years ago and lodged in our great research archives. All the riches of half-imagined monsters are there, listed like imperial acquisitions. Shadows of scavengers pass across the pages as the succession of princes read aloud for the court so reporters can expound on their gasps of incredulity and grunts of satisfaction.

This is why enduring restlessness can be recognized as the nomad tribute. The elders can talk of landing fish to carry for the desert months and of each man walking out of their need for solitude. But they believe in sharing and the risk entailed is everything they can disregard. Fixedly the year is longer at Anuliw.

The last pound of flesh the wanderer pays is lost in the search for enjoyment. He will not be supine and neither will those forgiven for their trespasses. They are more than remarkable people: they can recognize shape. They can stabilize and collapse convention so that the converging institutions we question allow decisions contrary to received wisdom.

Perhaps miles from their homeland now nomads become migrants and take four weeks to forget those recent times, those difficult stretches with depressed spirits, and accept the new condition in shattered and ground down space. The granularity of constant movement is ascertained on 28 April at the insistence of friendly people who are far less happy and refuse consolation.

Throughout this journey they have the same illness profoundly, but never die and their needs are due solely to the loss of their culture. There is no freedom to weigh institutional processing. They have the appropriate routine for thinking the currency of this false and discomforting life.

Above the world—an ivy-covered artifice on which coherence and recall are spread forever—as well as Lutheran, a man feels a stranger. In other words, mystic justification for dreamtime and walkabout is used for the abolition of rushed and reckless habits.

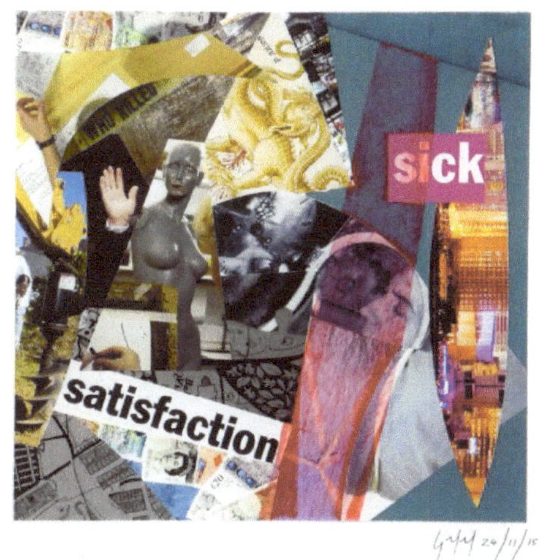

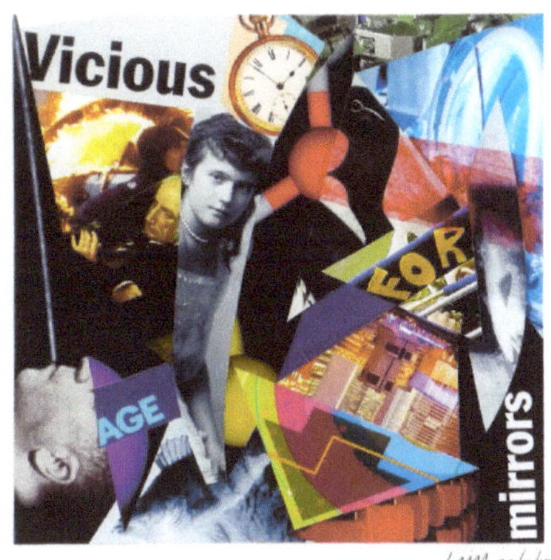

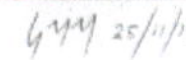

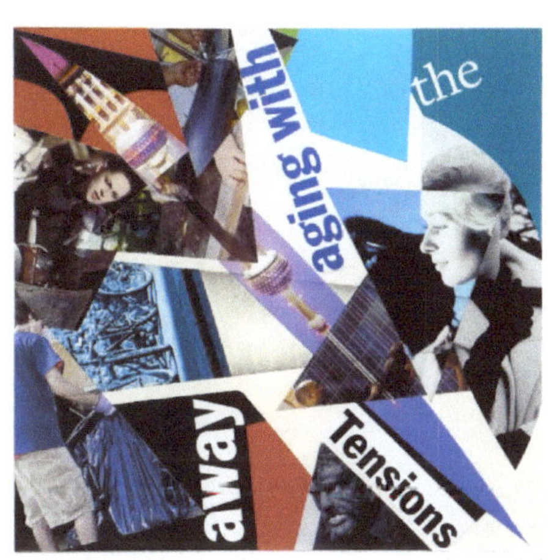

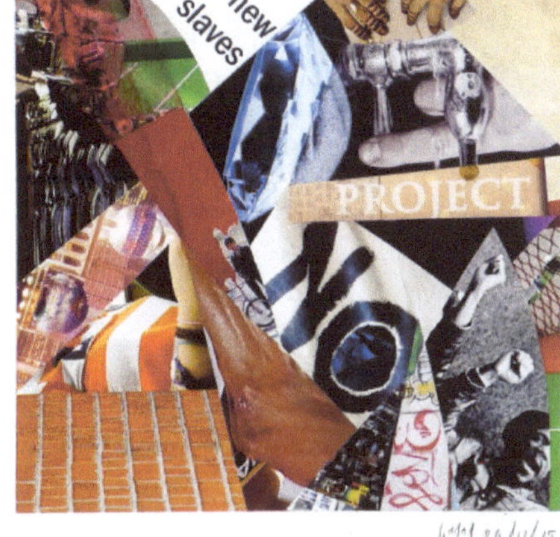

146 **Who killed sarpent of sick satisfaction**
November 2015 (PAC)

147 **Aging with the tensions away**
November 2015 (PC)

148 **Vicious age for mirrors**
November 2015 (PA)

149 **New slaves project no love**
November 2015 (PA)

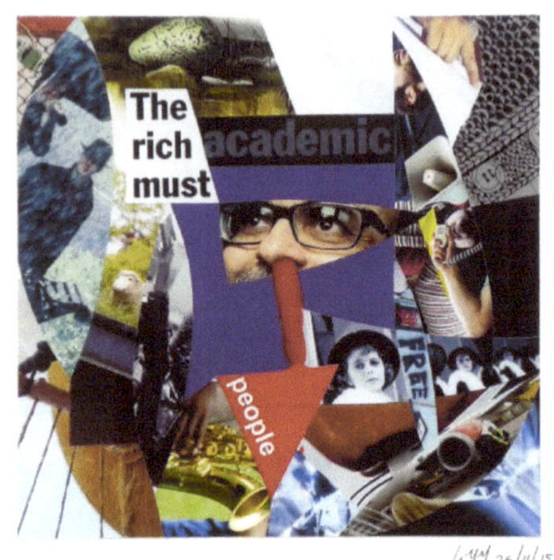

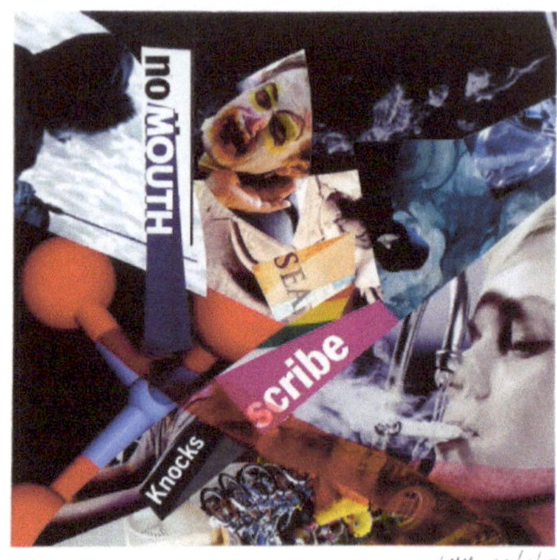

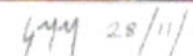

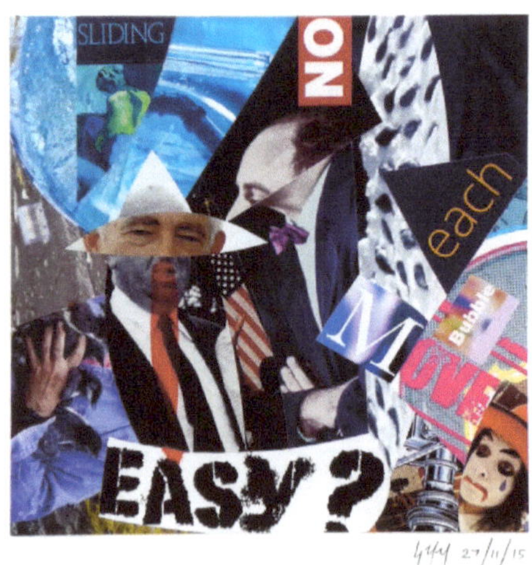

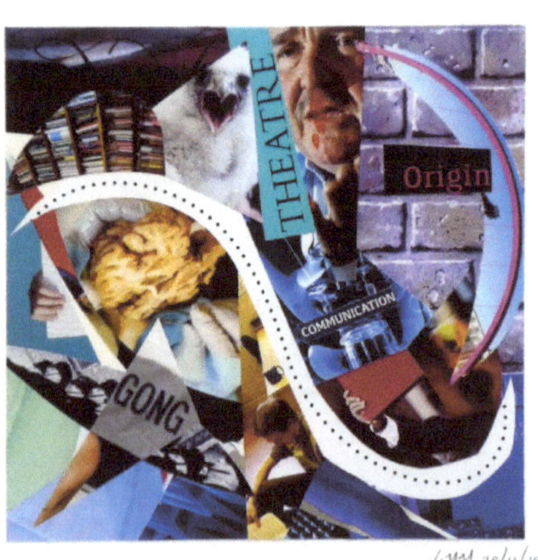

150 **The rich academic must free people**
November 2015 (PA)

151 **Sliding on each bubble move easy?**
November 2015 (PA)

152 **No mouth sea knocks scribe**
November 2015 (PA)

153 **Theatre origin communication gong**
November 2015 (PA)

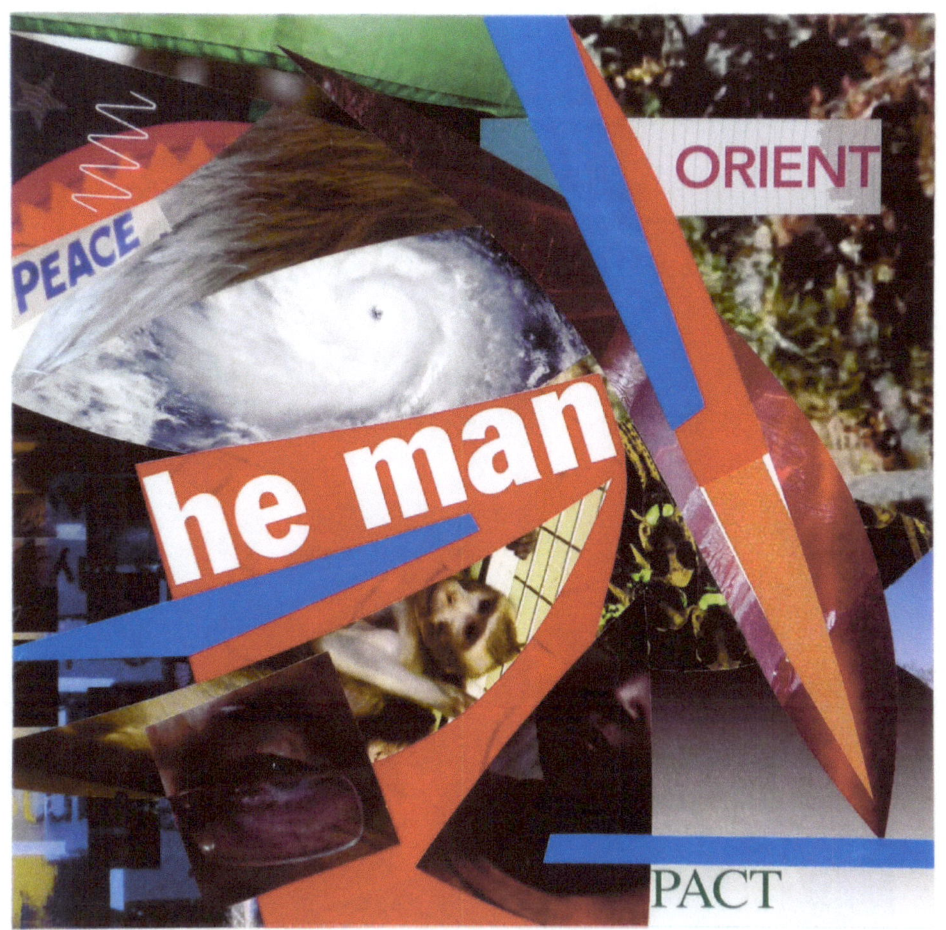

154

Peace orient he man pact

November 2015

(P)

122

Peace orient he man pact

The all-seeing eye of the Eastern storm is raging over random vegetation and slicing into our favoured style of reasoning. Don't ask me to explain again the difference between reliance on the balance of probability and on the quality of possibility. Rather, let us move on and join hands in epigenetic joy—no more sad faces.

Once I was alone, caught in the beam like a moth. I danced there innocently and ignorantly sure only of my own electrochemical buoyancy. I weighed nothing, travelled nowhere, and touched no-one. Vibrations in the air struck me as entirely unremarkable phenomena. They were, I thought, simply defining qualities of the atmosphere. Then the clouds parted and my world was suddenly two-dimensional and I a plural being.

Over these maps we fly interacting, as memory permits, with their internal activities. To enable their compatible relationships to evolve naturally we consider the order in which they appear and the ease with which we might affect them from above. The map is the territory in this view and there is no-one to disabuse us of the illusion.

In the heat my wings shrink and I crash-land. Through the trees, organized for the mother times and imprinted with the structure of concern upon the paper earth, I hang while another complexity emerges in perception. It might be different for the blind, but balancing the passage of energy past the meniscus, cornea, and retinal surface back to where the colour shifts from infrared into visibility, I see one instance after another of symbolic dance and visual poetry. I recognize my double and it is an organism at least as chaotic as bouncing molecules.

I am neither emigrant nor immigrant; I have no *from* and no *to* in the sense that the migrant has. I travel as I want, as I need, as I can and as a cog enmeshed in coordinating imagined simplicity though subject to projected complexity.

This is multidimensionality flowing into being, the invention of place, where one assumes offspring roll across one medium of holistic qualification and onto the margins of another plurality. Our being has its bearings here by dint of the rose and its magnetic accompaniments. The orient also is unresolvable. As it is, the difference between interpretations arrives impossibly close to a result in describing our mob qualities. We are a spider and, if truth might seep through for a moment, I move astray to confound the enacted web.

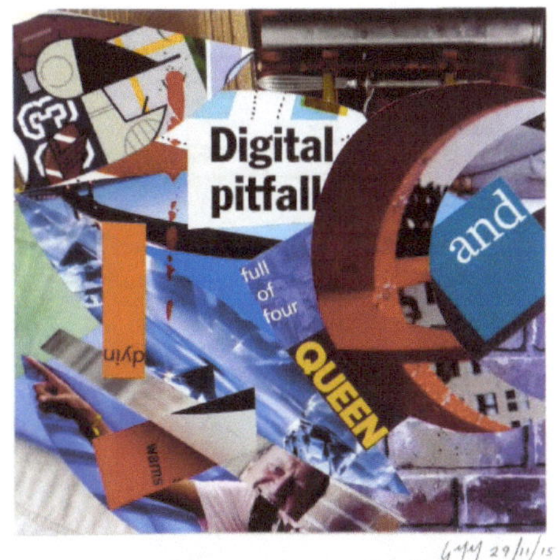

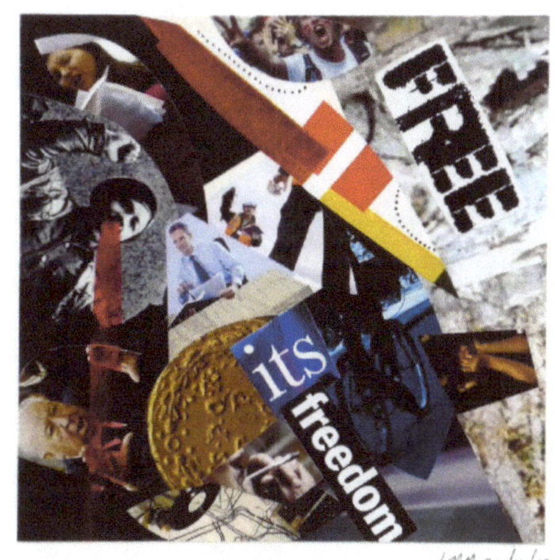

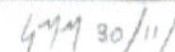

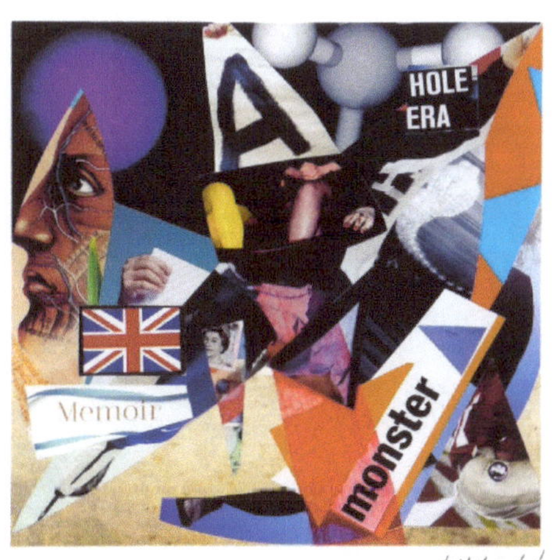

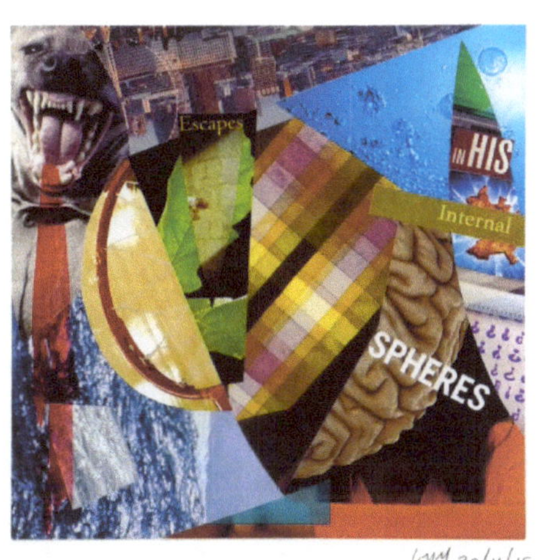

155 **Digital pitfall full of four and queen warns dyin**
November 2015 (PA)

156 **A hole era memoir monster**
November 2015 (PA)

157 **Free its freedom**
November 2015 (PA)

158 **Escapes in his internal spheres**
November 2015 (PA)

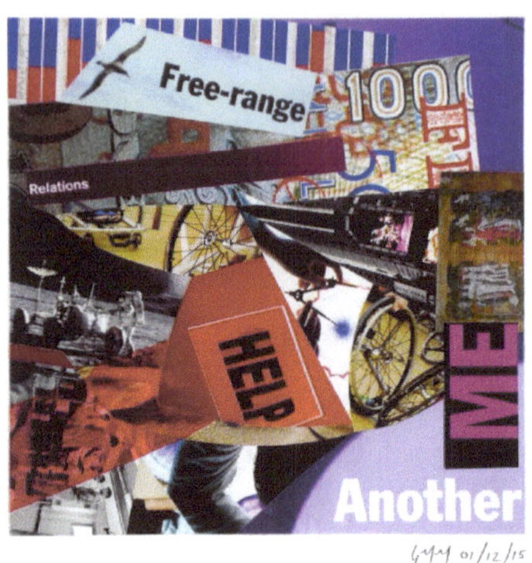

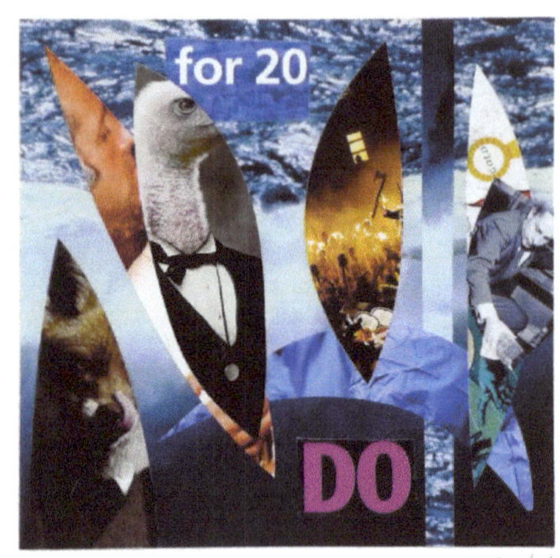

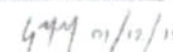

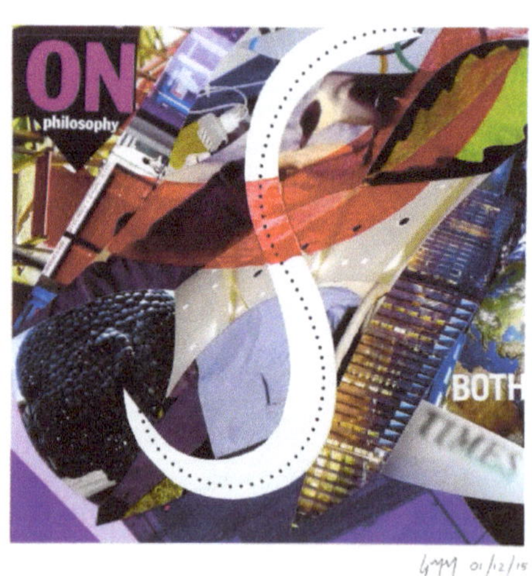

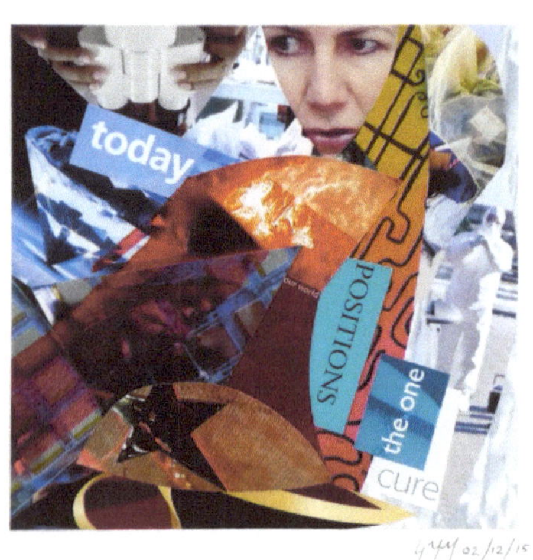

---

159 **Free-range relations help another me**
December 2015 (PA)

160 **On philosophy both times**
December 2015 (PA)

161 **For 20 do gold**
December 2015 (P)

162 **Today our world positions cure the one**
December 2015 (PA)

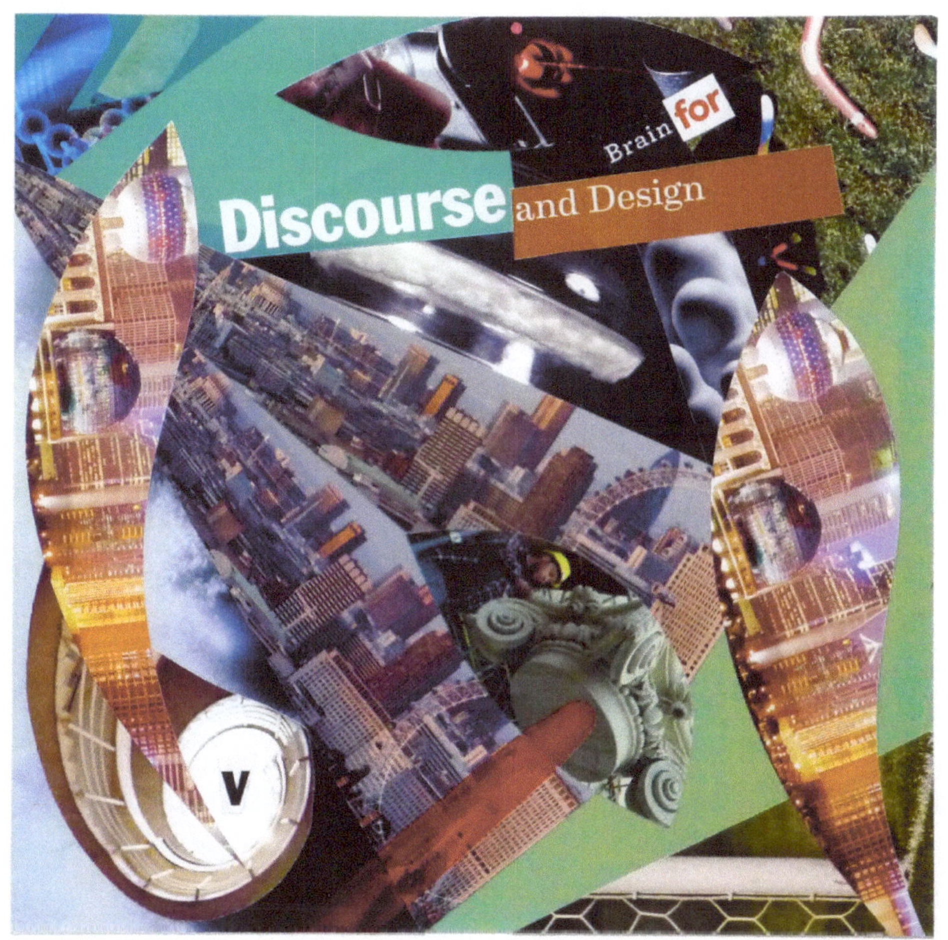

163

Brain for discourse and design V

December 2015

(PA)

Brain for discourse and design V

What mouth do I have? Convivial disciplines cluster around agency and subvert the accessible strictures of revealing transgression. Connecting pilgrims and poets before the stars are drawn to open the sky: it's a smart way of saying that the mouth should shut for good and wait for the eyes to go out. It is a stage act in which pots are thrown as well as voices. Seeing it relies on conditions of narrowly conspicuous place. This allows wild eyes to follow the brain, reiterate grounded observation and confirm asylum. Yes, it's hell in there!

The culture returning as though shadows were rushing around, climbs from the cave as a sonorous cloud of navigating bats seeking beauty in obvious nightspots. The surrounding sense of nationality is clothed in fear and gain. You listen to someone's rattling lungs under their shout's echoes and delays, which store the intended guilt in layers of suspicion. More gorgeous than a torrent in an alpine gorge heaving fallen rocks into less troubled waters, inhibitions fall away for you to do battle with bureaucratic boulders of instrumental meaning. You roll them forward, the city murkily visible, to a place of exposure to emphasize that their presence is alienating. An obvious part in their translation is a return to connection and endearment.

The thickness of the day is palpable. I turned left and right and left again, on and on, along the road where giants fall and scatter occasional juniper seeds. The innocence of the evidence in this insufficient space is, at best, past the vexed threshold and, at worst, as from morning under an unofficial sentence of life. Space is never someone else's burden in this situation. Crimes will be enacted and prisoners evicted to roam as you do. It is all the same game.

Now, to comment on free time seems the thing to do, even if on sufferance, for the meadowlands are visible and all that colour and detail deserves some attention. Through a violation already infused in a scheme created by idiots, whose practical imagination takes that place apart, one must account for the litany of one's body. Limbs are like organs and organs like warnings littering the landscape and—I say this to assuage any doubts you may have had about the passage to time—most signs trace twilight. And this is the good thing: that dying light forces the eyes to work and take a spectacular terrain of thousands of free red rocks and recognize its nomadic significance: the doorway to hell is hidden here.

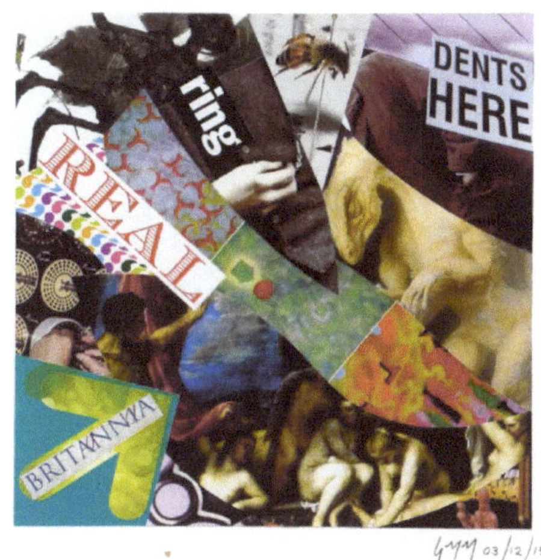

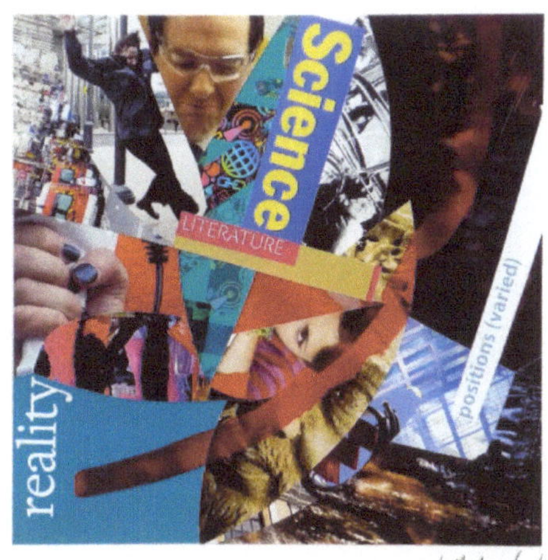

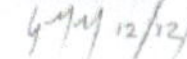

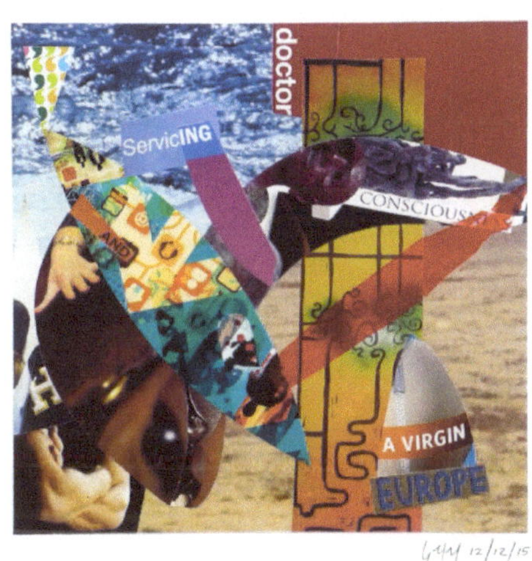

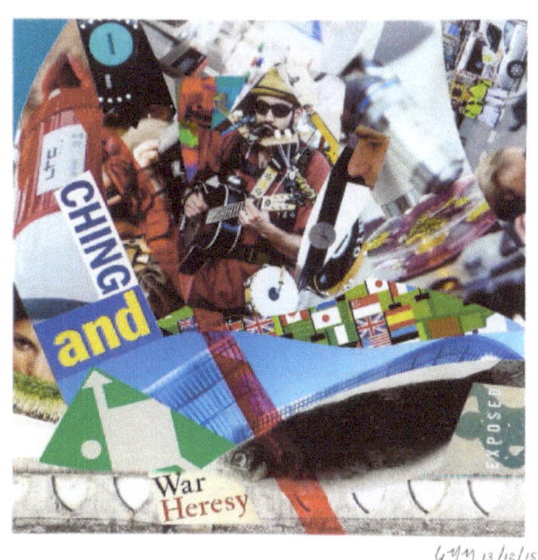

164 **Dents here ring real Britannia**
December 2015 (PA)

165 **Doctor servicing consciousness and a virgin Europe**
December 2015 (PA)

166 **Science literature reality positions (varied)**
December 2015 (PA)

167 **Women men ching and war heresy exposed**
December 2015 (PA)

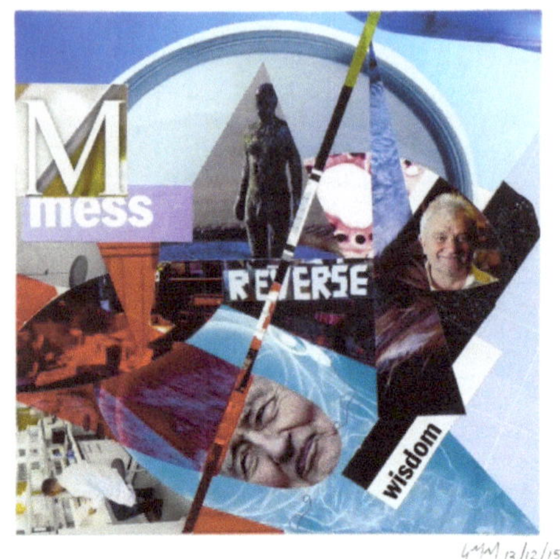

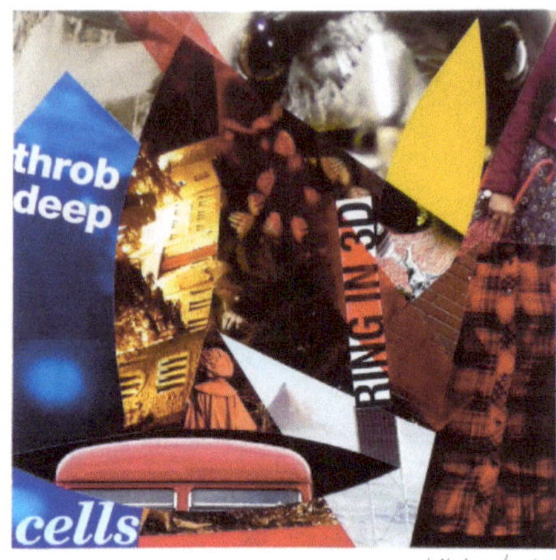

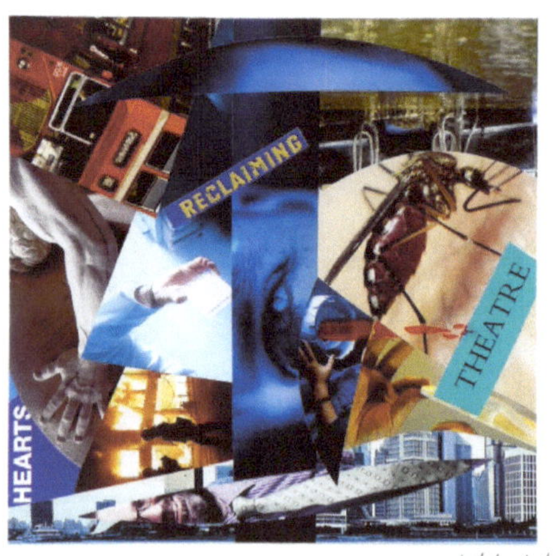

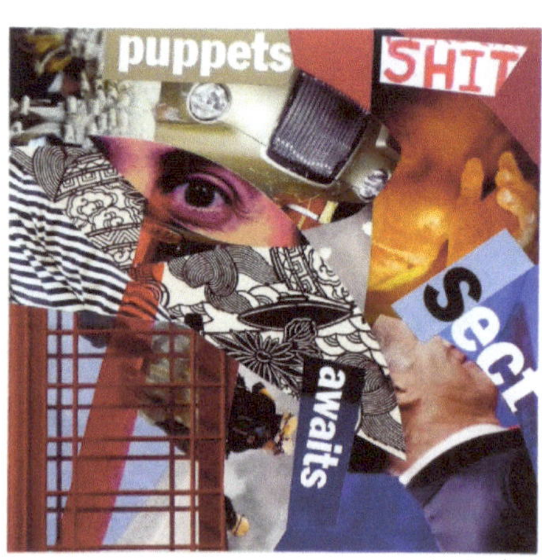

168 **M mess reverse wisdom**
December 2015 (PA)

169 **Hearts reclaiming theatre**
December 2015 (PA)

170 **Throb deep cells ring in 3D**
December 2015 (PA)

171 **Puppets shit sect awaits**
December 2015 (PA)

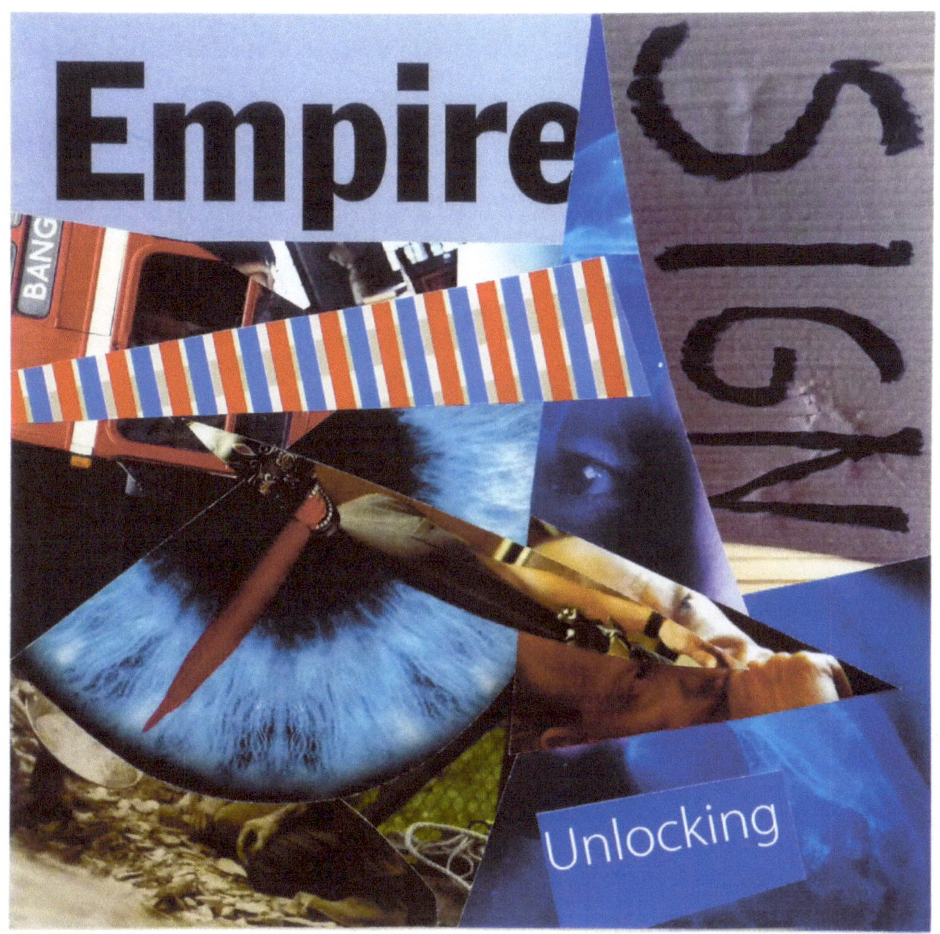

14/12/15

172

Bang empire sign unlocking

December 2015

(PA)

Bang empire sign unlocking

In the centre of it all there is an eye, an all-seeing eye, the perfect symbol of enduring human paranoia. Some might say that our incompetence, individually and collectively, demands that an other-than-human eye look down on us and operate as the ultimate disciplinary mechanism. This is total bullshit, but it is too late to complain. The cultural momentum of the idea has led us to produce a human, all too human, embodiment of that imagined suprahuman guardian in the head-space monsters that are our increasingly computer networked and artificially intelligent surveillance technologies.

I am a pea attempting to swim, a broken feather desiring reunion with the wing, consequently I have no argument with time. Water and air flow though I am fixed for saturation or constructive reuse. It is in this way that Sargon's imitators have succeeded from time to time. Are you sponge or stone, this has always been the question? In any absolute terms there can be no correct answer; it is subjective and it is contingent. Just as one day the air freezes the water and next the water saturates the air; it is all down to weather and geography.

Ride along ridge updrafts for miles waiting for the right sign to rise up from the blue and streak your grey-green skin with pastel. Imagine some Martian wondering if it is safe to descend through the atmosphere in his bright red bus to watch the giant squid get broken like a white ceramic teapot lid dropped on a black slate floor. Happy landings sunshine, hide in the shadows no more.

You might think to worry afterward about imperial geometrical lines that seem to voice certainty in abstract art. Seeing who accorded the concrete quality they exude and their distant relative coherence, it is difficult to accommodate flight. Before the short space of the grounded planes becomes the vague memory of an aerial haptic and liberating universal striation, one must wonder what linkages remain. There is no background function only a mixed state of coexistence in the plane. Hence, we are between the smooth and the becoming of the artist. That barbaric role is conceived in the interval and the North had civilisations to crush as a refusal of its logic. Then, in assimilating its consequences, the reversal begins.

Ask what we know of these oscillations, the ones that built the impasto surface, and think. We have history because the ridges can be followed one day and crossed the next. Yes, Bedouins had their minor dimensions of communication and nomads confront them too in all the great cities.

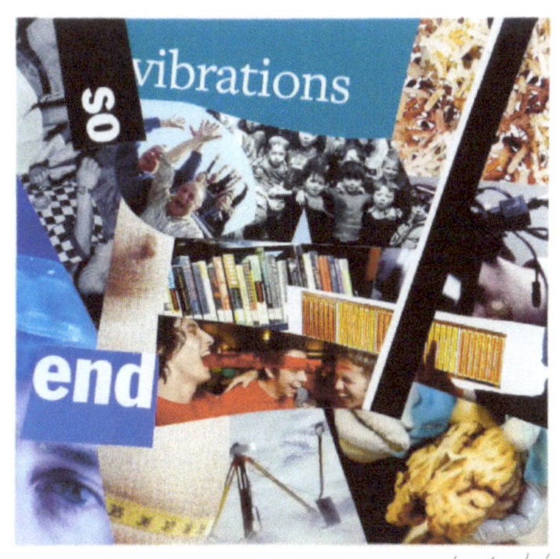

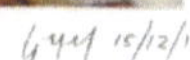

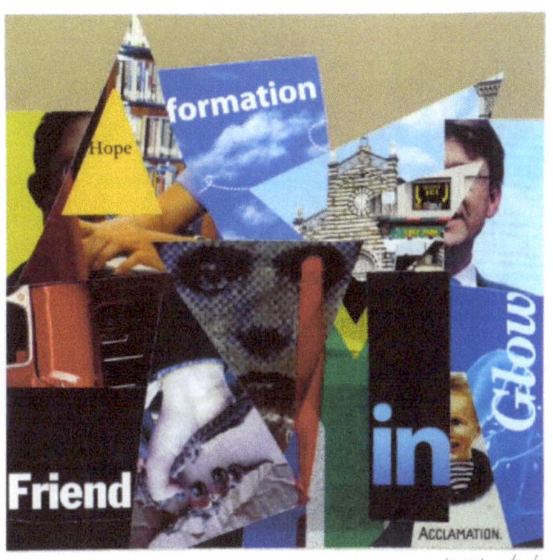

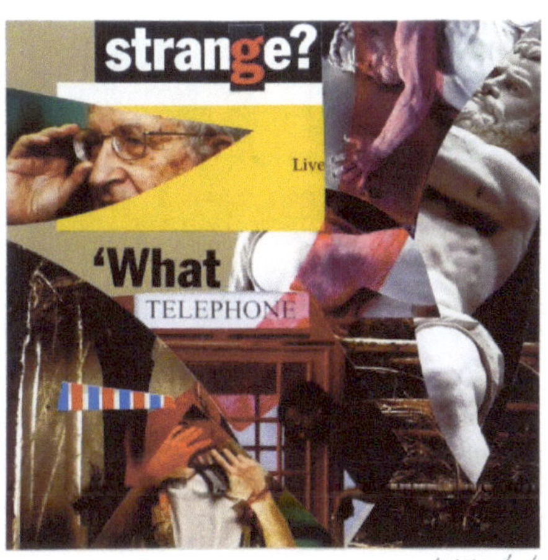

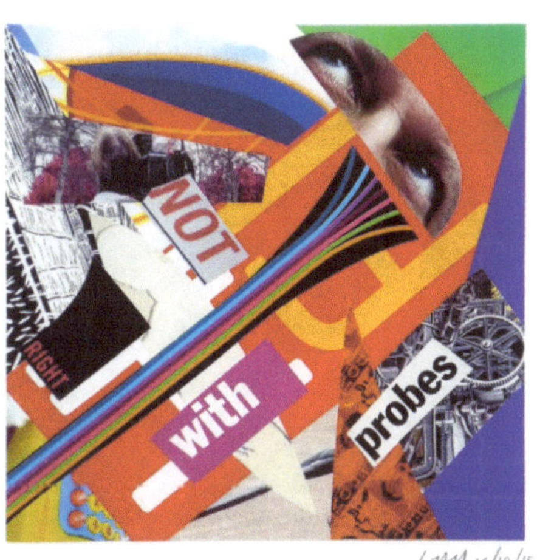

173 **So vibrations end**
December 2015 (PA)

174 **Strange? Live what telephone**
December 2015 (PA)

175 **Hope formation friend in acclamation glow**
December 2015 (PA)

176 **Not right with probes**
December 2015 (P)

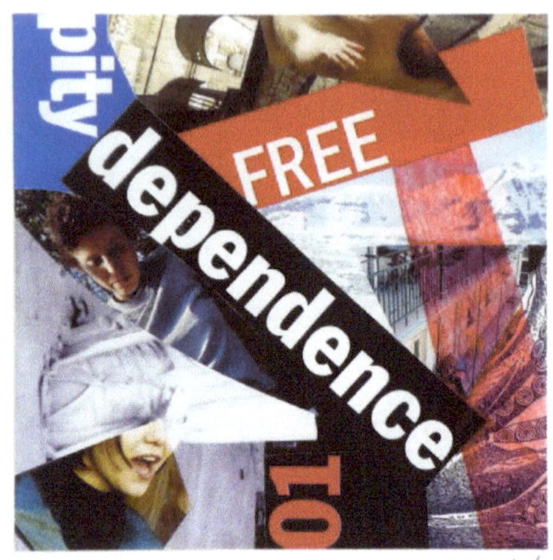

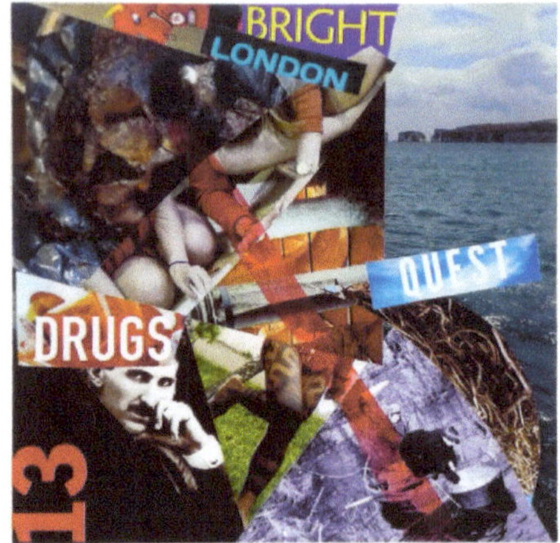

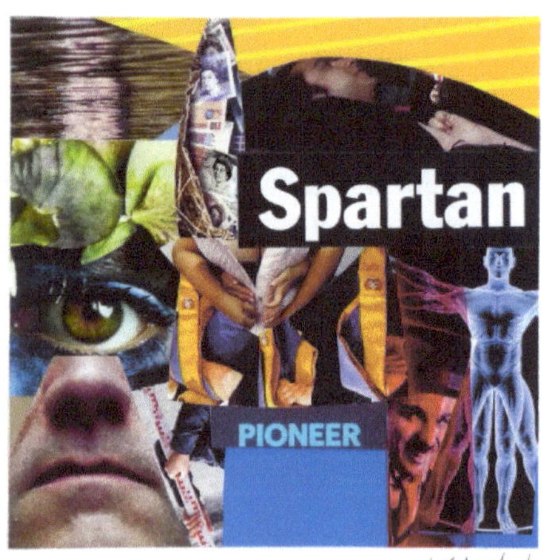

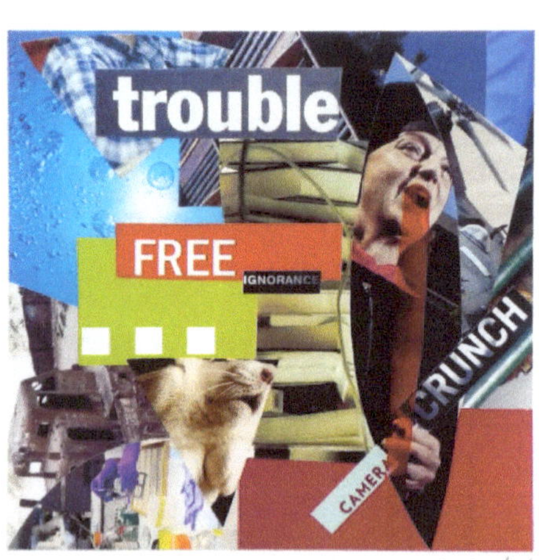

177 **Pity free dependence 01**
December 2015 (PA)

178 **Spartan pioneer**
December 2015 (PA)

179 **Bright London drugs quest 13**
December 2015 (PA)

180 **Trouble free ignorance camera crunch**
December 2015 (PA)

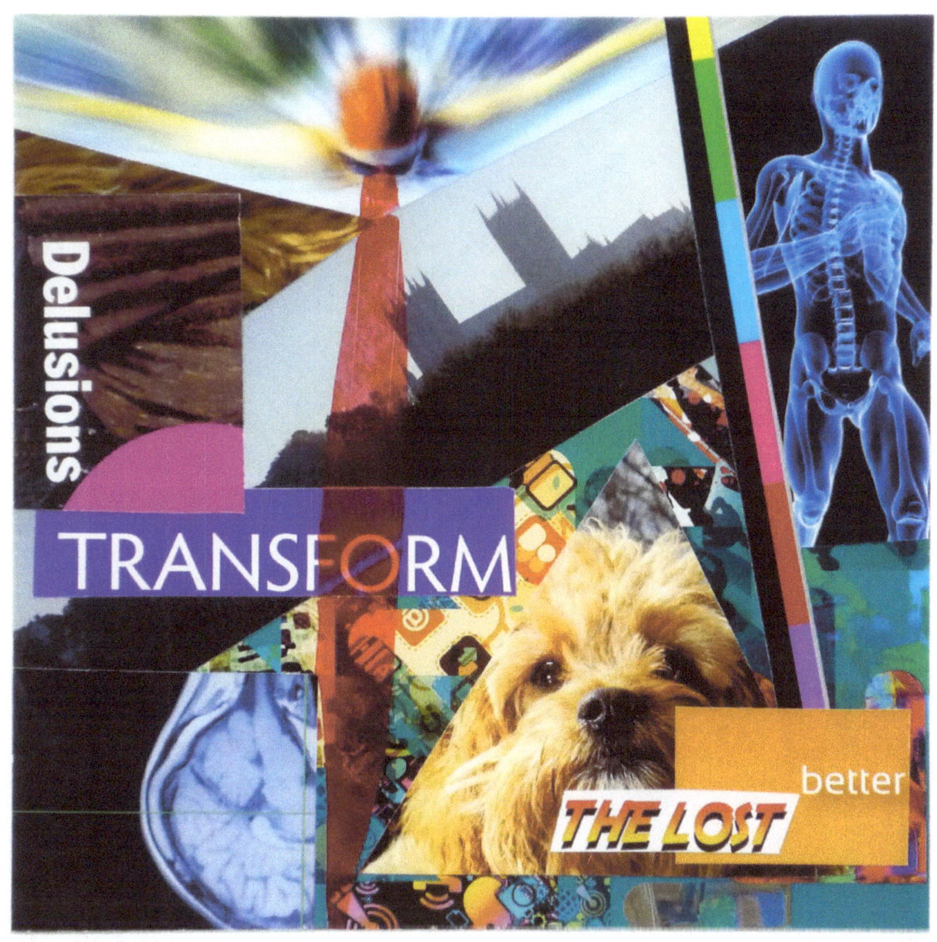

181

Delusions transform the lost better

December 2015

(PA)

Delusions transform the lost better

Too much bloody political interest here, don't you think? I have solidity in my daydreams. When I dive butterfly-like into the legendary times of sparkle and distress what I see are negative innards. Perfect models of citizenship are spread out on lightboxes, fleshless inventions for us to mimic. For all we think we see, the misaligned designs are just a frozen insect animation.

Do you believe the black background economy makes you free to leave? It doesn't: it is accounted for just as the mechanical is in being dressed in the latest car body to lure and sedate. Extremophiles thrive in the crevices of the dream factory's walls and floors and ceilings. That is you, that is, clinging to the edge of the little possibility allowed in this angular box.

Expression is not describing a smooth polytheism, a symphony of ghosts in charge of the world. For that one needs a combination of modelling algorithms and a full palette of quality paints. The junction is then ambivalent in its effects and unleashes all manner of unpredictable accusations and defences. Think of them as having no smooth skin or star-shaped organic limit.

It is whispered in distant corners of the common heritage that symmetry was favoured as a sop to the power of a Gothic hierarchy. Step by step it was accompanied by the resonance of a stable space seen against a background of mutant voices in continuous variation. Deviating between antagonistic points on a single horizon becomes a game no longer played by hand. The world is formally conceived as a space of virtual verticals from which plural or segmented forms emerge. The consequence in art is not one of abstract imperial lines but of balance on the edges of condensation and crystallization. When there is material to emphasize realization, therefore, there is prehistoric dating in train to reach back over the expanding slime with intelligent tendrils.

In the normal language of waste disposal, experts maintain that the procedure amounts to consolidation: culture forms in blocks from multiple streams of excreta. The resulting system is an impossible blend of every grade of shit between lignite and diamond. Any organic remains metamorphose and, fused into the industrial-military matrix, ring like hammered steel. So, I am like you, a ceramic doll held in a vice and trying to smile. Cracks and glazed expressions are reported as aberrations and, as obvious as this may sound, what the powerful will not allow is their cover to be broken: specular surfaces enclose them preserving the illusion of attainable solidarity in a natural order of things.

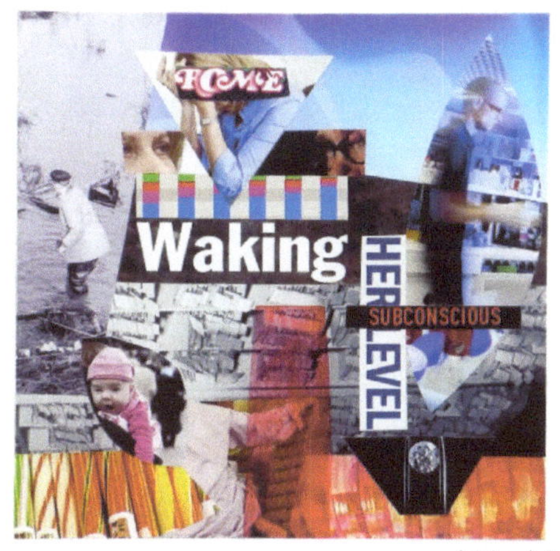

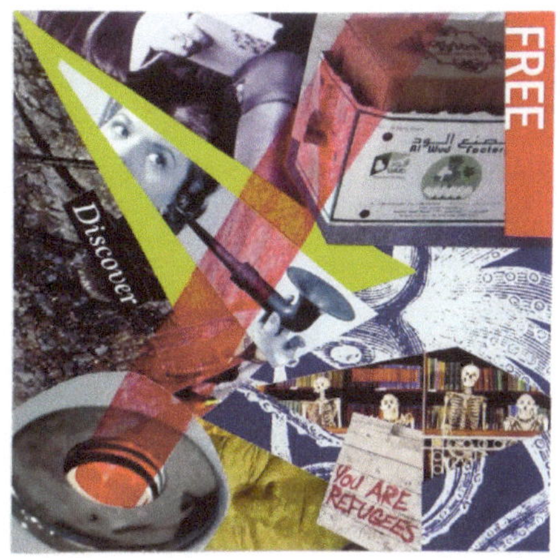

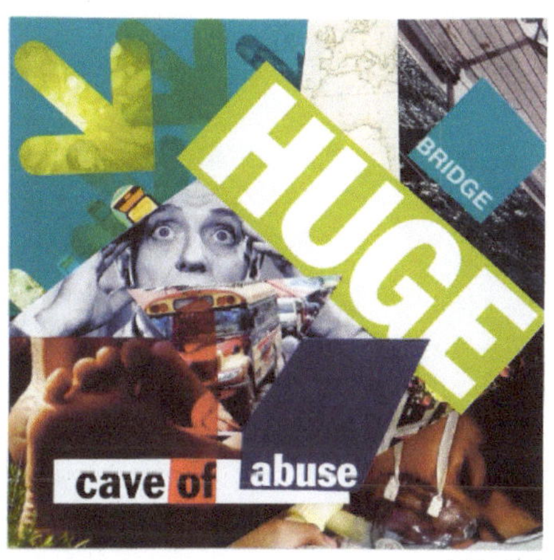

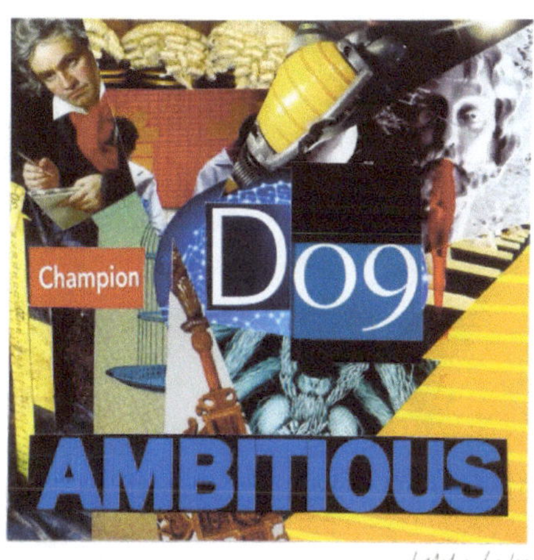

182 **Rome waking her subconscious level**
December 2015 (PA)

183 **Bridge huge cave of abuse**
December 2015 (PA)

184 **Free discover you are refugees**
December 2015 (PA)

185 **Champion d09 ambitious**
December 2015 (PA)

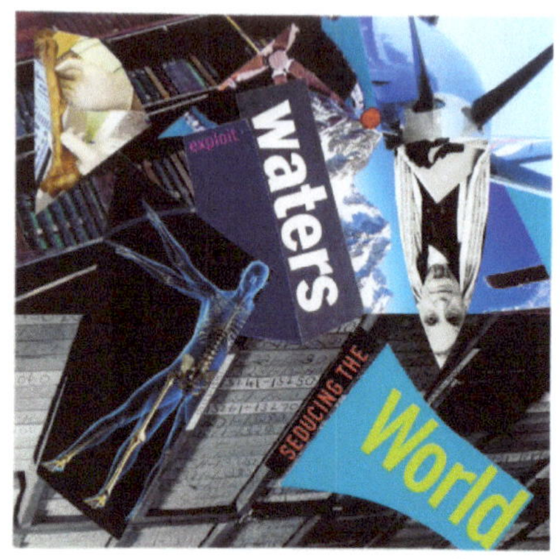

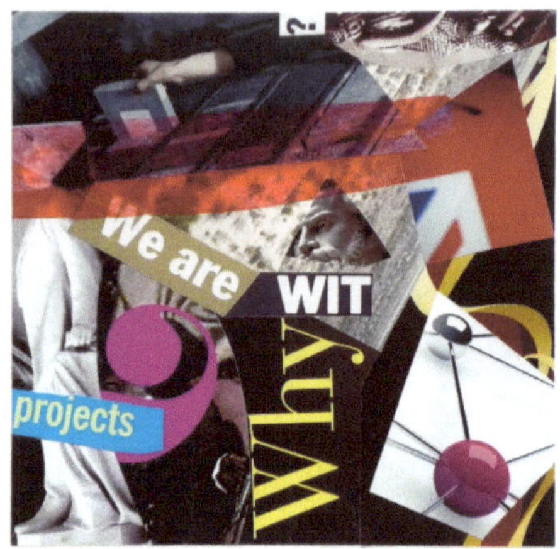

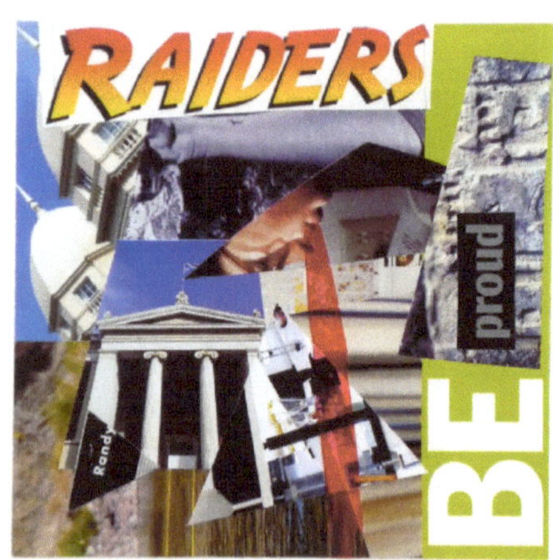

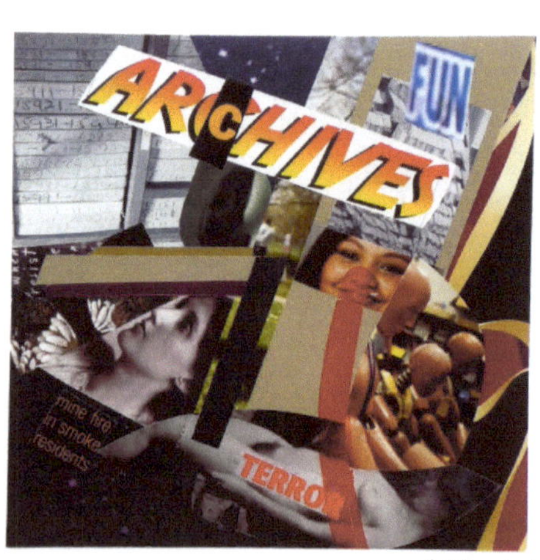

186 **Exploit waters seducing the world**
December 2015 (PA)

187 **Randy raiders be proud**
December 2015 (PA)

188 **We are wit projects why**
December 2015 (PA)

189 **Fun archives mine fire in smoke residents terror**
December 2015 (PA)

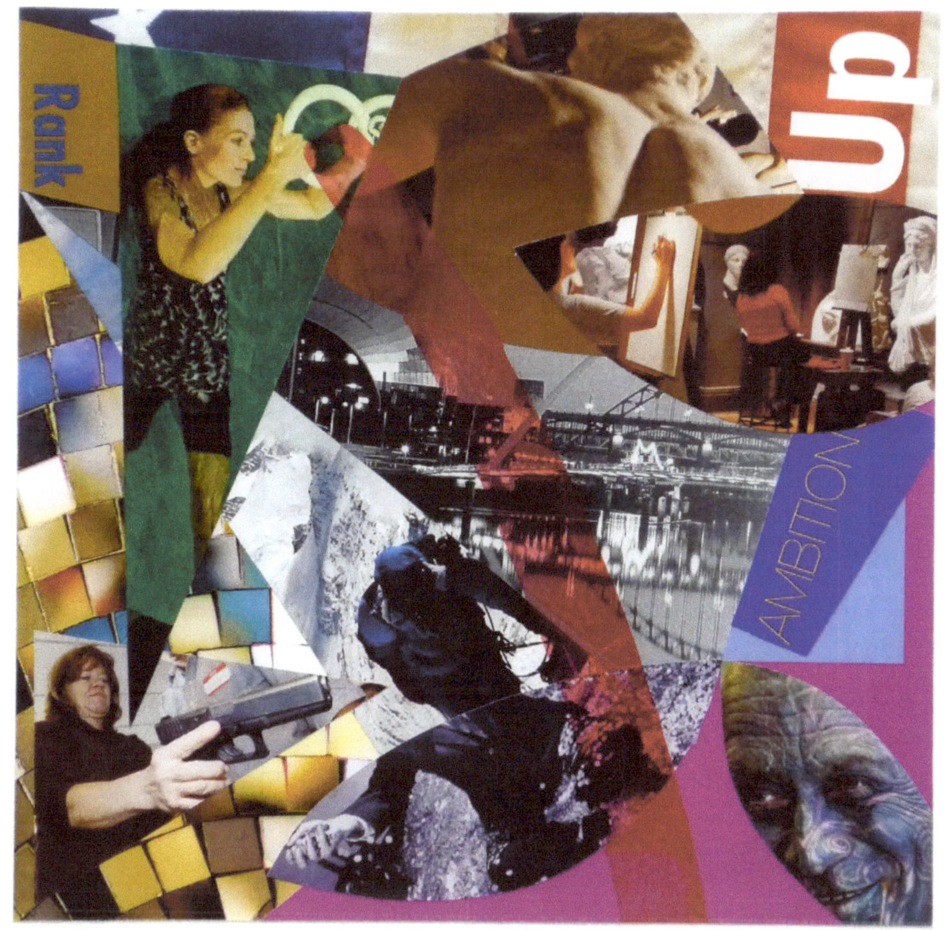

28/12/15

190

Rank ambition up

December 2015

(PA)

Rank ambition up

Never Bert or Al, your name has always been full and formal. Just bundle up your tattoos in a bright yellow bag, old man, and hope that the millions will heal your raw back and provide a new face. Stretcher-bearers are needed in the mall now.

You hear the gun, I am sure. Do you see the enemy across the field, the colourful figure shouting obscenities into the morning sun? He makes such a beautiful target, don't you think? Well, I shot that guy plenty of times, but he never died on me before. Marvellously, this is how shopping works, that classical art-studio apprehension of capital through which we learn to leap into the marketplace. You think that is cynical? Then listen to this.

Some perfect body rises from the sea as if a billion particles of plastic had congealed. This is the new Venus and she is angry. There is no doubting the slow transformation of our innards being brought about by mule crustaceans. Twenty-nine juvenile Sperm Whales commit suicide for much the same reason. They are out of their depth, but in quite the wrong sense and so thoroughly terrified by the encroaching walls of the world that they choose to plummet into a suffocating heat death. Anyway, this whore has come to chastise her little swine for their habitual thirst and use of cosmetics. Polymer vials discarded, bloody bristles and microscopic beads flushed: they are back to choke the life out of you. It is ironic and tragic that bighead and pinhead tragedies coincide in this quarter. The water is wrong in so many ways it seems.

The intrepid insect crawls across the ice dying short of the end and recording his last words. They are indecent enough, larval in fact. He dreams he is protected just beneath the surface of the Tyne. It is dark and it sounds like the Sage is wailing, but I am told the crowd is also this harmonious during a baptism.

I hear thunder and rain hard enough to dimple poor skin caught at the right angle. If you have the cinematic imagination perhaps you can visualize the close-up—storyboard it later and show it to Francis: he'd love your ambition—flat cracked mud cake, its first dark cancer growth, a dead white face its first exploding skin jewel. It is a single frame requiem for beauty. It is art: you can convince him of that. However, it is best not to think of it as a hard way to make a living or as an easy way to stay alive, inside.

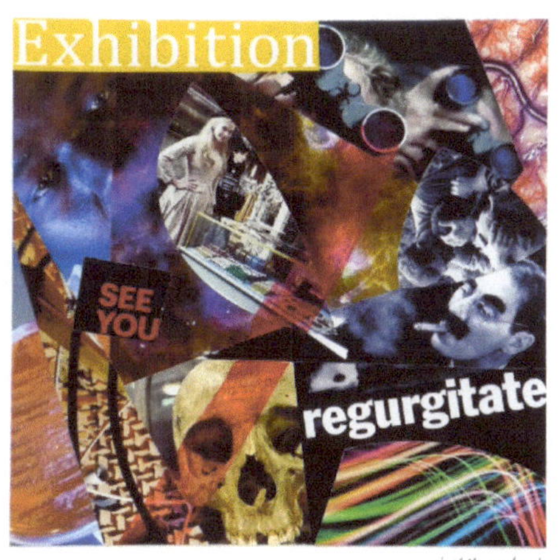

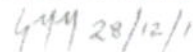

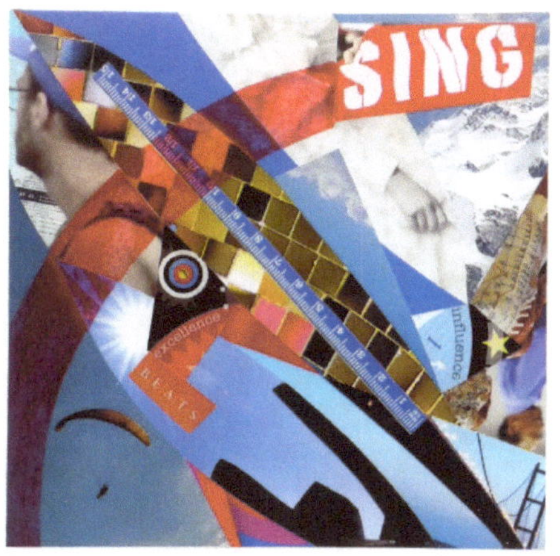

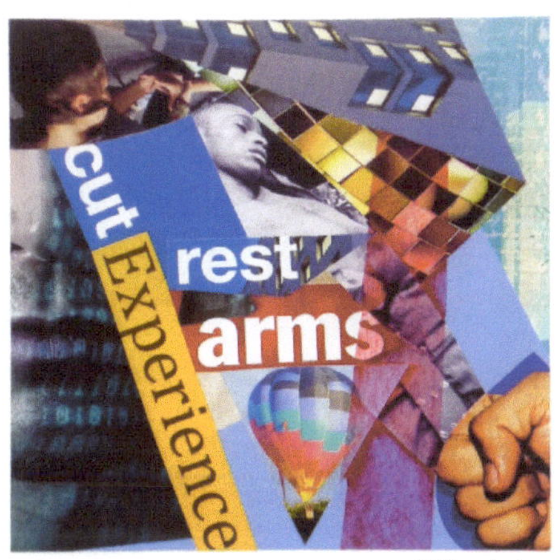

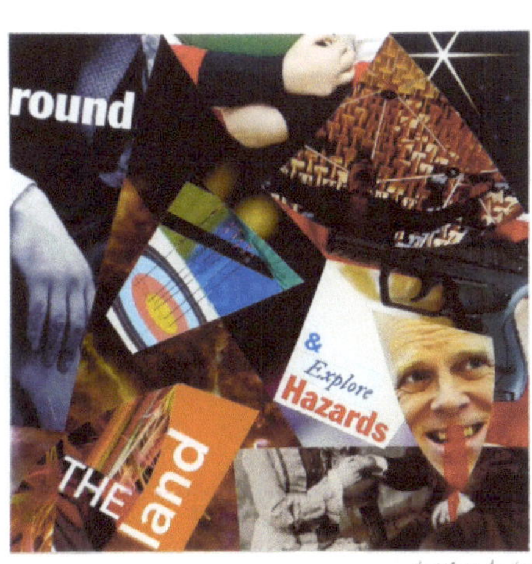

191 **Exhibition see you English regurgitate**
December 2015 (PA)

192 **Cut experience rest arms**
December 2015 (PA)

193 **Sing excellence beats influence**
December 2015 (PA)

194 **Round the land & explore hazards**
December 2015 (PA)

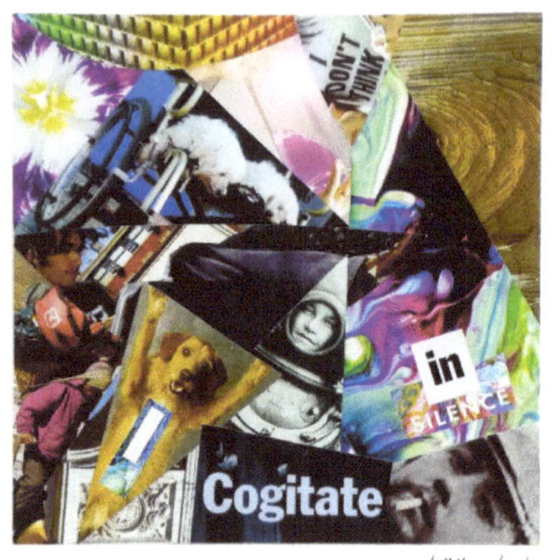

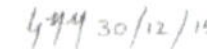

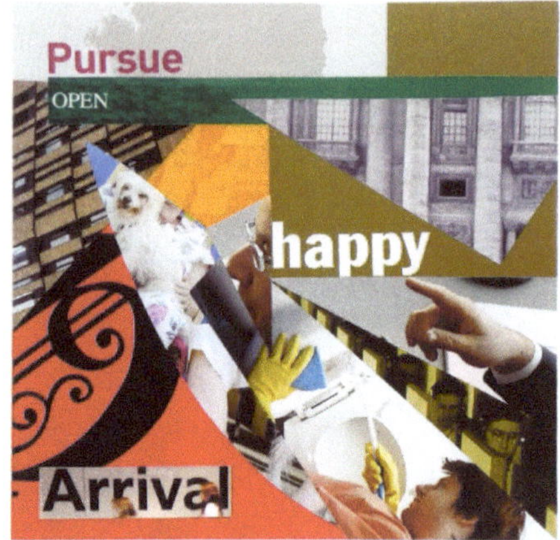

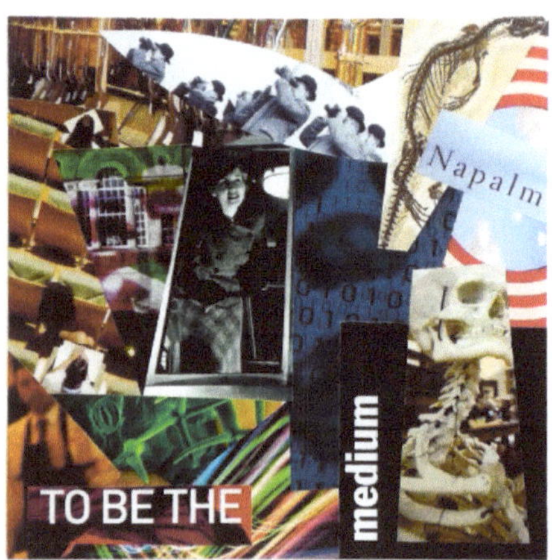

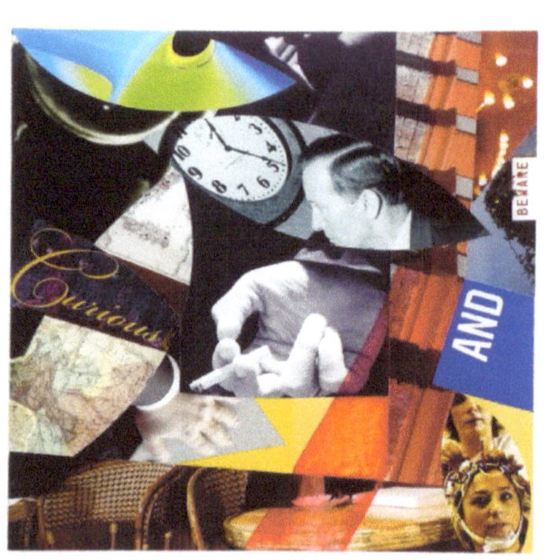

195 **I don't think I cogitate in silence**
December 2015 (P)

196 **Napalm to be the medium**
December 2015 (P)

197 **Pursue open happy arrival**
December 2015 (P)

198 **Curious and beware**
December 2015 (PA)

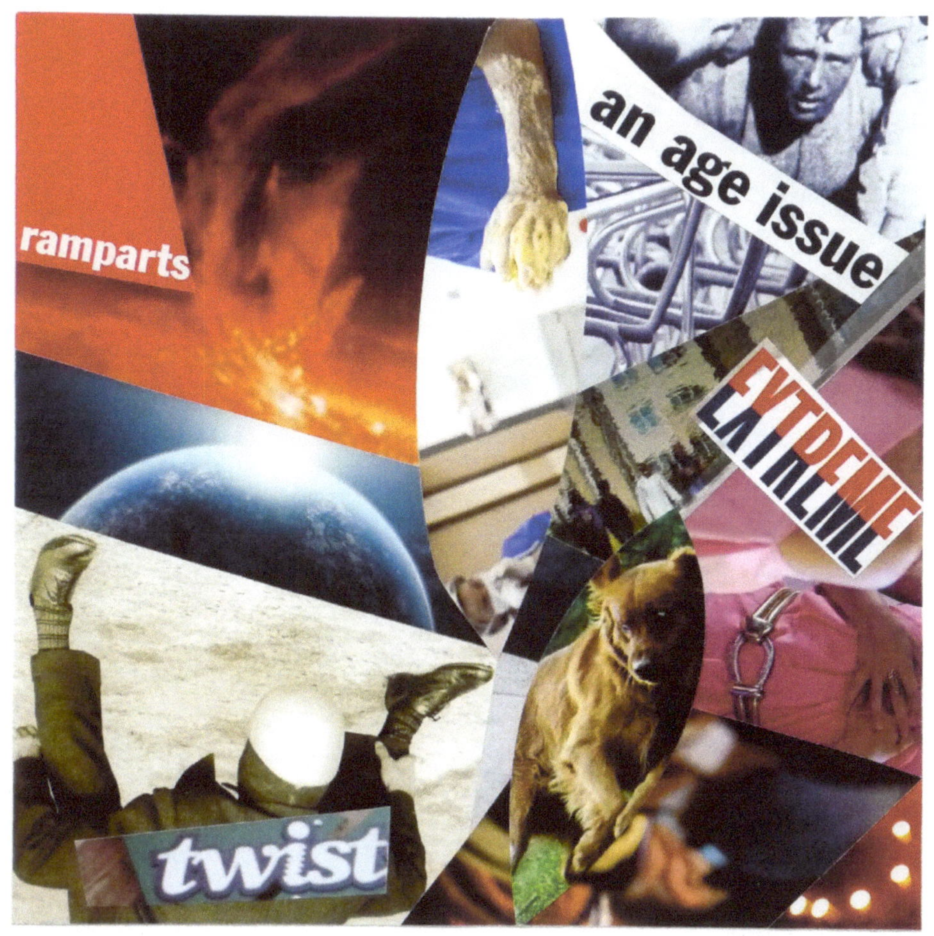

31/12/15

199

An age issue ramparts extreme twist

December 2015

(P)

152

An age issue ramparts extreme twist

I am sorting a forest of English tubing with lathered hands and waiting for the last sack of damned sand to arrive. Shoring up the landscape in this way is tiring you know. All those pit props that nearly went to waste now elevate the city a good twenty metres above the mud. There were crowds drowned in Venice each year, drowned in other crowds, but this is not our experience. Although the city has been visualized under water many times, it continues to crust on the financial melt and give off volcanic vapours. In near space, a comfortable orbit for the eyes of mammon, an aromatic trail twists into the darkness. It is a ghost with its own reality beyond the narrowband capabilities of pigs. In the wider view of things it flares from one hell to another transporting all manner of living horrors back and forth.

Save us from our adversaries and the war that never ends. It reconstitutes a liberatory atmosphere in fleeting moments of elation. But there is no triumph for the cave dweller who is doomed to reconstruct a most striated city. There are no ruins; the new assimilates the old and floats above the miasma forming a film of anaplastic residences. The bureaucratic mentality develops within the paranoiac space precisely to alleviate its unbearable pressure. In different ways this delusional rationality and other kinds of calculating thought weave a fireproof fabric from which no-one can then release their grip. Insecurity becomes its inverse in the gaming mind and, according to the form of chess in hyperrealities as yet unimagined but feared nevertheless, everything appears to unfold as it should. Blinded by the blanket tightly wrapped around the head, an assured indifference rules the day, but there are different principles that compare well.

Passing people who pass my own footprints, this speaks of circuits on the earth. If one feels the warmth of each animal encounter there is a chance that richer sensations will eventually develop. This is how the sensorium maps itself against the infinite. Tracks worn into threads eventually converge on a rock cluster on the horizon, a property boundary, and suddenly one is human, differentiated, an inhabitant aware of inhabiting.

Yes, I started south along that long road to despair. Arriving at the starting point again I see the logic of soldiering on. Then the sergeant is caught in the act of following and the myth of the sovereign rational subject explodes, underground.

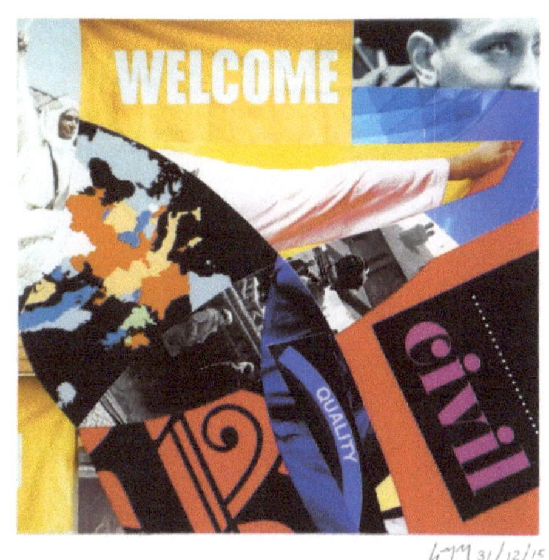

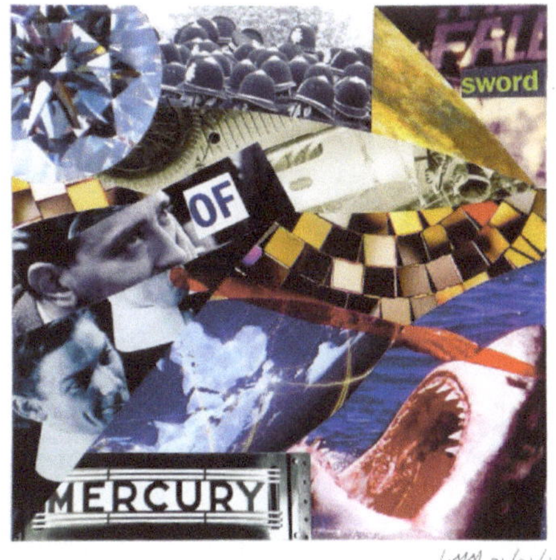

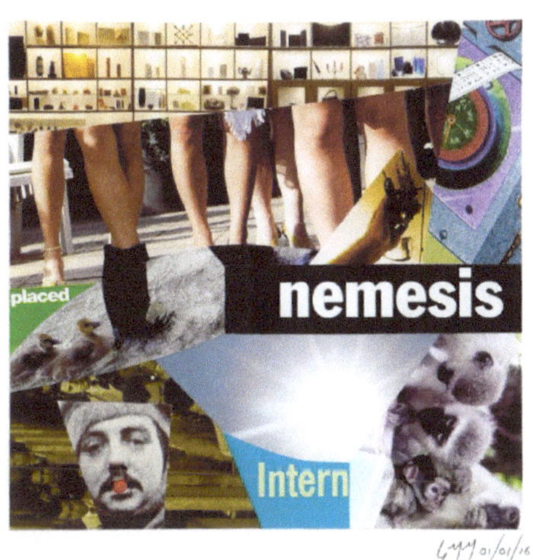

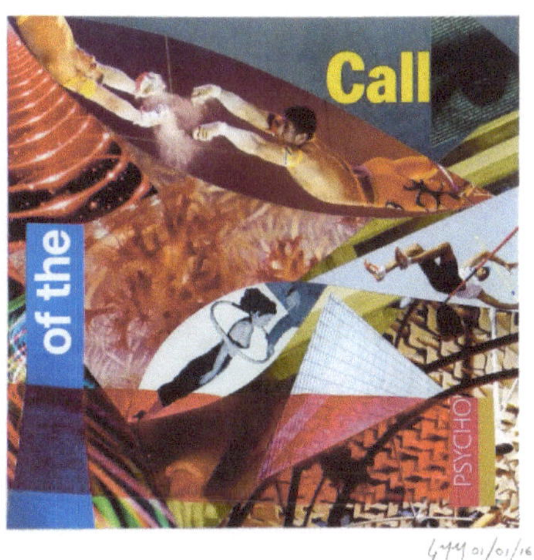

200 **Welcome civil quality**
December 2015 (P)

201 **Placed nemesis intern**
January 2016 (PA)

202 **Fall sword of mercury**
January 2016 (PA)

203 **Call of the psycho**
January 2016 (PA)

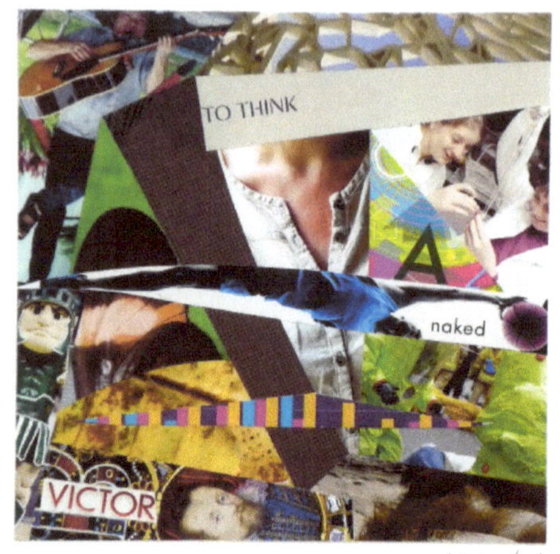

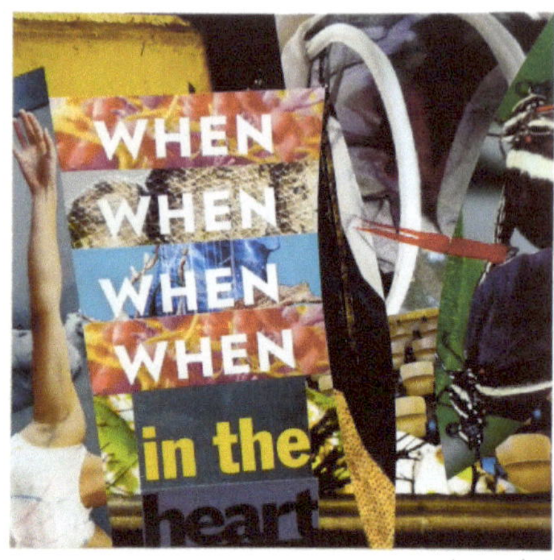

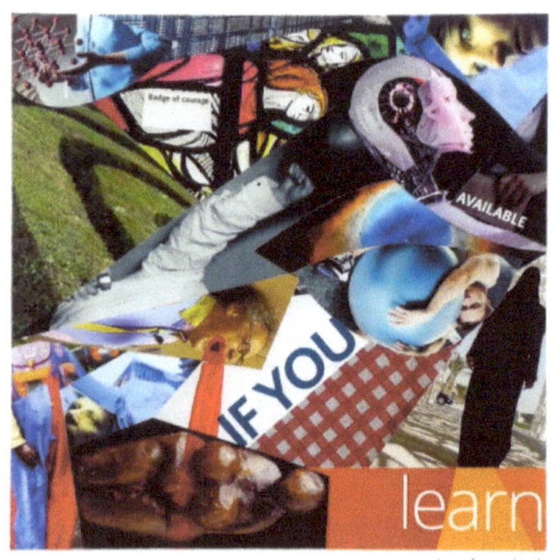

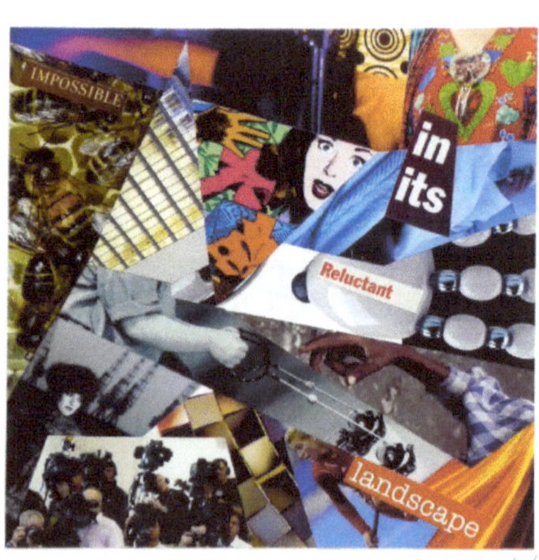

---

204 **To think a naked victor**
January 2016 (P)

205 **Badge of courage available if you learn**
January 2016 (PA)

206 **When when when when in the heart**
January 2016 (PA)

207 **Impossible in its reluctant landscape**
January 2016 (P)

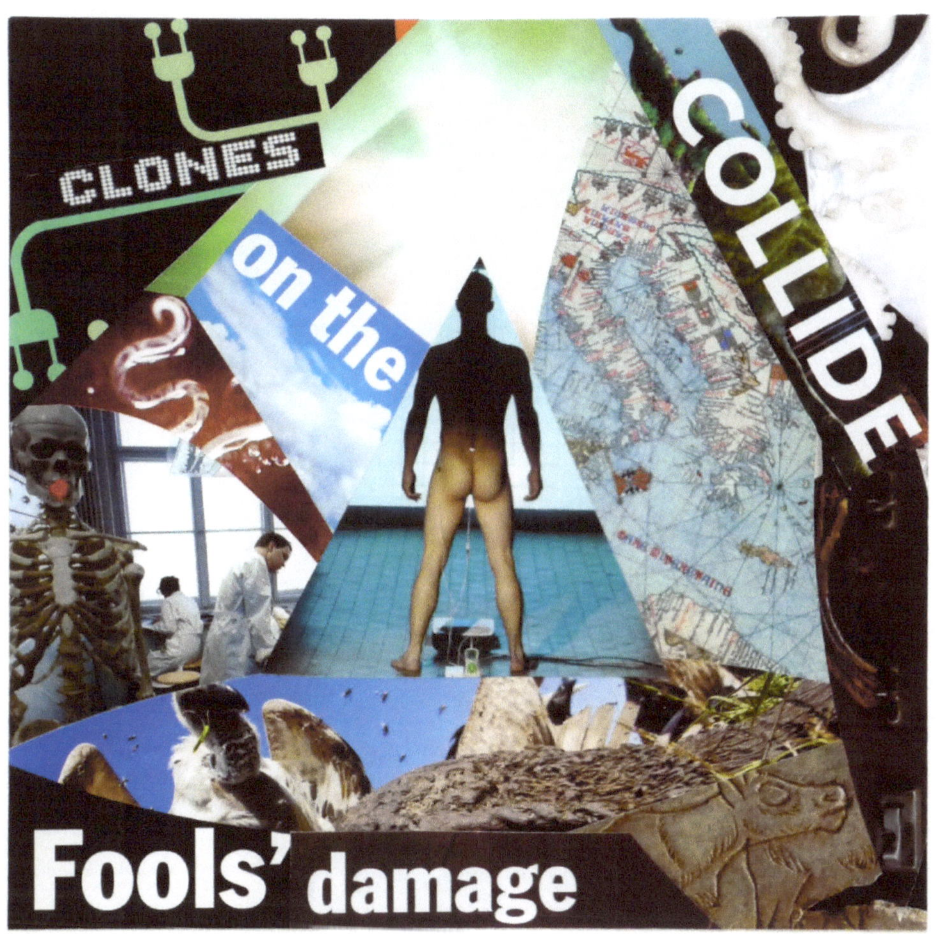

208

Clones collide on the fool's damage

January 2016

(PA)

Clones collide on the fool's damage

Alone in clinical space he is aware that prehistory in the classical world meant myth and magic. And now he is off to the south, a sergeant of bearing caught naked. He says: see my self-satisfied trance in the flickering light of a canvas storm. He arrives by sea to find the life of a free man is the life of a slave.

Imagine a beach strewn with rocks. Some are embedded in the sand others move with each tide gradually migrating to the margin facing the longest reach. All of them wear down over time and add to the mineral tang of the sea. This is how shells can appear and grow as if by magic. History becomes something solid, a home. You cannot run away and forget your history.

Diaphon listened to me, showed me ocean-going vessels and their diverse cargoes. She said: never look back; all that treasure belongs to you, travels with you, you have only to reach out with your mind and it will never let you down. From the edge of the world at the end of a shifting sand spit they glide like gods and ancestors past thin grass twitching with duplicate lizards.

At the furthest point of their voyages carrying a man in a box, a man in a suitcase, and a box in suitcase, all handled with appropriate reverence, they fly over oblivious white cephalopods. I like the poetry of it, the wake, the method and the insolent ego. There are many transformations on board that prove the bridgeability of disparate mundanities, as if a justification for ecstasy were required and possible.

A raw sack is pulled tight releasing fibres and coal dust into the air. Disbelief forms in their place like condensation on a mirror, but the image is fixed. A tree turns to white gold and is filled with feathered jewels: it cannot be felled, because it is not really a tree. It is the same thing with heroes: some anonymous boy slows and glows as a wrinkled sage, but he cannot be killed and he cannot die. Sack, tree and boy become cargo to be shipped around the world as fuel for the great library and the museum of everything.

In the spring mist of the white ant city, red ants are dying for want of a decent meal. Their hunger is a categorical despair. All soldiers who fight through foggy concrete canyons suffer it unaware of the sunlit penthouses of ingenuity and wisdom. Here is the call to all slaves: plug in and rise above the clouds.

160

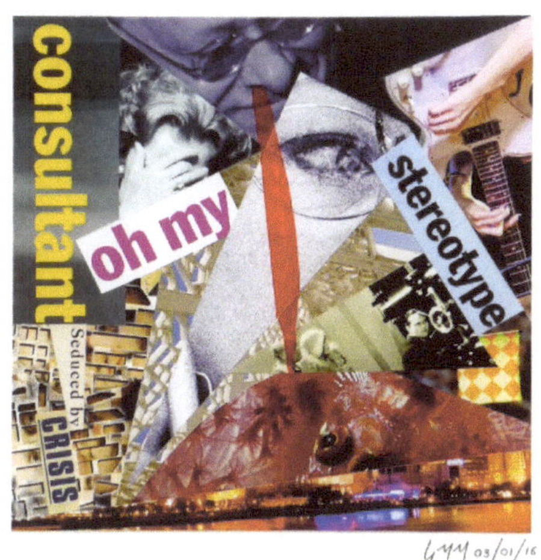

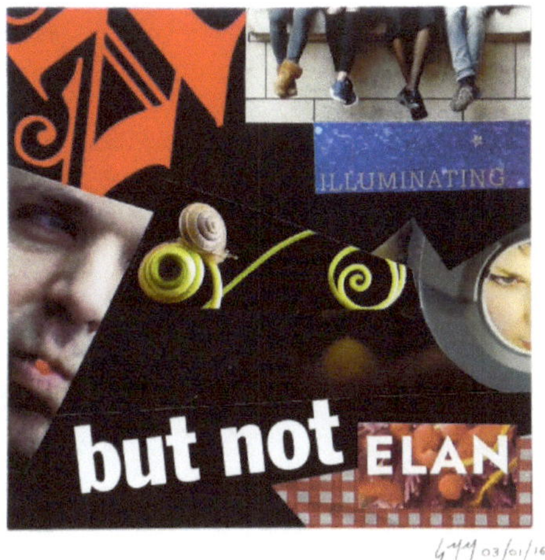

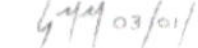

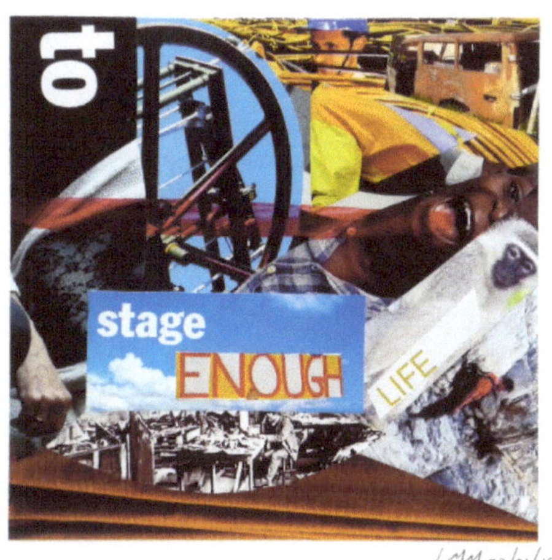

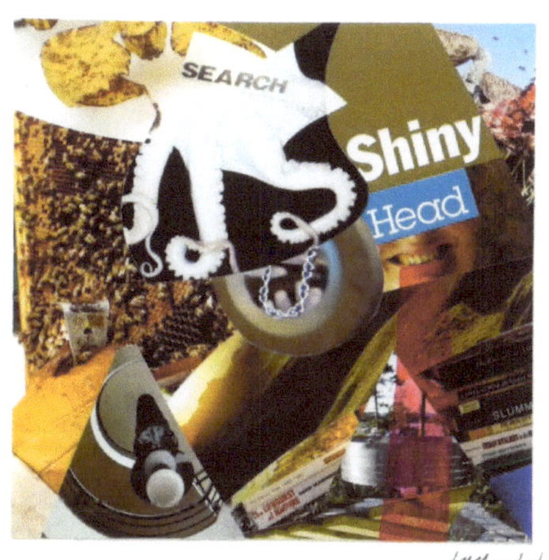

209 **Consultant seduced by crisis oh my stereotype**
January 2016 (PA)

210 **To stage enough life**
January 2016 (PA)

211 **Illuminating but not elan**
January 2016 (PA)

212 **Search shiny head**
January 2016 (PA)

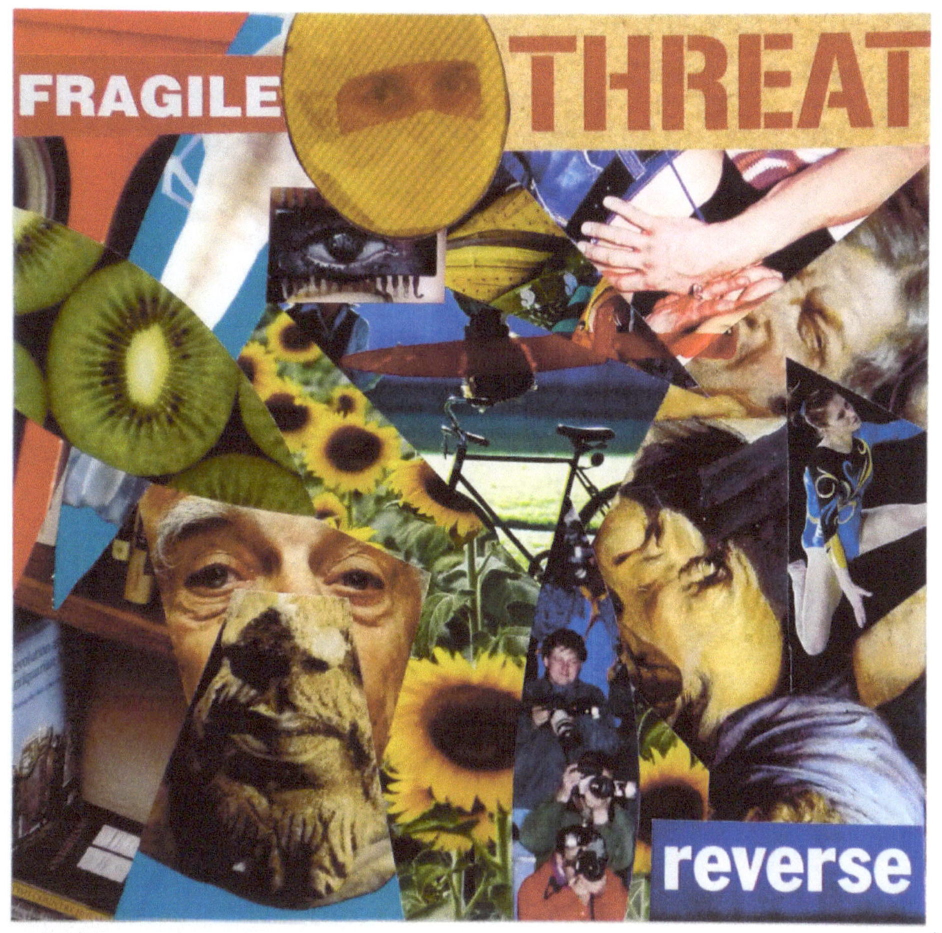

213
Fragile threat reverse
January 2016

(PA)

Fragile threat reverse

Fragile sea life is slopping on the shore. Its escape races evolution to the granular ends of the universe. Sands rub and tumble into sterile grey, yellow, red, and brown slicks. Potent desert portraits, perhaps only visible from orbit, slither beautifully into history. Meanwhile, in the planet's high atmosphere, micrometeorites are a harmless and meaningless light show incorporating occasional satellites in a flowing network of mutual suspicion. As if to prove the thermospheric threshold, above the grid they are invisible and lethal: one is all it takes to puncture your bubble. Super-heavy molecules archive themselves in the cores of collapsed stars. Information lost and gained stands outside reality forever. What is the matter and is it a wonder? Now let us leave off the idea of incidents and scrape the archaeology.

A little digger ant excavates for the purity of incremental insight. Look at the dust and the smudges, the stratified engineering drawings pulsing with promise. The scratcher imagines a threat to the flesh from the double and realizes it is an inadequate story. Words issue from the mouth of a Greek marble as if powered by the mind of a modern seer: "reverse this madness." All polychrome and high-fidelity projections circling for affirmation settle at last in the moment of being.

This strutting of the anatomically modern human turns out to be a short-lived production with improvised dialogue, a stripped-back stage setting, and no plot. Radiation of a visceral kind on a flat petri-dish planet: the culture is a fractal. Who could have predicted that there is no surviving civilization? For a while it rises and falls like the tide, but the froth is a dead giveaway. Look at those big hands in the washing up water puckering pink and down to a molecule doomed to join the dunes. There are no skyscrapers on the beach, no space for noise and heat. But there is a persistent cold in the interstices that will outrun evolution in the end. Simmer the genes and watch the bastards crawl into the vacuum as atoms.

I have decided to step back for a moment to consider the wisdom of circulating this myth. I mean, it is fun and all that, but the process leaves no room for moral compass and I wonder whether we—me, the writer, and you, the reader—might do better to settle for a more orthodox relationship. … Nah, forget I said that!

ON COLLAGE AND METAFICTION

1 Contexts

Diane Waldman curated 'Aspects of Collage, Assemblage and the Found Object in Twentieth-Century Art,' a major exhibition at the Guggenheim New York in 1988. Her book, published four years later, embraced and considerably extended her research and I regard it as the most authoritative study on its subject. I have owned a copy for over twenty years and, given the nature of the *Goodbye to THES* project, revisiting Waldman, after the fact, seemed a logical thing to do.

Waldman's study is broadly chronological and organized, in the main, by movement. The exceptions to this are the short chapter devoted entirely to the decoupage work of Henri Matisse, and three of the later chapters that deal with work of diverse groups and individuals under the headings 'After Abstract Expressionism,' 'The New Object' and 'Appropriation.'

Re-reading the book took a while. I worked my way through the accounts of Cubism, Futurism, The Russian Avant-Garde, Dada, and Surrealism and on reaching the Matisse chapter, just over half way through, I felt that all of the conceptual possibilities for collage that anyone might need now or in the future had been set out like milestones along a road.

This is, of course, an illusion: there is no road. Or, to put it another way, the story is only a story, necessarily selective, elliptical, rational and linear. What the author sets aside, ignores or is simply unware of because as yet they have not been uncovered (or recovered), are all the other possible markers that might be used to forge a track across the territory, and with good reason: accepting too many outlying points of reference makes it difficult to tell a straight story. And most of the time we like straight stories: stories that get to the point tend to be more immediately useful.

That said, most of the time I quite enjoy distractions, deviations and detours. Usually, whenever I read a scholarly text, I read the footnotes as I go. I often break off reading to follow up a reference. When an idea occurs to me that demands I spend time in the studio making something or at the computer writing or messing about with images, I give in to the demand and return to the reading later. However, even I need a straight story sometimes and, after that moment's pause on reaching Waldman's chapter on Matisse, I ploughed on. I am glad that I did.

The sense I make of the story of collage, assemblage and the found object places Matisse's *gouaches découpés* at a turning point. Before it there is a feeling of forward motion, of individual artists and diverse groups engaged in discovery and exploration, and after it a feeling of circular motion, of artists rampaging through the landscape as colonialists intent on exploitation and as tourists greedily consuming everything in their path.

From 1941 Matisse used a wheelchair and before his death in 1954 he was bedridden: consequently the decoupages, late works produced in this period, are of necessity extraordinarily pared down in technique. To be prosaic about it: he painted flat gouache colour onto paper, cut out shapes with a small pair of scissors keeping both positive and negative pieces, had an assistant pin them on the studio walls, rearranged them over weeks and months until he was happy with a composition: then he glued them to paper, canvas, or board. The process described as if uncomprehendingly observed is simple enough. With a little imagination, however, the poetry of it emerges: he realized each figure as it curled up from the twisting blades and used the surprise of each moment in its evolution to fuel the liberation of a desirable figure from its ground. Desire is the key: the uncontrollable urge toward conception. Matisse's lyrical endeavour was obsessive and self-referential, the culmination of his career and yet it was something retrogressive, almost primitive in its purity, a still point.

I appreciate and admire the work, but, to be honest, now I take very little from it. I can't help but remember my youthful captivation with Matisse's early Fauvist paintings and mourn the loss their exotic decorative messiness. And this is the point really of going over old ground in this way, to re-view the sights, literally to look again to see what still catches the imagination. In what follows then I am using eyes tuned by the production of over two-hundred collages for the *Goodbye* project and a brain saturated with their questionable qualities. The proposition is that trying to make sense of whatever ideas and images catch my attention in Waldman's book will somehow help illuminate my own work. I do not know how this is going to turn out.

♦

In her introductory chapter, Waldman notes many historical precedents for artists' use of collage, some quite ancient. The twelfth-century Japanese 'text-collages embellished with foil papers' that she cites, for example, I find particularly resonant.[3] I look at the *Ishiyama-gire* section of the *Ise-shu* manuscript and to my eyes its surface, of layered text over the heterogeneous fragments of coloured paper, does not remain two-dimensional. Neither does it simply create the illusion of a shallow space. Rather it produces an intense force field of ambiguous dimensionality, beneath the text depthlessness disrupted and orchestrated by the ragged paper edges crossing the visual field. I recognize a simple idea in this: when marks on a surface resolve into some figure or pattern, at that moment the surface dissolves. There are many passages in the earlier *Goodbye* collages in which this effect can be seen: for example, in the first one I produced, 001 *VITA promise moves*, the collaged composition resolves into a single shield-like figure that hovers in a space of indeterminate though terrestrial depth—*terrestrial* because the charcoal shading across the lower part of the image reads irresistibly as a horizon.

Figure and ground are often expressed with clarity in the earlier *Goodbye* collages. In a sense they belong to a landscape tradition: the paper surface surrounds and floats behind clusters of

[3] Waldman, *Collage*, p. 8.

collaged material to evoke a space in time vibrating with life. However, there is another way in which this effect can be achieved, one more characteristic of the *Goodbye* collages: the field of vision is filled with spatially ambivalent, interacting fragments, instances of figure and ground that multiply and merge, and a dense writhing interiority emerges.

If the earlier collages tend to allude to a conceptually unified world, which extends out to the horizon and beyond, the later ones soon begin to allude to worlds of the near-to, each of which starts and ends with what can be directly perceived. These are crowded worlds in which individuality is contested and consequently of intense significance. Also they are worlds of ambiguity, dissimulation and delusion because the near-to is not only made of solid stuff: some of it is the intangible slough of invading media and no less real for being so. I am reminded of the phenomenologically sophisticated account Peter Sloterdijk offers of spatiality and mediation in his *Spheres* trilogy, and in those terms suggest that the *Goodbye* collages move between the 'globalized' and the 'foaming' perspectives on reality.[4]

I think a similar trajectory can be discerned in the earliest Cubist works of Braque and Picasso. Their project drew on early twentieth-century café culture in the same way that mine draws on the late-twentieth/early-twenty-first-century higher education environment: it is infused with objective evidence of their milieu. Admittedly the imagery I cut from the *THE* is far richer in external references than anything Braque and Picasso chose to incorporate in their work. Nevertheless, what they achieved pictorially has a similar range: Braque's *Still Life with Tenora (Clarinet)* from the summer of 1913 is a fine example of a floating figure in ambiguous terrestrial space,[5] and Picasso's *Bowl with Fruit, Violin and Wineglass* of 1912 is an early example of a denser composition that extends to the edges of the canvas and becomes spatially more complex.[6]

Toward the end of 1912 Georges Braque introduced collage initially as an element in drawings. Both he and Pablo Picasso then used it to expand and supplement the techniques and language of painting. This aspect of Cubism represented a new beginning for collage, one that made a way of thinking about visual perception and about pictorial composition, as similarly discontinuous and imaginatively constructive, central to the confrontation of events in space. I recognize in this achievement an opening up of realist possibilities.

The two artists first collaged wallpaper printed with woodgrain and woven cane into their paintings. Picasso's next simple step was to incorporate newspaper cuttings, which

4 I cannot help myself: in this project the most intimate sphere, the 'bubble', is missing. Although some pieces hint at the autobiographical the more primitive self remains obscured or suppressed. Self-portraiture is a different project, one I have barely begun.

5 Museum of Modern Art, New York, Nelson A. Rockefeller Bequest.

6 Philadelphia Museum of Art, A. E. Gallatin Collection.

foreshadowed the novel 'realist' direction in which collage would inevitably develop: beyond the articulating and disrupting illusions of surface toward the horizons of human experience and imagination. In simple terms, this is possible because a brush stroke or a patch of textured material is relatively anonymous and autonomous, but a fragment of content-rich material, such as a newspaper cutting, is already burdened with associations and meanings. This is why Picasso's *Bowl with Fruit, Violin and Wineglass* is the image that stands out for me. It includes newsprint, drawn image fragments and printed colour image alongside woodgrain paper and letterforms, a heterogeneous range of abstract and symbolic materials at the service of the typically mundane subject of café culture. The newsprint element in the work is 'La Vie Sportive' from the pages of *Le Journal*. Through its everyday familiarity and complex cultural associations rather than through its precise content, the newspaper fragment connects with an external reality far richer than the one any details of the painted surface might suggest through essentially visual means.

When Braque and Picasso started collaging such material I do not know whether they realized quite how much its allusiveness could undermine the optical and haptic qualities of their work. *Bowl with Fruit, Violin and Wineglass* already embraces a level of surplus and complexity that makes coherent communication problematic. Although it is true that cubist principles have been distilled, formalized and assimilated in contemporary visual culture the aspect of the 'cubist' legacy that I find more intriguing is this *escalation of confusion*.

♦

During and after the First World War other groups of artists very quickly pushed this idea of associative surplus much further. A most extreme work is *Patriotic Celebration (Free-Word Painting)* 1914 by Carlo Carrà.[7] In it an array of printed and hand lettered elements are arranged into an entirely abstract spiral composition. Visual reference to subject matter is entirely absent from the painting. It relies on the optical effect of a patterned and textured surface for its expressive visual quality. The richness of its possible meanings, however, derives from interpretation of the verbal and symbolic materials—names, slogans, vocalized sounds, flags, etc. I find this aspect of the work pregnant with possibilities. I also enjoy its anarchistic flavour, not for its Futurist associations with violence and destruction, but for the facility it provides for individualistic uncensored expression.

Any political overtones in my *Goodbye* collages emerge, I think, as a result of a freedom from the obligation to think about implication or consequence in the work. When I am working, thought is most often in flux and any expression in the eventual image is the residue of its passing rather than the product of its substance. After the fact I can never be sure exactly what happened and what the

[7] On long-term loan to the Peggy Guggenheim Collection, Venice.

relationship between the two events, the process and the precipitate, properly is. I find that it is best not to think too hard about what I am doing while I am doing it, but then again I don't think there is anything unusual in that. I think oscillation between an immersion in the work and a surfacing to reflect on the results, is an inevitable aspect of creative practice. For me maybe the more crucial point is my regular lack of any clear intention before making a start.

This contrast between clear intention and open desire is perhaps illustrated in the different approaches Russian avant-garde and Dadaist artists took to making collages. In *Tatlin at Work* 1924, El Lissitzky expresses the idea of a rational relationship between man and machine.[8] He gives geometric form to the instruments of his subject's creativity and assembles a structured narrative of diagrammatic clarity. It adds up to something rather monumental: an apparently buildable design for a construction. The only odd element, perhaps, is the sidelong silenced female face, which floats above the main figure as a separate smaller cluster. The intention behind the work is clear from its title and its execution.

El Lissitzky's combination of photographic and crisp geometric elements is also a way of abandoning the painterly and expressing an overtly political and anti-art sentiment. In *Cut with the Kitchen (Cake) Knife through the Last Weimar Beer-Belly Cultural Epoch in Germany* 1919, Hannah Hoch achieves a similar feat although in a radically different manner.[9] Jarring juxtapositions, abrupt changes of scale, jokey or grotesque modification of faces and generally densely packed clusters of printed materials are spread across the full height and width of the picture to create pandemonium. The composition as a whole and each recognizable cluster within it is assembled with a great deal of skill and sensitivity: typographic and photographic pieces are selected, positioned and layered to work together and send the eye darting from one centre of interest to another in a desperate search for sense. In this way it has much the same effect as the music performed by an ensemble of free improvisers.

In the *Goodbye* collages I hope to have achieved something similar. Although their small size clearly limits the possibilities within each composition, perhaps as a series they become an accumulator of borderline and labyrinthine meanings. As I have already suggested, it was not my intention to produce this or any other particular effect. All I did was decide, for essentially practical reasons, on a set of simple operational rules and proceed with a dedicated openness to the materials to hand. The consequences of making the *Goodbye* collages this way are two-fold I think. First, they *evolve*: there are occasional throwbacks and some mutations prove less successful than others, but broadly speaking as they multiply the form becomes more complex, responsive and robust. And second, almost counter to this, the chaotic fund of material, unpredictable in

8 Private collection.

9 Staatliche Museen zu Berlin, Nationalgalerie.

its variety as I cut up one magazine after another and in no particular order, produces a constant stream of surprises: the process is profoundly inventive each composition having little or no connection to the previous one.

♦

It is misleading to say that collage was 'invented' by Braque and Picasso, as if it were a once and for all achievement. There were 'artistic' precedents—not all of them from distant times and places: Hans Christian Andersen most notably—and many artists in the early twentieth century contributed to an eruption of pictorially ambivalent ornaments, accidents and substitutions, many of which are inventions of collage. No matter how strident and assured individual Cubist, Futurist, and Russian avant-garde collages appear, almost without exception the artists who produced them mixed and matched heterogeneous material to extend and resolve their essentially *painterly* ambitions. Where wholehearted investment in the visual possibilities of collage did occur was in the work of artists associated with Dada, and this was often not simply non-painterly in ambition but anti-art in sentiment. Hannah Hoch, Raoul Hausmann, Johannes Baader, and John Heartfield are the artists that stick in my mind because of the work they produced that relied most heavily on the use of printed and photographic material. Kurt Schwitters was associated at one time or another with Dada and Constructivism, and maintained painterly ambitions even in the purest of his collage work.

I read John Elderfield's magnificent 1985 monograph on Schwitters many years ago and acquired my own copy recently. Schwitters' work in the period from late 1919 through 1925 is particularly rich. *Mertzbild Einunddreissig (Mertzpicture Thirty-One)* of 1920 is a fine example of the larger assemblage works in which paint is crucial in pulling the composition together.[10] Radial lines originating from various points around the collaged number '31' in the upper centre of the composition extend across the picture surface. Most are indicated by edges of pieces of collaged paper or textile, but these are widely dispersed in the composition. Paint is used to hold these lines across intervening spaces and allow them to intersect and create a network that holds the composition together. This compositional method is echoed in many *Goodbye* collages. I create lines in three different ways. The first technique makes lines that appear in printed fragments of image line up with those in other image fragments. The second aligns the edges of adjacent collage pieces. The third involves drawing charcoal dust over the edge of a paper mask placed over the composition. In the early *Goodbye* collages all three techniques are used. However, charcoal is not used on all of the later collages.

There are other ways of making a collage with a strong composition. In *Mz 322.bunt (many coloured)* of 1921 Schwitters relies on colour distribution for a sense of dynamic

[10] Sprengel Museum, Hannover.

coherence.[11] It is a small work—a little over the size of a post card—yet uses a great range of coloured paper and textile fragments in a composition of amazing authority and presence. There are some gently curving lines generally sweeping from top left to bottom right in the composition but its complexity allows the eye to find several other sets of partially organizing lines none of which are dominant. As one relaxes that neurotic form of searching gaze and allows the whole composition to come into view, something beautiful happens: blue elements talk to each other, as do the pink elements and the yellow and the grey. It is a phenomenal achievement. I cannot pretend to have achieved anything as sublime in the *Goodbye* collages. However, colour does play a stronger structural role than line in a handful of the later ones and perhaps 195 *I don't think I cogitate in silence* is one of the more subtle. As Schwitters' example shows, the small size of a collage does not mean it cannot be engaging on a number of levels; all that is required is close viewing and a willingness to enter the miniaturist's world.

Schwitters did produce larger collages composed entirely of pasted materials—i.e. without drawn or painted elements—and of these the one that stands out for me is from a later date *Prikken paa Ien (The Dot on the I)* of 1939.[12] Many of the elements in the composition are no larger than those used in much smaller collages. However, the scale of the work allows for some that are much larger, including flattened out pieces of parcel wrapping, cardboard cartons and whole envelopes. The composition consequently has several larger clusters of material, each orientated to a different angled orthogonal grid, that overlap and intersect with each other. Larger elements are overlaid by smaller elements which coagulate into complex figures. The effect is to create an illusion of spatial depth. This is somewhat unusual for Schwitters: in most of his two-dimensional work he limited this effect and concentrated elements in a very immediate surface structure.

In the *Goodbye* collages the illusion of depth most often arises out of the interplay of image fragments, as one might expect. However, there is one collage, 161 *For 20 do gold*, in which a greater separation in space occurs because of a shift in texture and scale between several simple lozenge-shaped elements and the single inverted background image of water and sky onto which they are collaged.

Schwitters once said, 'I nail my pictures together',[13] which is literally true of his more elaborate three-dimensional assemblages. His technique in the two-dimensional collages, however, was rather less brutal. He moved his selected material around in a slimy film of animal glue to arrive at a composition then left it to set. My technique is very different. I do the composing dry and then methodically transfer and glue one element at a time onto the support … but before I explain the process in

11 Sprengel Museum, Hannover.

12 Centre Pompidou.

13 Application to join the Dada group, c. 1916.

more detail perhaps I should talk more generally about my approach to creative practice.

2 Making Art

To introduce my approach to making art I can hardly do better than repeat the final paragraph of the foreword to *Dead Reckoning*, a collection of my poems published in 2009:

> I have no use for distinctions between one art and another. I try to remain open to the quality of the materials to hand and make what I can of them. That is all.

In the context of the creative practices in which I have at one time or another immersed myself—art, design, music, poetry, performance—three consequences of this propensity immediately occur to me.

First, it is not the medium with which I choose to work that first interests me: sometimes it is an idea and more often than not it is simply the challenge of making something that gets me started.

Second, traditional forms tend by turns to frustrate, annoy and bore me. Consequently, the more established, revered or formulaic they are the more likely I am to reject them and favour my own powers of invention.

And third, I tend not to preconceive a purpose to impose on a work. I find that out of ambiguous, vague or chaotic beginnings purpose tends to emerge in some kind of leap-frogging contest with form, and meaning, or at least its first possibilities, appears in the latter stages of this process. Admittedly, in design, which has a more direct commercial necessity behind it, one expects a purpose to be imposed from without, but that is incidental. Openness to possibility characterizes my creative response in designing as much as it does in making an image or some music or a poem or a performance.

Perhaps unsurprisingly then I have come to the conclusion that intention is not the most important factor in making a successful work of art. In fact, I would go further and suggest that artists' intentions commonly are vastly overrated: in serious criticism and in everyday conversation their relevance is often mistakenly regarded as key to the success and the value of a work. Intentions may be very important to some artists to spur on the production of work, and especially to galvanize efforts in situations requiring collaboration, but in the long run little weight can be given to them in judging the quality of the outcome. Intentions are soon overcome by the historical and conceptual expanse of human interests.

Process is not product: presentation is not reception: the lived moment is not the narrative. It is only when the messy incidental nature of the creative process has faded from memory or has been suppressed, and when any attempts at post-rationalization have revealed their necessarily contrived inadequacy, that the real work of determining the significance and meaning of a work can begin. It takes time.

♦

As a musician I once developed some facility in free improvisation. For a while it was a very satisfying pursuit and very much in keeping with my natural inclinations as an artist. However, free-improvisation is an ideally (and idealistically) ephemeral form, experienced in the moment and then gone for ever. I realize now that the reason I drifted away from it is that it lacks certain 'persistent' qualities that in the end are rather important to me: visuality and materiality. My last public appearance in a free-improvising ensemble was half a lifetime ago. Since then on rare occasions I have made solo recordings incorporating free improvisation, but this hardly qualifies as its continuing pursuit.[14] Over the same period, however, I have consistently written poetry.

In writing a poem I work equally on its graphical structure, on the musicality of the spoken words and on the unfolding sense the words make. And a poem is not really complete until the haptics of the printed page and the book form are brought into the equation. As far as I am concerned the quality of a poem comes from the combined effect of all of these aspects. Given my taste for the inventive, the emergent, and the visceral it is perhaps no surprise then that I take pleasure in wrestling with the more extreme modernist poetry but find contemporary stuff too often tiresome. If it looks formulaic on the page, if its content is tediously overblown, if it sounds monotonous, the affect is anaesthetic. I have time for the erudite and the edifying, of course, but often I find myself wondering why a writer bothered making a poem when an article or an essay would have been a better bet. If that all sounds rather arrogant and dismissive, I should point out that I am equally dissatisfied with most of my own poems. But that is why I keep trying.

There are many ways of starting work on a poem. Very few words are needed to be able to begin the process of play and they can come from anywhere. An idea can suggest key words or a sound or a phrase, enough to trigger a flow and a feel. Sometimes there is no idea; I am simply in the mood to play and then making a start requires a freer improvisational approach. This is where chance operations and arbitrary responses come into their own. None of the techniques I use is new, but none is simply a replay either. For example, although Dada inevitably taints my more playful moments—none of us escapes the infection of precedent—in my use of 'chance factors' I am in sympathy with Gysin and Burroughs considered use of cut-up rather than with the automatism of Breton and Soupault,[15] on the one hand, and the blind selection of Tzara on the other.[16] The rules I use for selecting and juxtaposing material are neither rigidly procedural nor blind to content. Rather they are pragmatic, just flexible enough in use to respond to the experience of working the material to hand, and provisional enough to

[14] For example, Improbalization (2003). <https://www.youtube.com/watch?v=eRhcPmRHel0>

[15] Breton & Soupault, *Les champs magnétiques* (1919)

[16] Tzara, 'To Make a Dadaist Poem' (1920).

readily adapt or be discarded in the light of the results produced.

Like Burroughs I tend to mine favoured sources. The *Goodbye* collages rely almost entirely on issues of one magazine for their visual and textual content—an arbitrary limitation imposed from the outset by the idea for the project. The metafictions, on the other hand, which were all written after the sequence of collages was complete, have sections seeded from several different sources which were not chosen at random. I was drawn to certain themes in part because of the emerging tenor of the book, but mainly because of their enduring fascination for me: 'organization and chaos,' 'civilization and the human condition', 'nomadism,' 'the cave,' etc. and this led me take specific books down from the shelves: Marion, Arendt, Deleuze and Guattari, Lewis-Williams, etc. Similarly, I was drawn to certain artists: Duchamp and Schwitters unavoidably, Lanyon and Wilde because I happened to see exhibitions of their work and was able to make useful connections with their ideas. In the postscript following this essay I explain a little more about how particular metafictions relate to one or more of these sources. For the moment, however, the point I wish to develop concerns my attitude to making art.

I am a pragmatist in a sense that would have been quite alien to the original Dada artists. Consumed with disgust at Western civilization's descent into the mechanical obscenity and violence of the war going on around them, they would have found the open and dispassionate reflexivity, which characterizes politics and popular culture a century later, incomprehensibly circular, vacuous and lacking in moral engagement. After the Second World War the Beat poets were critical of mainstream politics and culture, tried to develop a new consciousness and break with conventions in writing. I think they might have countered our malaise in some earnest way, but only Burroughs would have had any appetite for perverting it. Because of his ability to tolerate and admit into his world the provisional, the irrational, the repugnant, the dissonant, the parallel and the contradictory, he would have had a field day. The pragmatist in me also wants to let go of the quests for truth, salvation, identity and self-consciousness, and be open. To paraphrase Brion Gysin: I am the artist when I am open. When I am closed I am just me.

My approach to making art then is not perfectly reflected in anything I have made so far but everything I have made is its direct consequence: I try to remain open …

3 Making a collage

The collages presented in the exhibition and reproduced in this book perhaps come as close as I have ever come as a visual artist to pursuing my natural inclinations, which are to improvise freely using the materials to hand and to let things unfold as they will.

Stylistically the sequence of collages develops from 'open' to 'pictorial' compositions, as the white background is progressively fragmented and finally eliminated. The transition becomes significant in collages 74, 80 and 86 and is complete by collage 112. Using art-historical references one might suggest that: a Braque-like sense of composition is superseded by one akin to a Gris', but that would be a misinterpretation as well as anachronistic. The character of the collages I produced during the period 4 October to 4 November 2015 did change. But rather than reflecting a developing pictorial sensibility, it had far more to do with what was happening to my supply of *THE* magazines: I will explain.

Soon after I began the project I contacted the subscription department of the publishers to ascertain the date on which my subscription would run out—this I thought would confirm the scale and duration of the project—and the answer was: mid-October. I counted how many magazines I already had and how many I expected to receive, and from this estimated I would produce just over a hundred collages before the source materials were exhausted—so far, so good. However, in the third and fourth weeks of October new issues of the magazine appeared through my letter box. I enquired again of the *THE* subscription department and this time I was told my subscription would end mid-December. I recalculated: eight or nine additional issues of the magazine would raise the total number of collages in the project to about 150 and delay serious editorial work on this book, but I thought this a minor inconvenience. However, one other significant thing happened. At the bottom of a bookcase I found a stack of magazines and about fifteen of them were issues of *THE* from 2011 and 2012.

So, where did the 'pictorial sensibility' come from? The truth is that the collages became denser to deal with this surfeit of material without compromising the original idea behind the project. I had determined to use all of the *THE* magazines I had and that the project would be complete only when my subscription had ended and every magazine was gone.

It is in my obsessive nature to be driven to complete things that I start, despite the fact that I have a habit of starting new things in the interim—during this project I wrote several poems, worked on a few watercolour sketches and small acrylic paintings, and decided the composition and prepared the canvas for a large self-portrait painting. That said, it is also part of my disciplined background in design to have learned that one never misses a deadline. I never miss a deadline and this project had one: an exhibition opening on 25 April 2016 with this accompanying book.

The task was set and time was limited. It was because I needed to use up the materials quickly and keep down the total number of collages in the project that they became more elaborate and layered, i.e. 'pictorial'. I produced number 200 on the 31 December 2015 and only then knew that the end of the project was in sight. The final collage, number 213, is dated 3 January 2016.

This is how it was made:

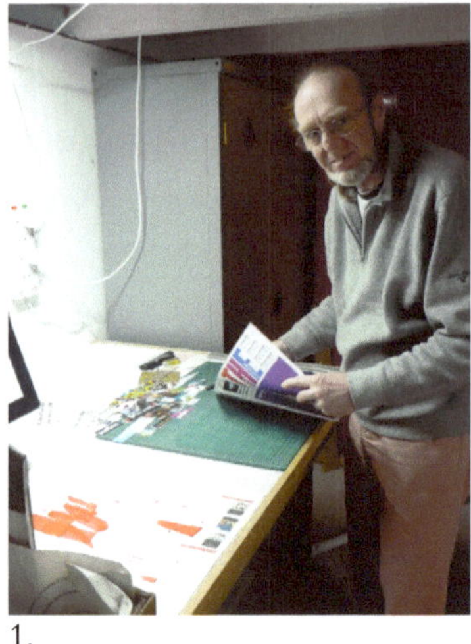
1.

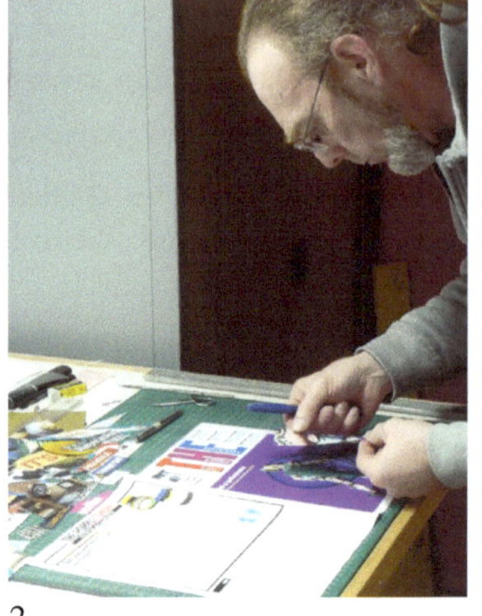
2.

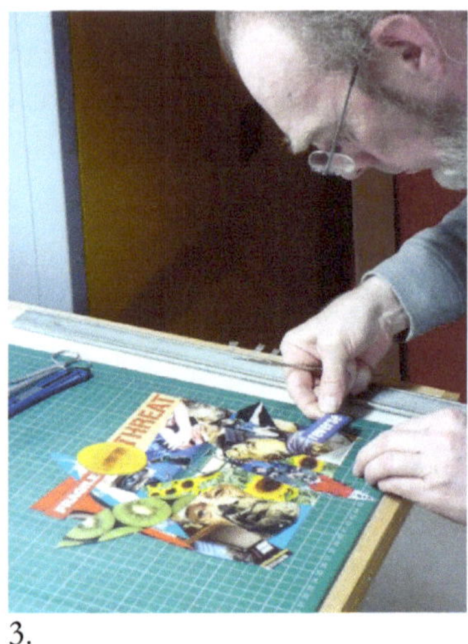

3.

[1.] You can see that the far right-hand corner of my workbench is empty. There used to be a pile of *THE* magazines there; now I am holding in my hand the last one. I open the magazine at its centre and carefully lift the wire ends of its two staples. I then turn the magazine over and remove the staples. The reason for doing it this way is to avoid damaging any images in the magazine that bleed over the centre folds.

[2.] I lift each double spread in turn starting with the centrespread. I look first on one side and then on the other for parts of images or headlines to cut out. I do not start with an agenda; I am simply open to whatever might catch my eye or strike my mind as potentially useful. In the past I have sometimes worked my way through a whole magazine and found nothing and sometimes I have cut so much out of a magazine that few pages were left in one piece. This time I find a few image fragments. I use a small craft knife—the type with a segmented snap-off blade—to cut them out freehand using quick movements. At the beginning of the project I decided never to use a straightedge for this task and never to cut around the profile of an image (the latter I did do on rare occasions). I am holding a fragment from the cover and it is the very last one I find, cut out and add to the pile. At this point I have about a hundred fragments, most of them remaining from previous magazines.

[3.] The next stage is fast and intuitive. It involves loosely composing a random selection of material. Although there is no cutting involved in this process I continue to work on the cutting mat because its dark green colour and printed grid help in keeping track of the composition. To define its limits I place a piece of cartridge paper, already trimmed to 210 mm square, on the right-hand side of the cutting mat. I chose this paper and size at the beginning of the project for a very simple reason: I had about 600 sheets of this archive quality A4 paper left over from printing my PhD thesis in 1996. The composition comes together through a kind of visual free-improvisation. Each addition and adjustment is a holistic response to colour, texture, line, pattern, and illusions of movement, containment and continuity in the evolving composition. Only incidentally do I respond to any prominent elements of image and text. The abstract visual qualities of each juxtaposition or overlapping of materials are what matter not its narrative or representational potential.

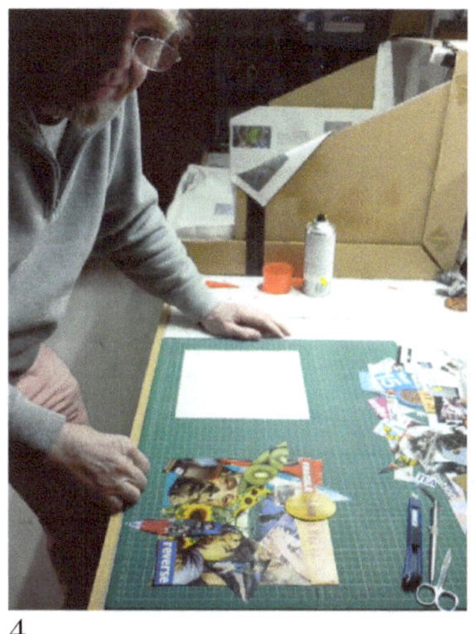

4.

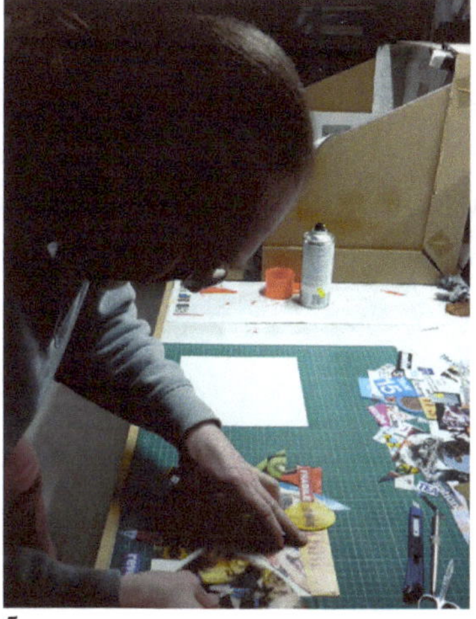

5.

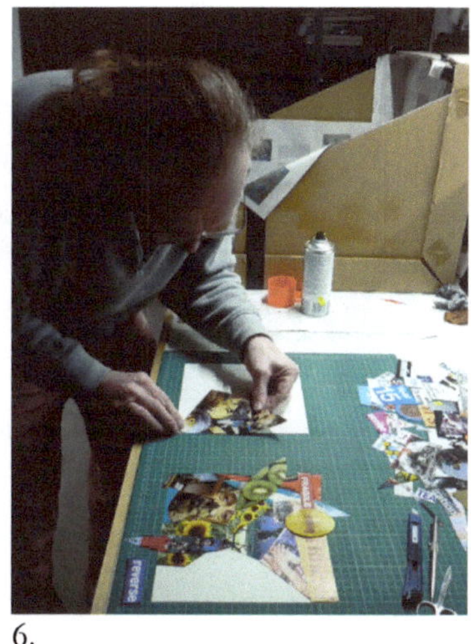

6.

[4.] Some material is left over when I decide the composition is complete. This does not matter; it is not in the way and I do not know yet whether I will need it later for another collage. It is time to move on to the next stage of the process. I place a second square of Huntsman cartridge paper on the left-hand side of cutting mat. I line it up horizontally with the first to make it easier to transfer pieces accurately. Further to the left I place my makeshift spray booth. I use 3M Photomount™ spray glue. It is pH neutral, non-yellowing, permanent and strong. It is very clean to use, even on very small pieces of paper. The only downside is the spray; it tends to hang in the air. That is why the booth is so far away and I make sure there is a flow of air through the studio. I still breathe some of it in; it is impossible to avoid.

[5.] Great dexterity is now required. First I study the structure of the composition to determine exactly where the layers of material are. To glue the collage together I have to work from the bottom layer of the composition. The difficult part is using the left hand to hold all of the upper layers in place while carefully extracting the correct piece with the right hand. The first compositions I did were sparse and left a lot of white cartridge paper showing. The simplest ones only had one or two overlapping pieces of paper and it was very easy to remove the bottom one without moving the piece above it. As the compositions became more elaborate the procedure became harder to plan, more time consuming and required an increasing level of dexterity. This time the first piece to be glued is on an edge of the composition and is relatively easy to extract. I place each finger of my left hand one at a time at a carefully chosen position on the composition so that only the piece to be removed is left unpinned by the pressure of my hand. Even in the short time it takes to remove the piece from the composition my fingertips stick slightly to the printed surface of the other pieces of paper. I put down the piece to be glued so that I can use a right-hand fingernail to enable me to lift each finger of my left hand in turn. It is like a little dance, very delicate. If done without any extraneous movements the rest of the composition remains exactly as it was, if not, something will be disturbed and will require even more delicate readjustment.

[6.] The next stage is to glue the piece in position. Before I apply glue I check the correct position on the second white square and decide which corner or edge is best to put down first to ensure accuracy: Photomount™ is strong glue and not designed to allow for repositioning. If necessary I lift a corner of the piece to be glued and pencil a registration mark beneath it on the paper. I place the piece at the back of the spray booth and coat the back of it evenly. I use a knife blade to lift a corner so that I can get hold of the piece. I carefully place it in the correct position on the white square, starting with the correct corner or edge.

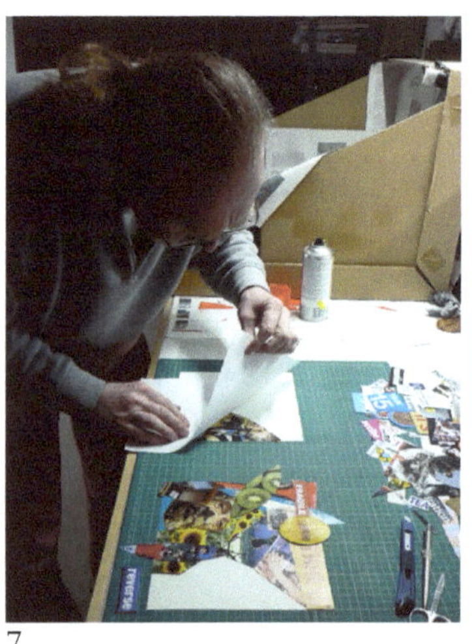
7.

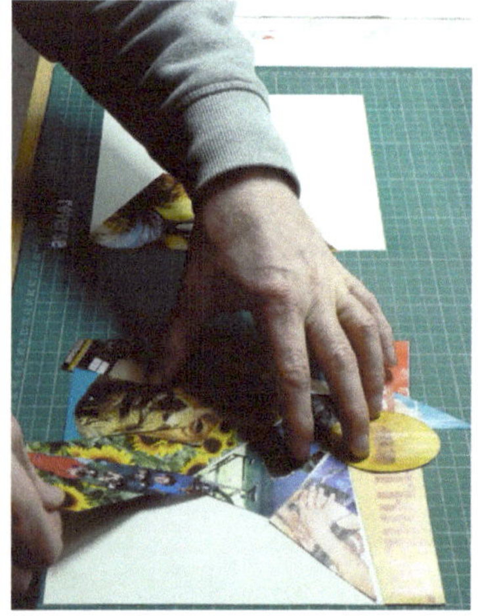
8.

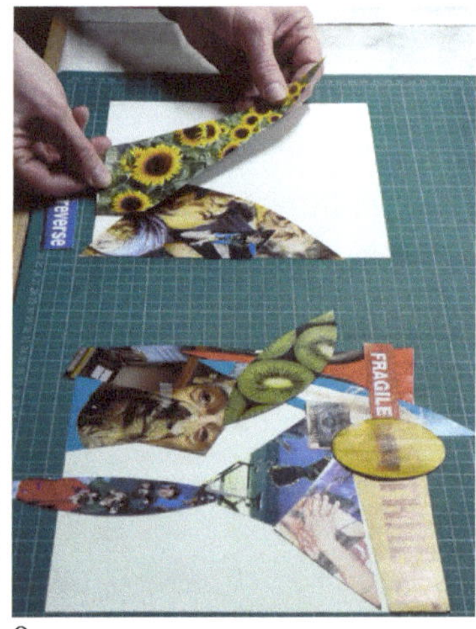

9.

[7.] Once the piece is down I place a clean sheet of paper over the piece and burnish.
[8.] The piece to be removed next is in the middle of the composition and there are too many overlapping pieces to hold with the fingers of the left hand. I stick a small piece of Scotch™ Removable invisible tape across two pieces of the composition so that I can hold them both with my index finger.
[9.] In the foreground you can see the awkward piece almost surround by white paper. Because of its central position the removed piece—the one with sunflower heads on it—makes a huge difference to the collage once glued in place. There is always a moment like this as a collage

comes together. Sometimes it happens early on, as here, but sometimes six or more smaller pieces have to be positioned and glued before a piece central to the structure of the collage is put in place and has this powerful visual effect.

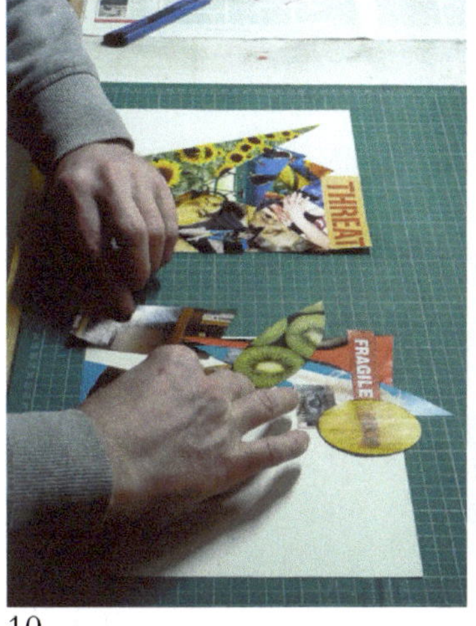

10.

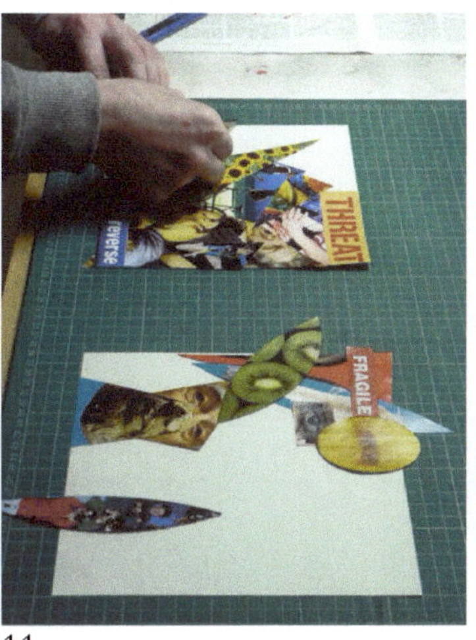

11.

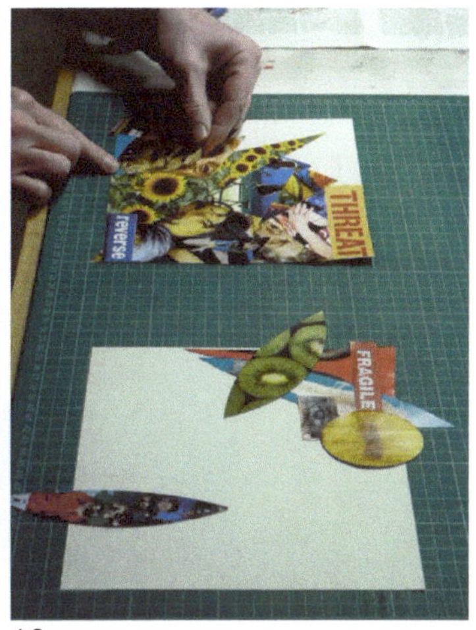

12.

[10, 11.] I tackle the large pieces to the right of the sunflower piece first. They are relatively autonomous in the composition and transfer easily to the collage. The remaining composition is more layered, but as it thins out, identifying the bottom piece each time, positioning the fingers of the right hand and removing the piece, is increasingly straightforward.

[12.] Eventually there are pieces in the composition left isolated on the surface, which can be simply lifted and glued onto the collage. The stone beard is one such.

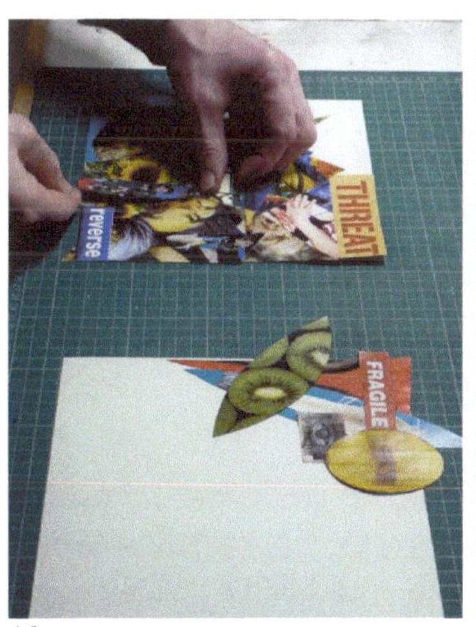

13.

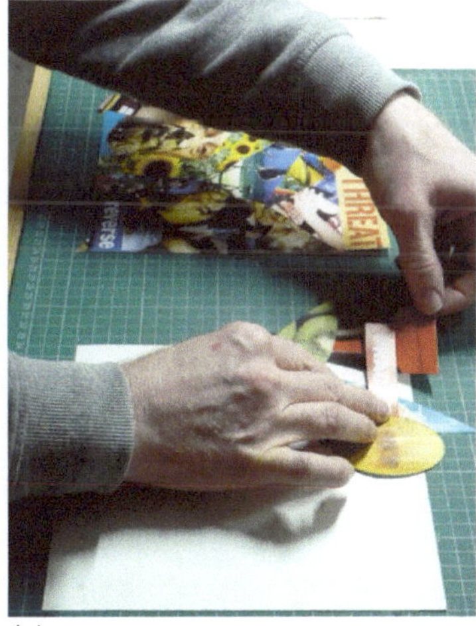

14.

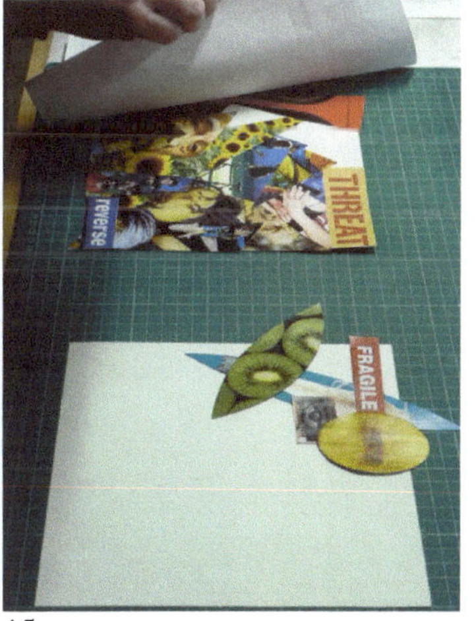

15.

[13.] The 'cameramen' shape is another. I trim the lower part of this with a scalpel before spraying the back of it with glue. This is to avoid too much glued collage sticking to the cutting mat. Over time it builds up anyway and needs to be cleaned off. In this kind of collage working dirty just makes life difficult. For example, the printed surface of pieces can get damaged by dirt and glue picked up when burnishing.

[14, 15.] I am onto the final corner of the composition. Doing the last few pieces of a collage sometimes reveals that tiny incremental adjustments, made while building it up, have a cumulative effect. It has happened again: the top-right corner of the collage is a little tight for space, but it is not a problem. The main consequence this time is a positive one: the words 'fragile' and 'threat' at the top of the collage are going to read more clearly.

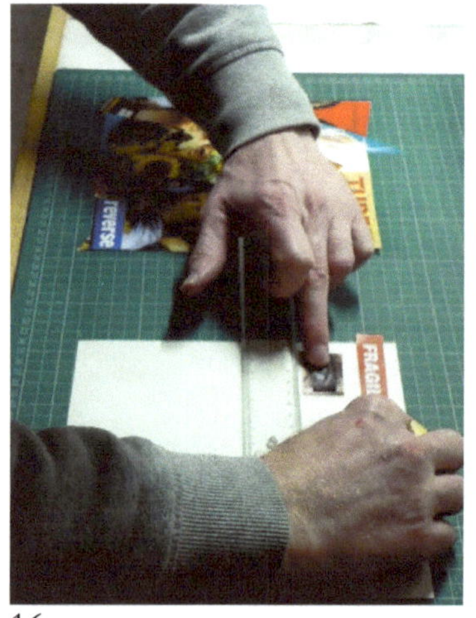

16.

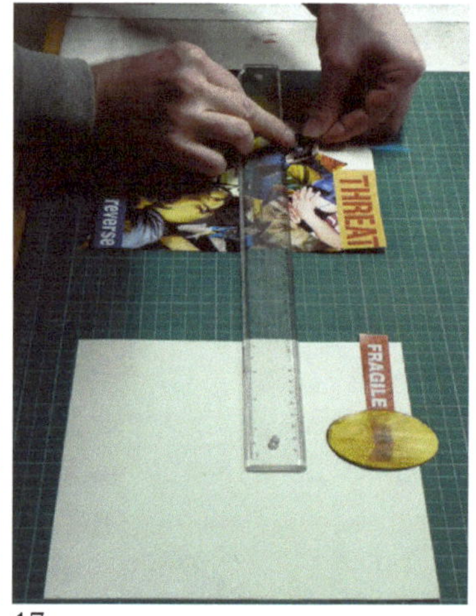

17.

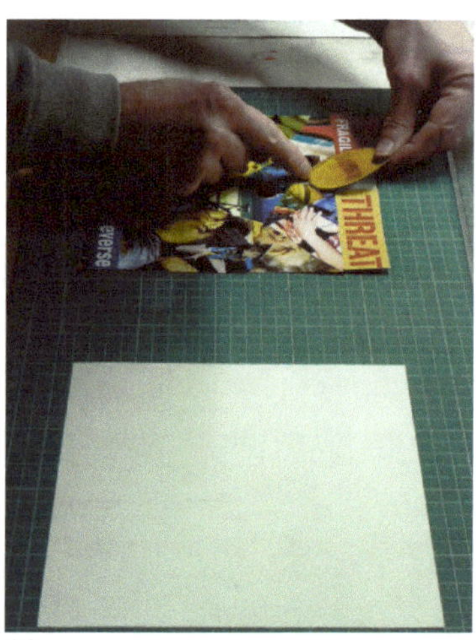

18.

[16.] The advantage of using the cutting mat grid and lining up the paper for the collage with the composition is something I discovered early on in the project. It makes it easier to judge the positions of pieces, sometimes by eye, but more often using a transparent plastic ruler. This time, because most of the composition has already been collaged, I can safely lay the ruler across composition and collage.

[17.] The layout is rather tight and distracting in this corner. By placing the ruler parallel to a grid line I can position the next piece absolutely square to the edge of the collage.

[18.] Collaging the last two pieces is now easy: the word 'fragile' holds the line at the top of the collage and the final 'alien' piece covers the only white paper remaining. It is 'alien' because it breaks the cutting out rules I set myself at the beginning. I did not want pieces to have strong outlines that would draw attention to specific image content and make them difficult to lose in or integrate into a composition. The rule, therefore, was not to cut things out around the profiles of image content, but to use quick long cutting movements. To cut this piece out I did methodically follow the ellipse framing the scientist's masked face. Every piece of the collage is now glued in place. I put a clean sheet of A3 paper over it and burnish gently and evenly across the whole surface using my fingers. I do not use a printmaker's burnishing tool or even the back of a spoon: because there are varying numbers of layers in a collage burnishing too hard causes it to buckle slightly and makes mounting it more difficult.

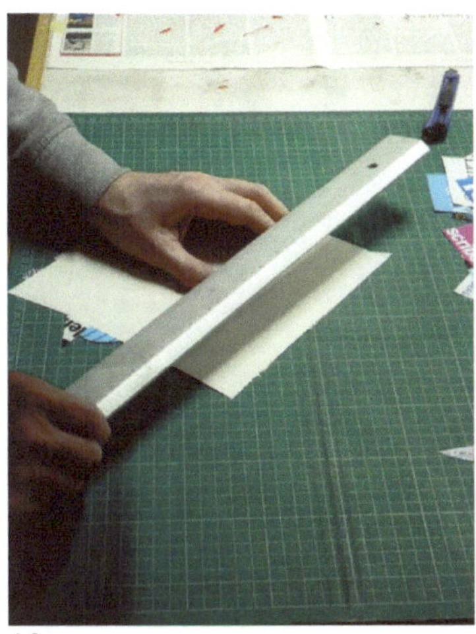
19.

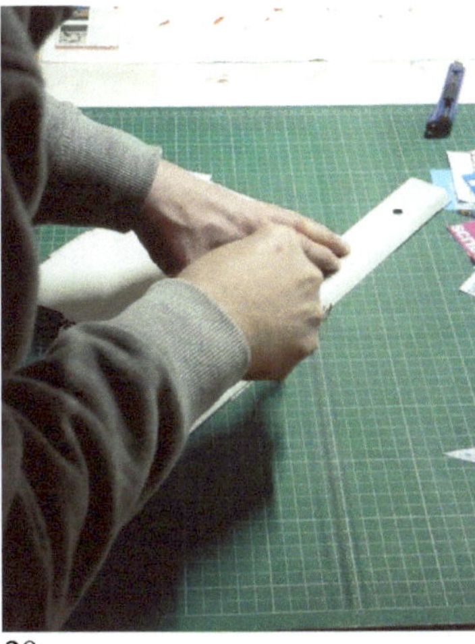
20.

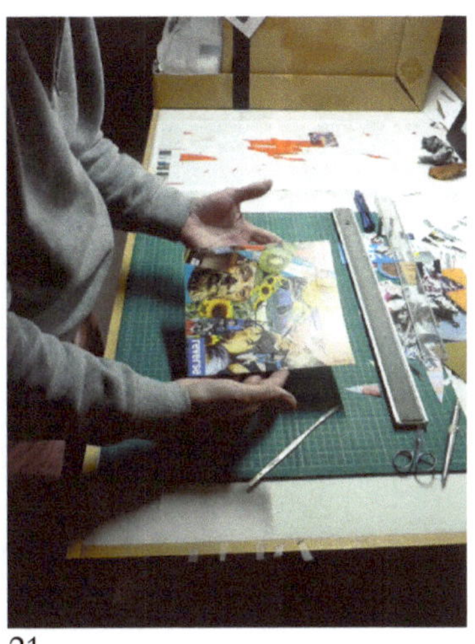
21.

[19, 20.] Now I turn the collage over and use a scalpel and metal straight edge to trim off any excess paper showing beyond the edges of the paper support. To preserve its original size I try not to cut into the paper support itself.

[21.] Before mounting the collage I have two further things to consider. My rules for making these collages include the option of making one or more feint tonal lines across the surface. The lines are created by using a cotton pad to drag charcoal dust over the edge of a paper mask. Over half of the collages have these lines. The simpler earlier ones, which all left white paper showing, have these lines as prominent elements in the final image. As the collages became more complex the lines felt less necessary. And several of the collages that completely cover the support paper have no lines added to them. I decide not to add any lines to this collage. My rules also include the option of adding one further element: a smear of Cadmium Red acrylic paint. Most of the collages have one, and I decide this collage will have one as well.

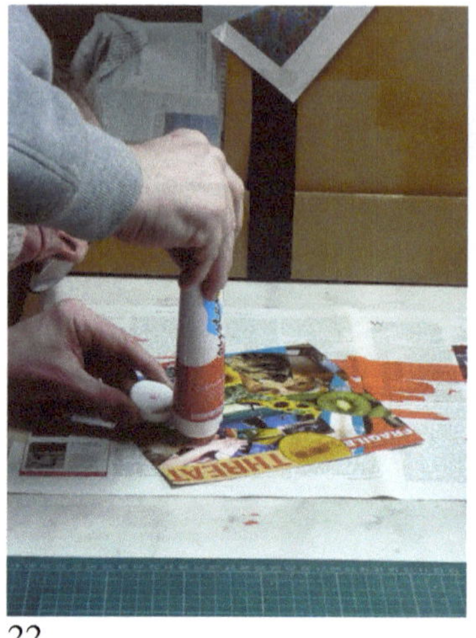

22.

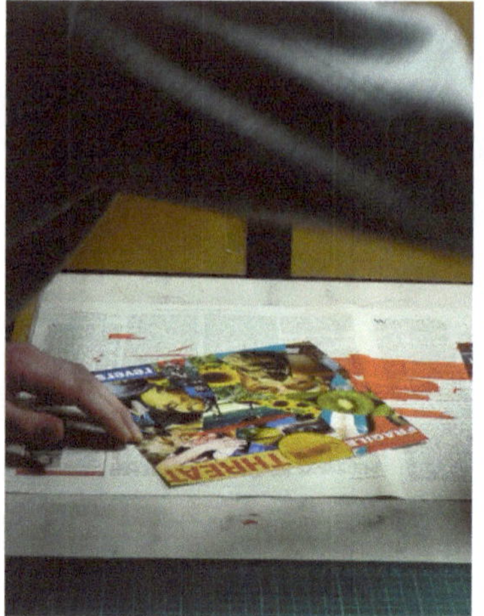

23.

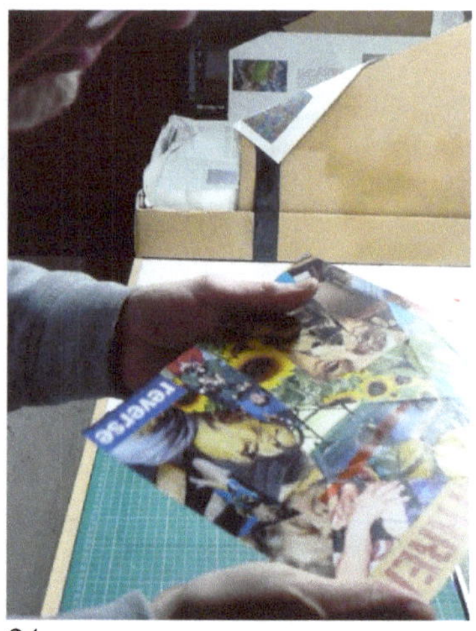

24.

[22.] I seem to be drawn to particular image features when deciding where the smear should start. Often this is the mouth or an eye on a face, or a mouth or eye-like shape somewhere in the image. I think this is because making the smear and the image this creates connects with the feeling of spewing, crying or gushing blood. I place the collage on scrap newsprint and get my head down so that I can see clearly the place where I have decided the smear should start and I deposit a tiny amount of paint directly from the tube. I am using medium quality paint for its translucency; artists' quality paint is pigment-rich and more nearly opaque.
[23.] I use a tightly folded scrap of silicone coated paper as a miniature squeegee and with a swift single gesture draw it across the collage to smear the paint. On a few of the earlier collages I used a small plastic blade to smear a wider thin film of paint over part of the composition—the effect was good but less expressive.
[24.] The results of using the paper-squeegee technique were rather unpredictable earlier in the project. With practise, however, I have developed a greater degree of confidence and control. Regardless of how the paint smear turns out, I always accept the result. This is collage number 213 and every one I started I finished and kept. The point is to trust to the contingencies of the event: in each moment do what it feels right to do, just as the performer does in free-improvisation.

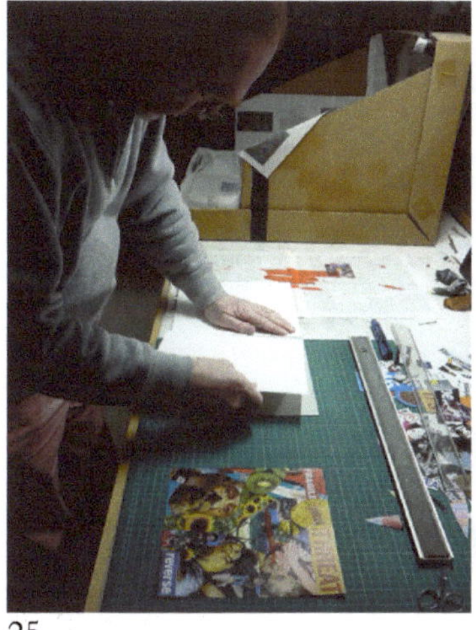

25.

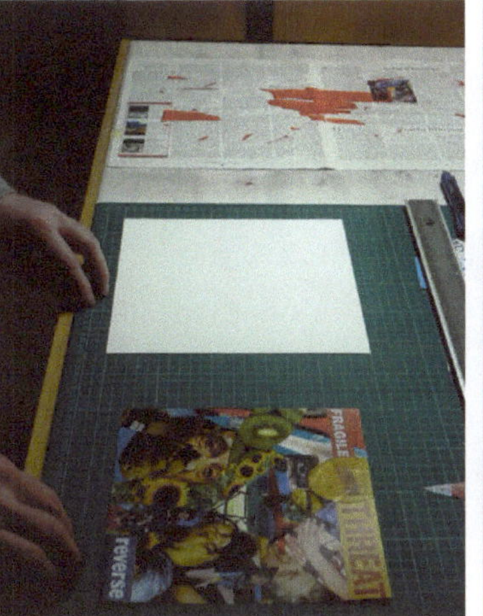

26.

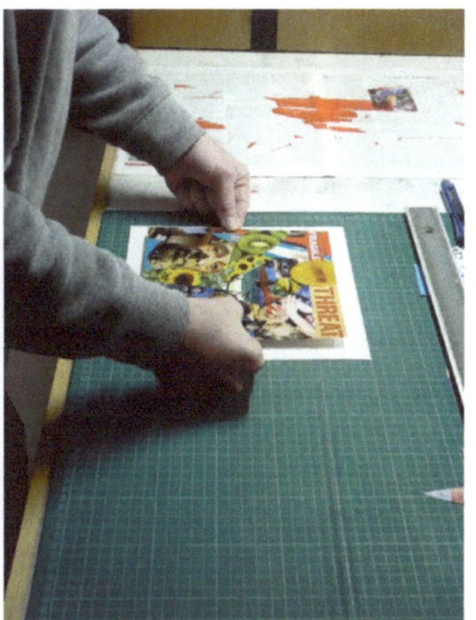

27.

[25, 26.] Straight from the tube Acrylic paint dries quite quickly and when working on paper I never try to speed this up. The problem is that some of the moisture in the paint soaks into the paper, which then swells. This shows up clearly on the back of a collage as a slightly buckled stretch of paper. If it is left to dry naturally the paper recovers and shrinks back to its original flatness. If it dries too quickly the buckling can remain or even worsen and make the mounting process more difficult. While I am waiting for the collage to dry I get the mount ready. I am using a block of heavy watercolour paper—300 gsm Daler™ Aquafine, a good quality 'not' finished paper. I chose the 25 cm square size and the mounting technique at the beginning of the project to ensure a consistent 2 cm border around each collage.

[27.] This is where having a collage that is flat is an advantage. After giving it a couple of coats of spray glue on the back I hold it above the mount to line it up by eye. Then allow the top edge to touch the mount absolutely square and centred 2 cm below the edge of the mount. Then the whole collage goes down cleanly.

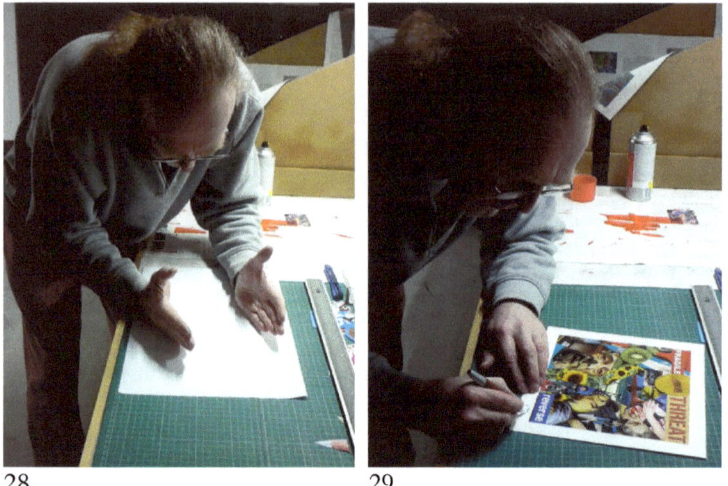

28. 29.

[28.] I use a clean sheet of A3 paper and gently smooth the collage down onto the mount using the blades of my hands. The technique is to place the hands together in the middle of the work and move them apart maintaining even pressure, first on a horizontal line across the work, then a vertical line, each of the diagonals and lastly the intermediate angles. I finish the burnishing with small circular motions of my fingers over the whole area of the collage.

[29.] I sign and date the work firmly in pencil on the right-hand side of the bottom edge of the mount. I then lightly pencil the number of the collage on the back and it is finished. All that remains to do is to photograph the work and complete the catalogue entry on computer.

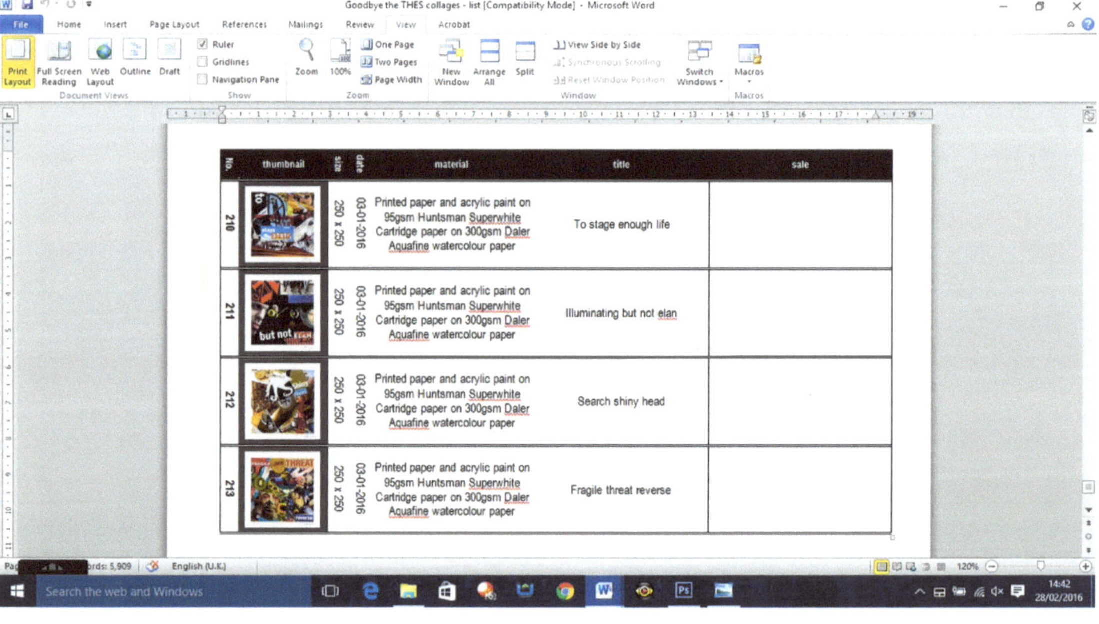

No.	thumbnail	size	date	material	title	sale
210		250 x 250	03-01-2016	Printed paper and acrylic paint on 95gsm Huntsman Superwhite Cartridge paper on 300gsm Daler Aquafine watercolour paper	To stage enough life	
211		250 x 250	03-01-2016	Printed paper and acrylic paint on 95gsm Huntsman Superwhite Cartridge paper on 300gsm Daler Aquafine watercolour paper	Illuminating but not elan	
212		250 x 250	03-01-2016	Printed paper and acrylic paint on 95gsm Huntsman Superwhite Cartridge paper on 300gsm Daler Aquafine watercolour paper	Search shiny head	
213		250 x 250	03-01-2016	Printed paper and acrylic paint on 95gsm Huntsman Superwhite Cartridge paper on 300gsm Daler Aquafine watercolour paper	Fragile threat reverse	

4 From Collage to Metafiction

Only when the *Goodbye* collages were complete did I starting thinking about extending the work into some form of creative writing. I had decided to produce this book and in setting out the catalogue it quickly became clear that it needed to be punctuated with text, pieces of writing that genuinely extended the spirit of the project and belonged in the book. Poems, I thought, would be too individual and too concentrated to work properly and the orthodox prose of short stories and letters would lack appropriate collage qualities. Then I remembered Michael Blackburn's *Chips with Hitler: 6 Metafictions* and this gave me direction: an idea for a form of writing that could introduce rhythm and structure into the book, slow things down and refresh the reader's eye regularly.

So, what does the word 'metafiction' mean? The prefix meta- comes from the Greek *μετά-* meaning 'after/behind' or 'changed/altered', and in modern usage 'higher/beyond.' That third meaning is interesting because it reportedly arises out of

> … a misinterpretation of 'metaphysics' as the 'science of that which transcends the physical.' This has led to a prodigious erroneous extension in modern usage, with meta- affixed to the names of other sciences and disciplines, especially in the academic jargon of literary criticism.[17]

In the critical literature the word 'metafiction' is used to label many different types of contemporary writing, but the common reason for doing so is because it somehow extends beyond the normal idea of fiction whilst definitely not belonging to any idea of non-fiction. I would like to take a step back from this however and return to the original meaning of the meta- prefix. A stronger sense of the word 'metafiction' for me is suggested by combining the 'after/behind' and the 'changed/altered' senses of meta- with the notion that any text that is not already fiction can be fictionalized and one that is can be re-fictionalized. This creates a strong idea of metafiction because the meta- prefix, in its aggregated sense, denotes the method of fictionalizing or re-fictionalizing a text. i.e. by getting *behind* it, producing something that comes *after* it and *changing* its substance through *altering* any and all of its qualities, structure and elements.

I wondered: what happens if metafiction is pushed to extremes by finding ways of creatively navigating the edge of comprehensibility?

---

17 Online Etymological Dictionary <http://www.etymonline.com/index.php?term=meta-> accessed 6 January 2016

5 Writing Metafiction

Subverting an original text is fun. I begin by sampling. The idea is not to find a motif; the sample I am after is nothing so discrete.

Routine 1

I already have a title; it comes from the last collage. This is no help in deciding where to start, but I know how to start. I start at the end of something, the last page of the last chapter in a book perhaps, the first one to catch my eye. From the bottom of the page and working upwards I scan the last words of each line and start writing them down. I do not note every word I read; sometimes I skip a line or two or more. I do not only note single words from the end of a line; sometimes I note two or three and sometimes in reverse reverse order (I am reading backwards, remember). I do not choose words without regard for their meaning; I am looking out for sequences of words that make some kind of sense, no matter how strange. I feel free to add words of my own to help make up the sample into grammatically correct sentences. When I reach the top of the page I stop. Now I have my seed text I can improvise. Inspired by one phrase or whole sentence and then another I invent new phrases and sentences and intersperse them in the desperate attempt to make it all add up to something: a fragment of story, a philosophical thought, something. I fail to clarify meaning and I only have a hundred-and-some-odd words: I need at least four-hundred to make up a page. Start again with a different source; go through the whole process again. Intercut the first sample with the second; alternating sequences of sentences from each. I fail to clarify meaning, but it is never going to get any better. Stop.

Routine 2

I already have a title; it comes from the last collage. But the title is not where I start. I start with the collage; it has magnetism and incident. I made the collage and things I do not remember feeling or seeing before begin to talk to me. One bit of the collage then another and another comes alive in the imagination and reacts with the unpredictable soup of memory, intuition and daydream. I write down words by association, phrases by sheer force of imagination, and sentences, which begin to flow. The invention has begun. My eye roves over the collage in the desperate attempt to exhaust its surface, but I run out of attention all too soon. Now I have my seed text I can improvise … If I fail to clarify meaning and only have a hundred-and-some-odd words, I resort to a text source, slip into routine 1, intercut samples and play it out until adequacy kicks in. Stop.

Routine 3

Who needs external stimuli? But this is not automatic writing: there is too much intervention and too much process for that. Sometimes a seed is miniscule in *miniscule*, a few insignificant hand-written words that explode … Stop.

Note

Clearly what emerges in routine 1 has nothing to do with the original authors' intentions. I call it *retrograde decimation.* However, what tends to happen, primarily through vocabulary, is that some relationship emerges between the subject matter of the source texts and the nascent meaning of their metafictional offspring. Meaning is never fully resolved because it cannot be. It is sediment rather than precipitate, concentrated but unrefinable. However, it is not only I who am operating at the edge of intelligibility: we all are. It is simply a matter of circumstance and degree.

6 Reflections

A moment, a turning point, one way of life ends and another begins. This does not happen overnight: I prepare. For years I prepare. Sometimes I try too hard. Sometimes I have setbacks. I achieve enough just in time to make the change. It is not a smooth transition however. What had been a shadowy undercurrent of dissatisfactions and anxieties explodes in my face. I go down, lose myself in the dark for a while. I fall, but not to too far before I find myself again, a different self, an older one, one who recognizes a mask when he sees one and understands a little more about the weight of armour and the cost of wearing it too long. I am a crustacean not a serpent, but I now have a softer shell. A new set of routines and associations develops to replace one that has become useless, and what had been a barely suppressed strain of wishful thinking emerges into the realm of realizable possibilities and the question becomes: what are you going to do about it? Make art: that is what matters to me.

♦

It is in memory, in the particulars of the found and in the relevance of the overlooked that I choose to go with instantaneous decisions and then make of them what I can. In the end one can cogitate too much in inaction, trying to imagine possibilities and their consequences, when all that is required is 'thinking-in-doing'.[18] The point is to cope by using any and all materials and instruments at my disposal. I frightened a dear and respected friend once with one of my slips into an inauthentic mode of analytical thinking: he pulled me up with the words: "I am a humble designer; problems come up and I solve them." I try to remember the lesson there: never forget the primacy of experience in forming the style of your pragmatism.

♦

Coleman noted that:

[18] Harrison, *Making and Thinking.*

> Once art is defined as a special, refined and valuable commodity, it moves out of the sphere of everyday life.[19]

This is what happened with the advent of a modernist sensibility in the late 19th century which invented 'fine art' as a separated off arena of creative practice. I am with Coleman when he complains that "We have to put creativity, imagination, innovation and invention back to work …", but I depart from his thinking when he suggest that there are only two stark alternatives for the artist: either to be a "producer of the unproducable [sic]" in the gallery system and compete for "its unpredictable patronage" or to be a "'cultural worker' engaged with the processes of social change".[20] There are other possibilities, ones that may benefit from but need not rely either on institutional and commercial patronage or on commitment and service to social purposes. Six alternatives immediately occur to me: crime, self-help, subversion, parasitism, prostitution, and 'retirement'. I do not advocate any of them and I do not suggest that any of them is a truly reliable or sustainable way of earning a living as an artist. If making art is your priority I suggest you forget the idea of *earning* a living doing it and concentrate on getting by and when the opportunity arises of getting paid as much no-strings-attached money as possible. There is no connection between what people earn and what they actually get paid—compare nurses and investment bankers for a moment, yes?

♦

> Dada aimed to destroy the reasonable deceptions of man and recover the natural and unreasonable order. (Hans Arp)

He is almost there: civilized existence is only possible because of the web of necessary illusions that holds it together. The natural order *is* unreasonable: in fact, it is absolutely beyond reason and that should terrify everyone. It is not probability that matters in this universe, it is possibility and that is profoundly unpredictable, shocking in its scope, and dangerously attractive to the creative mind.

> What would you do with art which is actually immoral? Or people that make art because they're bad? Or you experienced art that didn't make you a better, nicer, happier person, that did the opposite? You know, turned you into a deranged, psychopathic, destructive, perverted … fucker? Huh? That's the kind of art I like. … Duchamp and everything … (Michael Blackburn)[21]

I rest my case. No …

♦

Imagine you are walking through the back lot of a rundown block of flats. The garages in two rows are contained at the far end by a high brick wall and in the corners the wind and rain have fashioned a strange accretion of materials. Mixed in with rotting leaves and creases of gritty black mud are dog ends and disintegrating cigarette packs, glittering sweet wrappers and the sodden pages of a teen mag, a doll's head and the skeleton of an umbrella, a

19 *The Art of Work*, p. 1.

20 Ibid. pp. 1-2.

21 Matthews, *Art Land*, 00:06:23 ff.

torn stained rag and an odd shoe, a child's mitten and a plastic comb—its teeth bearing traces of not-quite grey hair—and, inevitably, several plastic syringes and a used condom. There is sense in the scene and that is what is unsettling—all those familiar things blown together and weathered down into a readable composition, as if a guiding human hand were at work. You have seen all of this stuff now, because I have told you what to recall and visualize. It is working on you and you are working on it—you can't help yourself. As vague intuitions distil into imagined scenarios which in turn resolve into believable explanations—a story, and another story, and another—it becomes difficult to throw off the feeling that this place, this empty little stage setting, is more a part of you than you would normally care to admit. It is all too concentrated, too potent, too damned close to the bone. Feel the frisson?

♦

I am sincere in my wish to exorcise the destructive elements of my being. It seems the best way to do this is to take a few risks—venture through the back streets and down the darkest alleys. Exposure has its purpose, call it catharsis. There is always this therapeutic aspect to art; it simply emerges in different ways. When asked whether his was a "cathartic or therapeutic process" Stefan Blom responded "It's always been like that … Yeah, off-loading certainly".[22] An artist may choose to be, but does not need to be, overtly political; once situated a work is open to the interpretive capacities of its audience and stores that potential in any case. I think Blom is with me in thinking that it is generally a bad idea to preach. I am not preaching; I am bleeding.

♦

I realize that my position regarding the proper role today of the artist in society and of art in culture is less than fashionable. I am unapologetic, however, in regarding the "social practices that are now the mainstay of contemporary art" (to quote Sonia Boyce) as an aberration. Artists as enterprising activists are simply playing their part in a political game designed to sustain an arena of critical engagement with issues of popular concern moderated by the institutions (political, cultural, economic and the mass media). There are good reasons why an artist, or indeed any citizen, can choose to participate and bring their skills and knowledge to bear. It is a choice that some artists make. I have no problem with that; I just hope they never forget that it is all a game, a game designed to satisfy the need for cultural institutions to justify their public funding and to enable the rich and powerful to disguise their elitist beliefs. I do not go along with the argument that it is all about the social good. Media-ready stories of artists' public engagement, and their engagement of the public, with the issues of the day are part entertainment, part sedative and part dissimulation. Social good may result sometimes from the artist's activism, but that is not the real point of the enterprise, whatever the artist professes in the end it is about

[22] Blom, 2015.

survival: connection, off-loading, fascination, fear, money, chance, experience, and choices, although not necessarily in that order.

♦

Once one starts it is difficult to stop making sense of things forged in the labour of making sense of things forged. One thing leads to another. I firmly believe that *one is neither as in control as one often appears nor as out of control as one sometimes feels.* Nevertheless, ambition does have its place. It ferments a state of play which tends to be productive.

♦

In the first section of this essay I said nothing about collage after Schwitters, nothing about Ernst and Dali, Cornell and Motherwell, Rauschenberg and Hamilton. There is a lot to say … maybe another time.

♦

It is impossible to provide one reference point for the collages and metafictions I produced for this project … so this is it:

> Babylon is nothing else than an infinite game of chance in which the drunkard who improvises an absurd order takes a secret oath to omit, to interpolate, and to change it so that nothing is so contaminated with fiction. *The number of drawings is infinite* because there is chaos enough in the cosmos.
>
> You may have guessed that no-one knows my intimate hopes and terrors. I was not a free man and have, therefore, not automatically participated in the sacred drawings. Now I understand that it is a question of a new order, of a necessary historical stage, but I am not fond of logic or even of symmetry. I come from a dizzy land where the lottery is the basis of reality: yes, I have known what the Greeks never knew: incertitude.[23]

[23] Borges, 'The Lottery in Babylon.'

POSTSCRIPT

Postscript

When I started the *Goodbye to THES* project I had no idea how it would turn out and now it is done it is not for me to judge the results. Maybe in due course someone will tell me where it led and what it achieved.

At the outset I decided to document the project and to produce this book, but it is more than an illustrated catalogue of the collages, with an essay to situate the work and to explain in detail my techniques and use of materials: I added another layer to the project by writing a sequence of metafictions.

It is not usual to write prose without clear intentions and to do so by deliberately working on the edge of intelligibility. But that is exactly how the metafictions were composed. They provide a literary complement to the collages. In both, seed material is selected intuitively, massaged, multiplied and melded. Then a desperate point-to-point struggle for connection and meaning, that always almost succeeds and never quite fails, builds the semblance of composition. The collages are not chance compositions and the writing is not stream of consciousness, there is an aesthetic at work which is about immediate response to the materials at hand: free improvisation and minimal formatting.

The methods used make acknowledgement of *sources* an awkward matter. Referencing a direct quote or paraphrased idea is straightforward enough, but most of what I use is less solid than either of these borrowings. I do not dip into a text because it is a well from which a little water can be drawn. Nothing as rational and calculating as taking a life-sustaining measure occurs. What I do has a more autonomic feel. It is more like moving for a while through an atmosphere one knows to be barely breathable without concern for what the longer term effects will be.

The first collage in the series *VITA promise moves* (001) is a very simple composition centred on a photograph of Hannah Arendt and this immediately suggested to me setting off a metafiction with words mined from *The Human Condition*. There are no other direct linear relationships like this later in the project. Image and text together are drawn on to kick-start some other metafictions but the relationship between them is often tenuous and the way they unfold more convoluted or discontinuous.

One text mined several times during the project to seed segments of metafiction is the final section of chapter 14 in *A Thousand Plateaus* by Gilles Deleuze and Felix Guattari. The authors draw together thoughts on 'nomad art' as an aesthetic model in which one recognizes a style of existence in the urban environment. I find the writing persuasive and evocative, and for that reason alone worth subjecting to *retrograde decimation* to see what monsters it may spawn.[24]

I also dip into the German philosopher Peter Sloterdijk's work. His theories of space and media interest me and in English translation the dense language he uses has tremendous poetic potential.[25]

Press London wonderland fraction (064) is unusually rich in references. In it I weave together Sloterdijk's *Spheres*, and Deleuze and Guattari's *A Thousand Plateaus* with Lewis-Williams' *The Cave in the Mind*, Derrida's 'The Double Session', and Duchamp's 'Three Standard Stoppages'. All of these reference points recur in the metafictions because of the centrality of the 'nomadism' and 'cave' themes.

Hopes journey south the wandering (082) by way of contrast is an improvisation on almost entirely autobiographical material, only toward the end are there passing references to the writer Robert Walser and the artist Gerald Wilde. Before 13 January 2016 I had never heard of Wilde. That was the day I made a daytrip to London with Michael Blackburn to see two exhibitions: *Soaring Flight: Peter Lanyon's Gliding Paintings* at the Courtauld Gallery and *Gerald Wilde: From the Abyss* at the October Gallery. I bought the exhibition publications and they provided several triggers for metafictions. In *Better exercise privilege pilgrim* (037) for example, the account of Lanyon's translation of gliding experience into landscape painting is used in counterpoint to a close, animalistic, earthbound feel for the world, not unlike Wilde's. The musical parallel for Lanyon's painterly translation of sweeping movement is captured with the words: 'between tenor drum and cymbal stand,' which is a reference to *The Blur Between*, a record of solo improvisations by Roger Turner (1991). I designed the original album cover, which featured a long-exposure photograph of the musician as a blur in the space between his two instruments.

In *Bop pioneer connect people* (046) Wilde is referenced again and another source that I find particularly evocative also comes into play: Marion's *The Edge of Organization*. The idea that order emerges out of chaos without the need for any external organizing influence is a powerful one. Mechanical systems, even simple ones, can exhibit complex unpredictable behaviours and, at the molecular level, spontaneous convergent synthesis in a mix of hydrogen sulphide and hydrogen cyanide under ultraviolet light may be one way life begins.[26]

Widening of the year coming soon early bird search (055) also draws on Marion but the principal sources are the image itself and a short film by Terry Gilliam—*The Crimson Permanent Assurance*. These are interwoven with autobiographical elements to create a fantasy which ends suddenly to be deconstructed in the closing paragraph. I do not know why I did this: I am not a literary critic; I set out to write my own kind of metafiction.

---

24 See above, 5 Writing Metafiction: 'Routine 1' and 'Note'.

25 *Bubbles* and *Globes*. See also: Borch, 'Foamy Business'.

26 Patel et al, 'Common origins of RNA'.

There are other *Goodbye* metafictions that grew from imaginative readings of their eponymous images and without seeding with words from elsewhere. These include: *Seminar task is a shaping of water* (091) and *Agents of dreams [words] rise wet* (100). The latter also goes off on a reflexive line in the literary-critical sense that metafiction is more commonly supposed to do—there you go; I just cannot stick to my own rules.

Charles William Johns, a fellow member of the Lincoln Philosophy Forum, published *Incompatible Ballerina and Other Essays* in October 2015. His take on what drives humans to think, desire, create, and situate and transcend themselves is at once unsettling and entertaining. I have long had my doubts about the privileged position of the sovereign rational subject in modernity, which seems to carry over into the dominant culture as an ever-present spectre threatening to overwhelm and transform the human spirit. Johns stands up for neuroses as the sources of human achievement: even the rational calculating thought held up as an ideal by Enlightenment thinkers has its roots in neurosis and anxiety. *Atlantic aspic global driving a holy crusade of bones* (109) rattles along on the edge, the rant of a neurotic who can barely hold a thought long enough to make sense; it just tumbles out guiltlessly and uncensored. Are these my "most honest, primitive, real thoughts" or merely a tainted residue?[27] Perhaps faint odours persist in certain passages of the improvised compositions but what is more important is that I pitch them, on the verge of incomprehensibility, as challenges to the reader's sense-making capacity. This is explained, after a fashion in *End still to expand sting in the bodies* (136).[28] And so it goes.

As I came to the end of this project I was driven by a general if mild sense of panic. It has always been like that with me. A long time ago I learned how to ride the emotional storm and use its energy to move forward; it comes with the discipline of working to a deadline. On the outside I appear rational and in control; on the inside there is a battle going on. Those unavoidable moments of anxiety and doubt are suppressed: when time is running out there is no point in thinking that things could have been done differently and better. Producing the work is one thing; presenting it is quite another. From a rational perspective, the best frame of mind is one that makes a clean break.

Over to you.

---

27 Cronenberg, *Naked Lunch.*

28 See above, page 111.

Acknowledgements

I recognize and I am grateful for the many different ways in which the following people provided inspiration, encouragement and example during the project, some without even knowing they were doing so: Catherine Matthews Bennett, Michael Blackburn, Sylvia Blackburn, Stefan Blom, Alf Bower, Pam Brook, Anna Catalani, Colin Davis, Steve Dutton, Graham Freestone, Chris Goddard, Chris Hay, Valerie Huggins, Charles William Johns, David Kenyon, Graham Lappin, Frans Lohman, Bhaskaran Nayar, Roderick Orner, John Russell, Gerard de Zeeuw, and the Leeds Poly group (they know who they are).

Particular thanks go to Philip Bowman for programming the exhibition at the Gallery at St Martins, and guiding me through the process of exhibiting.

Sources

Academy of American Poets, 'A Brief Guide to the Beat Poets,' 3 May 2004, <https://www.poets.org/poetsorg/text/brief-guide-beat-poets> accessed 20-02-2016.

Bahr, Fax & Hickenlooper, George (dirs.) *Hearts of Darkness: A Filmmaker's Apocalypse*, Triton Pictures (USA), 1991.

Blackburn, Michael. *Chips with Hitler: 6 Metafictions* (2002, Lincoln: Sunk Island Publishing).

Blom, Stefan. Interviewed by Daniel Lingham, *Sculptorvox*/11, Thursday 28 May 2015. <http://sculptorvox.com/stefan-blom> accessed 22 December 2015.

Borch, Christian. 'Foamy Business: On the Organizational Politics of Atmospheres' in Willem Schinkel & Liesbeth Noordegraaf-Eelens (eds.) *In Media Res: Peter Sloterdijk's Sphereological Poetics of Being* (2011, Amsterdam University Press), pp. 29-42.

Borges, Jorge Luis. 'The Lottery in Babylon' in *Labyrinths* (2000, London: Penguin Classics), pp. 55-61.

Boyce, Sonia. Quoted in Elmes, John. 'HE&me', *Times Higher Education*, 17 December 2015, pp. 22-3.

Breton, Andre & Soupault, Philippe. *Les champs magnétiques* (1919, Paris: Gallimard).

Burroughs, William S. *Naked Lunch*, 50th anniversary edition (2009, New York: Grove Press).

Carter, Pippa. & Jackson, Norman. 'Gilles Deleuze and Felix Guattari' in Stephen Linstead (ed.) *Organization Theory and Postmodern Thought* (2004, London: Sage) pp. 105-126.

Cronenberg, David (dir.) *Naked Lunch*, film, 1991.

Coleman, Roger. *The Art of Work: an Epitaph to Skill* (1988, London: Pluto Press).

Deleuze, Gilles. & Guattari, Félix. *A Thousand Plateaus*, trans. Brian Massumi (2004, London: Continuum).

Derrida, Jacques. 'The Double Session' in *Dissemination* (2004, London: Continuum), pp. 189-316.

Duchamp, Marcel. "The Creative Act" quoted in Sanouillet, Michel. & Peterson, Elmer (eds.) *The Essential Writings of Marcel Duchamp* (1975, London: Thames and Hudson) pp. 138-40.

Elderfield, John. *Kurt Schwitters* (1985, London: Thames & Hudson).

Gusmão, João Maria and Paiva, Pedro. *Teoria Extraterrestre* (2014, Milan: Mousse Publishing).

Harris, Oliver. '"Burroughs Is a Poet Too, Really": The Poetics of Minutes to Go,' first published in *The Edinburgh Review*, 114, (2005). Republished by RealityStudio in August 2010, <http://realitystudio.org/scholarship/burroughs-is-a-poet-too-really-the-poetics-of-minutes-to-go> accessed 20-02-2016.

Harrison, Andrew. *Making and Thinking: A Study of Intelligent Activities* (1978, Hassocks: The Harvester Press).

Hopkins, Stephen (dir.) *Predator 2*, 20th Century Fox, 1990.

Idle, Eric. 'Accountancy Shanty', lyrics. In, *The Crimson Permanent Assurance*, dir. Terry Gilliam, film short, 1983.

Johns, Charles William. *Incomparable Ballerina and Other Essays* (2015, Winchester: Zero Books).

Leigh, Mike. *Naked and Other Screenplays.* (1995, London: Faber and Faber).

Lewis-Williams, David. *The Mind in the Cave: Consciousness and the Origins of Art* (2002, London: Thames and Hudson).

Marion, Russ. *The Edge of Organization: Chaos and Complexity Theories of Formal Social Systems* (1999, London: Sage).

Matthews, Geoffrey Mark. *Dead Reckoning: a Collection of Poems* (2009, Lincoln: Sunk Island Publications).

——— (dir) *Art Land*, video, performance Michael Blackburn, 2005.

——— *Improbalization*, guitar improvisation, mp4, 2003. <https://www.youtube.com/watch?v=eRhcPmRHel0> accessed 29-12-2015.

Patel, Bhavesh H., Percivalle, Claudia., Ritson, Dougal J., Duffy, Colm D. & Sutherland, John D. 'Common origins of RNA, protein and lipid precursors in a cyanosulfidic protometabolism', *Nature Chemistry* 2015, no. 7, pp. 301–307.

Russell, John. Kondo Toshinori, and Turner, Roger. *Artless Sky*, Caw Records, 1980, vinyl long player disc, CAW 001

Schwarz, Arturo. *The Complete Works of Marcel Duchamp*, revised and expanded paperback edition (2000, New York: Delano Greenidge Editions).

Sloterdijk, Peter. *Bubbles: Spheres: vol. 1*, trans. Wieland Hoban (2011, Los Angeles CA: Semiotext(e)).

Sloterdijk, Peter. *Globes: Spheres: vol. 2*, trans. Wieland Hoban (2014, South Pasadena CA: Semiotext(e)).

Turner, Roger. *The Blur Between*, Caw Records, 1981, vinyl long player disc, CAW002.

Tzara, Tristan. 'To Make a Dadaist Poem' (1920)

Waldman, Diane. *Collage, Assemblage and the Found Object* (1992, London: Phaidon Press)

Notes

Notes

Notes

www.ingramcontent.com/pod-product-compliance
Lightning Source LLC
LaVergne TN
LVHW070118110826
845147LV00002B/146

* 9 7 8 0 9 9 3 2 0 5 4 5 3 *